# Fodor's InFocus

D1527636

# IN FOCUS DUBAI

1st Edition

Where to Stay and Eat
for All Budgets

Must-See Sights
and Local Secrets

Ratings You Can Trust

Fodor's Travel Publications  New York, Toronto, London, Sydney, Auckland
**www.fodors.com**

**FODOR'S IN FOCUS DUBAI**

**Series Editor:** Douglas Stallings

**Editors:** Brooke Barrier, Douglas Stallings
**Editorial Contributor:** Lindsay Bennett

**Editorial Production:** Evangelos Vasilakis
**Maps & Illustrations:** David Lindroth *cartographer*; Bob Blake and Rebecca Baer, *map editors*; William Wu, *information graphics*
**Design:** Fabrizio La Rocca, *creative director*; Guido Caroti, *art director*; Ann McBride, *designer*; Melanie Marin, *senior picture editor*
**Cover Photo** (Dubai Marina): Ludovic Maisant/hemis
**Production/Manufacturing:** Amanda Bullock

**SPECIAL SALES**

This book is available for special discounts for bulk purchases for sales promotions or premiums. Special editions, including personalized covers, excerpts of existing books, and corporate imprints, can be created in large quantities for special needs. For more information, write to Special Markets/Premium Sales, 1745 Broadway, MD 6-2, New York, New York, NY 10019, or e-mail specialmarkets@randomhouse.com.

**AN IMPORTANT TIP & AN INVITATION**

Although all prices, opening times, and other details in this book are based on information supplied to us at press time, changes occur all the time in the travel world, and Fodor's cannot accept responsibility for facts that become outdated or for inadvertent errors or omissions. **So always confirm information when it matters,** especially if you're making a detour to visit a specific place. Your experiences—positive and negative—matter to us. If we have missed or misstated something, **please write to us.** We follow up on all suggestions. Contact the In Focus Dubai editor at editors@fodors.com or c/o Fodor's at 1745 Broadway, New York, NY 10019.

# Be a Fodor's Correspondent

Your opinion matters. It matters to us. It matters to your fellow Fodor's travelers, too. And we'd like to hear it. In fact, we *need* to hear it. When you share your experiences and opinions, you become an active member of the Fodor's community. Here's how you can help improve Fodor's for all of us.

Tell us when we're right. We rely on local writers to give you an insider's perspective. But our writers and staff editors also depend on you. Your positive feedback is a vote to renew our recommendations for the next edition.

Tell us when we're wrong. We update most of our guides every year. But things change. If any of our descriptions are inaccurate or inadequate, we'll incorporate your changes in the next edition and will correct factual errors at fodors.com *immediately*.

Tell us what to include. You probably have had fantastic travel experiences that aren't yet in Fodor's. Why not share them with a community of like-minded travelers? Share your discoveries and experiences with everyone directly at fodors.com. Your input may lead us to add a new listing or a higher recommendation.

Give us your opinion instantly at our feedback center at www.fodors.com/feedback. You may also e-mail editors@fodors.com with the subject line "In Focus Dubai Editor." Or send your nominations, comments, and complaints by mail to In Focus Dubai Editor, Fodor's, 1745 Broadway, New York, NY 10019.

Happy Traveling!

Tim Jarrell, Publisher

# CONTENTS

# ABOUT
# THIS BOOK

## Our Ratings

We wouldn't recommend a place that wasn't worth your time, but sometimes a place is so experiential that superlatives don't do it justice: you just have to be there to know. These sights, properties, and experiences get our highest rating, **Fodor's Choice**, indicated by orange stars throughout this book. Black stars highlight sights and properties we deem **Highly Recommended**, places that our writers, editors, and readers praise again and again for consistency and excellence.

## Credit Cards

Want to pay with plastic? **AE, D, DC, MC, V** after restaurant and hotel listings indicate whether American Express, Discover, Diners Club, MasterCard, and Visa are accepted.

## Restaurants

Unless we state otherwise, restaurants are open for lunch and dinner daily. We mention dress only when there's a specific requirement and reservations only when they're essential or not accepted—it's always best to book ahead.

## Hotels

Unless we tell you otherwise, you can assume that the hotels have private bath, phone, TV, and air-conditioning. We always list facilities but not whether you'll be charged an extra fee to use them, so when pricing accommodations, find out what's included.

### Many Listings
- ★ Fodor's Choice
- ★ Highly recommended
- ⊠ Physical address
- ✛ Directions
- ⬧ Mailing address
- ☎ Telephone
- 🖷 Fax
- ⊕ On the Web
- ✉ E-mail
- ⬧ Admission fee
- ☉ Open/closed times
- Ⓜ Metro stations
- ⊟ Credit cards

### Hotels & Restaurants
- 🏨 Hotel
- 🛏 Number of rooms
- ⚲ Facilities
- ⦿ Meal plans
- ✕ Restaurant
- ⬧ Reservations
- ↘ Smoking
- 🍷 BYOB
- ✕⬚ Hotel with restaurant that warrants a visit

### Outdoors
- 🏌 Golf
- ⛺ Camping

### Other
- ⬧ Family-friendly
- ⇨ See also
- ⊠ Branch address
- ☞ Take note

# WHEN TO GO

Hotels remain busy year-round because of a constant parade of business travelers, but occupancy levels peak during large exhibitions and conventions. Resorts are busiest in the winter, with their highest occupancy levels from Christmas through the Dubai Shopping Festival in late January to early February, when prices reflect increased demand. Prices also increase during such major sporting events as the Dubai World Cup and Dubai Desert Classic. Many large hotels change their best-rate prices based on that day's demand.

During Ramadan, which varies but usually begins in August or September, hotel occupancy is lower than normal. Room rates may drop, or special offers, including extras like spa treatments, may be included in the standard rates. Daily life in Dubai changes during the Muslim month of fasting—restaurants stay closed during daylight hours and nightclubs shut their doors for the duration.

## Climate
During the winter months, December through March, temperatures are usually in the mid-70s °F; nights can cool into the 60s and, occasionally, the 50s. Almost all the annual rainfall comes during the winter. In the spring from April through June, temperatures rise into the 80s and 90s and precipitation is next to nothing. The real heat doesn't hit until July and August, when daytime temperatures soar to a stifling average of 105°F and can reach as high as 118°F. During the summer, tour activities are usually restricted to the early morning and late afternoon, and street life retreats into air-conditioned malls and hotels. September, October, and November are more pleasant, as the heat recedes and temperatures drop back toward winter's lows. The air is dry year-round, except during the brief periods of rain. During the day, temperatures are higher in the desert than on the coast, but at night the desert is cooler than the coast.

Dubai is subject to the *shamal* storm system, which arrives in the region from the northwest and can cause high winds, rough seas, and sandstorms. These storms can arrive at any time of year but are more likely in the spring.

## Dubai

# Welcome to Dubai

**WORD OF MOUTH**

"This is \$\$\$\$\$ with a capital \$ and it shows in just about everything and everywhere. Dubai dazzles, and it is an interesting place being that it has a polyglot of nationalities living and working there."

—LizzyF

By Lindsay
Bennett

**DUBAI SITS ON A GOLDEN SANDY COASTLINE** in the Arabian Gulf, where the warm azure waves of the sea meet the desert. A high-rise oasis, this city is a pleasure-dome surrounded by dunes; one of the most fashionable on the planet thanks to its ability to satisfy the needs of legions of demanding vacationers. Dubai is about having fun—and it's one big adult playground.

Nature plays her part here, with year-round sunshine, gorgeous beaches, dramatic arid landscapes, and warm waters, but it's the man-made attractions that make Dubai so alluring. You can launch yourself into high-adrenaline desert adventures, diving and water sports, and some of the world's best golf courses. The 5-, 6-, and 7-star hotels offer the ultimate in luxury, and the party scene is hot. Shopping malls are the biggest in the world and are packed full of high-class merchandise. And with hundreds of restaurants with cuisine from around the world, you can munch your way from Mexico to Malaysia.

Dubai is an Arab country with a long history as a trading port. Traces of its traditional life, customs, and architecture can still be seen and explored, but today and tomorrow are much more important than yesterday. Almost every building in this metropolis is less than 20 years old and the most dramatic developments—groundbreaking megaprojects—have just been completed or are still under construction.

The city is certainly unique. Islam is its anchor, but it has opened its doors to the rest of the world and has invited them in to work, rest, and play, which creates a truly international atmosphere. Unashamedly modern and materialistic, life here takes place at breakneck speed. The landscape is stark, the confidence is sky high, the can-do spirit is palpable, and the *bling* is in your face. Dubai produces strong reactions in people, but one thing is certain—love it or loathe it—you will not forget it. It is without a doubt, one of the world's true must-see destinations.

**SHISHA: SMOKE WITHOUT FIRE.** Emirati men love socializing, but as they don't drink alcohol they get together over coffee and *shisha* instead of a drink at the bar after work. The shisha, or *hookah*, is a smoking device, usually made of glass, that filters smoke through water before it reaches the smoker's mouth. Shisha tobaccos are aromatic and are often mixed with apple, cinnamon, or cherry, so their taste isn't as strong as other tobaccos. Smoking shisha is said to induce relaxation—but you'll have to decide if it's for you!

# THE MAKING OF DUBAI

The desert is one of the harshest environments on earth, and it's a testament to the ingenuity of man that people managed to settle in Dubai in ancient times. Archaeological digs at four sites around the city have unearthed artifacts that indicate a small population settled here as early as the third millennium BC. In addition, Dubai served as a port of call on the sea routes between the Mesopotamian region and the civilization of the Indus valley in India in the second and third millennia BC. Archaeologists also have discovered remnants of a mosque and other buildings, which suggest that a small port existed here at the end of the first millennium AD. However, Dubai didn't make much of a mark on world events through the second millennium. The only record of the port town is in Venetian ledgers showing they bought pearls from the traders here.

Even in the early years of maritime trade by the Europeans during the mid-1700s, the region around the Gulf had a reputation for piracy, and cargo ships stopping in Dubai were regular targets. Disputes between local, familial Arabic tribes resulted in numerous raids along the coast. By the 1820s the British government was fed up with the raids and negotiated a deal with the tribes that allowed it to act as arbiter in local disputes to help lessen piracy and improve regional security.

In 1833, after a family disagreement in the Bani Yas tribe in Abu Dhabi, the Al Maktoum clan packed its bags and traveled up the coast to visit the Al Abu Falasa clan (also of the Bani Yas tribe). There, they took a liking to Dubai Creek and settled on the Bur Dubai bank. It was a profitable move, as the business-savvy clan quickly assumed control of the pearl trade and other commerce in the tiny settlement. The Al Maktoums honored the accord with the British government, previously signed by the Al Abu Falasa clan, as it provided protection against piracy and the British had growing influence in the area. In 1853, the Al Maktoums and other local ruling families, known collectively as the Trucial Sheikhs, went on to sign a "perpetual truce" with the British. The relationship was further strengthened in 1892 when both parties agreed that Britain would act as protector of the Trucial States in exchange for exclusive

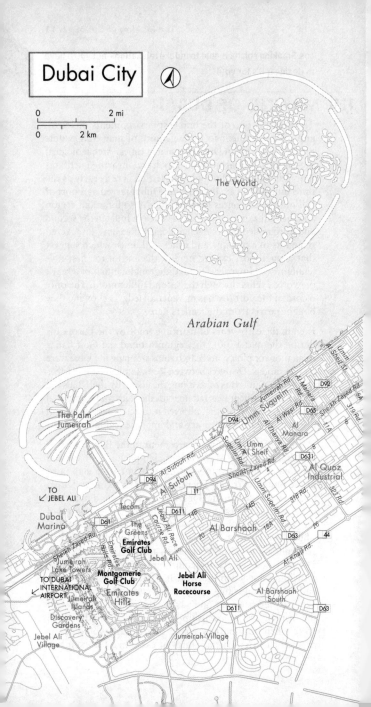

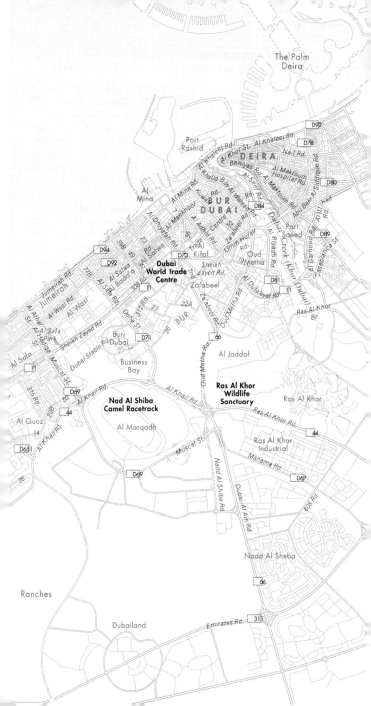

trading rights within the territory. However, the states remained self-governing entities—not British colonies.

In 1894, Sheikh Maktoum bin Hasher Al Maktoum assumed power in Dubai. He was the first clan member who hoped to expand the emirate and enforce the long-term goals of economic growth and security. He introduced tax and duty incentives that lured traders and merchants who might previously have used other ports, and also began rebuilding the family ties that had been broken in 1833—the first meeting between the sheikhs of Dubai and Abu Dhabi took place in 1905 just before his death. By the end of his short but action-packed reign in 1906, all commercial taxes had been removed on goods imported or exported through Dubai port. Furthermore, the city was growing. An influx of Iranians and Indians immigrated here and significantly increased the population. There was no question about it—Dubai was officially open for business and it was thriving!

However, two economic disasters brought the city's new prosperity to a sudden end. Although New York was far away, the Crash of '29 spilled over the world like a tsunami, and trade plummeted. Simultaneously, Japanese scientists announced a breakthrough discovery—how to control the growth of a pearl in an oyster shell. Cultured pearls became cheaper and quality control produced a more uniform result. The natural pearl industry in Dubai, an economic mainstay for generations, collapsed and the clans were forced to find more profitable ventures.

The economy saw little improvement in the 1930s through World War II. The region suffered from a lack of trade and supplies because its major trading partner, India, was a British colony and therefore was deeply involved in the war. Relationships within the Gulf were also becoming increasingly strained. The borders between the various Trucial States had never been formalized, and when a dispute between Dubai and Abu Dhabi erupted in fighting in 1947, Britain had to intervene.

But Dubai experienced a stroke of luck when Britain moved its Trucial State administrative headquarters here after the war. The emirate immediately was brought into the modern world. Electricity supplies revolutionized daily life, an airport allowed faster travel, and telephones extended communication beyond local seaways. Even so, the economy still was not healthy. The Trucial States seemed to be functioning at a minimal level, but a geological phenomenon was about to change all that. In 1958, oil was discovered in the waters off Abu Dhabi.

Dubai's Sheikh Rashid had only just succeeded his father, Sheikh Saeed, at the time of discovery and knew that his neighbor's good fortune would create opportunities for his fiefdom. Abu Dhabi had no port but would need huge amounts of infrastructure commodities, including steel and concrete, so Rashid dredged Dubai Creek to take the modern vessels that would be needed to service the oil trade and transformed Dubai into a shipping town. By 1966 when oil was discovered off the coast of Dubai, it was simply an added bonus for the vastly expanding economy. When the larger modern ships began to outgrow Dubai Creek, Rashid approved the building of Port Rashid, a man-made terminal on the coast at the creek mouth to increase its capacity.

Meanwhile, the British, dealing with domestic economic issues, withdrew from the area in 1968 and gave the Trucial Sheikhs three years to create a security plan. Sheikh Zayed bin Sultan Al-Nahyan, ruler of Abu Dhabi, and Sheikh Rashid of Dubai decided to create a federation of states and invited other local sheikhs to join them—hence, the United Arab Emirates was born in December 1971.

Throughout the 1970s as petro-dollars flooded into Dubai, Sheikh Rashid funded massive developments in the city's infrastructure. Port Rashid was expanded but the expansion quickly proved too small. Cargo ships were becoming bigger and containers were industry standard. Rashid decided to invest in a new port at **Jebel Ali,** which would become the largest man-made harbor in the world. The port would be surrounded by a tax-free, duty-free industrial zone that would attract trade from around the region.

By the time Rashid died in 1990, Dubai was on solid economic ground, but it was clear that the oil supply would not last forever. So Sheikh Maktoum, Rashid's successor, sought to diversify his small country's portfolio by encouraging tourism, which he believed was the fastest growing industry. He appointed his brother Sheikh Mohammed to manage the development of the country's tourism infrastructure, and the scene was set for Dubai's debut onto the world stage. In 1995 he was given the title Crown Prince of Dubai, which put him in line for the crown if Sheikh Maktoum were to die or renounce his throne.

Sheikh Mohammed, king of the megaproject, had already spearheaded the birth of Emirates airline. He followed that with investment in luxury accommodations, the creation of a Western-style leisure infrastructure (including bars and restaurants), and million-dollar giveaways in Dubai's shopping festival. Pioneering vacationers returned home with rave reviews about their adventures in Dubai. In 1999, the opening of the **Burj Al-Arab Hotel** brought even more attention to Dubai with its images of star athletes Roger Federer and Andre Agassi playing tennis on the hotel's helipad high above the coastline.

The government's goal was to bring in 15 million visitors each year by 2010—ambitious, to say the least. Developers were contracted to create several new offshore island communities, and the world's largest theme park would take shape inland, rising from the desert sands. In 2002, Sheikh Maktoum opened Dubai for property investors and kick-started a real estate boom. Dubai's leadership changed hands in 2006 after the death of Sheikh Maktoum, with a natural handoff to Sheikh Mohammed, who had long been the energy behind the throne.

# DUBAI AND THE UNITED ARAB EMIRATES

Dubai is an emirate, similar to such principalities as Monaco and Lichtenstein, and maintains a feudal form of hereditary rule that's been held by the Al Maktoum family since the 1830s. The leading male members of the ruling family are called sheikhs, which loosely translates to "prince," and leadership is passed down through the family but is not an automatic right of the eldest son. Rather, the current sheikh chooses who will succeed him from eligible members of the family.

Dubai is one of seven countries that make up the United Arab Emirates (UAE), a federation founded in 1971. The other six emirates are: Abu Dhabi, Ajman, Fujairah, Ras al-Khaimah, Sharjah, and Umm al-Quwain. The UAE's main legislative body (the Federal Supreme Council, or FSC), is made up of the seven sheikhs of each emirate, but Abu Dhabi is the preeminent emirate in the federation. The president of the UAE plays an influential role and is always the sheikh of Abu Dhabi, a hereditary post that's passed down to a member of the Al-Nahyan family—currently Sheikh Kahlifa bin Zayed Al-Nahyan. The sheikh of Dubai is vice president.

## Dubai's Ruling Family

1

In one of Hollywood's versions of aspiration versus seemingly insurmountable odds *Field of Dreams* (1989), Ray Kinsella (played by Kevin Costner) turns his dreams into reality and builds a baseball stadium in the middle of the corn belt. At the climax of the film a stream of headlights fills the screen as massive crowds clamor to view Kinsella's upcoming sporting spectacle.

You might wonder if the Al Maktoum family—rulers of Dubai—have this film in their DVD or Blu-ray collection, as it encapsulates the story of Dubai perfectly: an unprepossessing location with an inspirational leadership that can think its way out of the box and push past the boundaries of the world as we know it! In this case, it's not thousands of cars cruising down America's highways to see a baseball game. Instead, thousands of airplanes wing their way to Dubai International (DBX) carrying passengers who are eager to experience the 21st-century spectacle that's risen out of the desert. The Al Maktoums have transformed Dubai from an invisible locale to a super-cool tourist destination. And there's much more in the pipeline.

Each emirate controls most of its own domestic matters, including taxes, trade, and investment, but the federation oversees foreign policy and defense. The UAE cultivates friendly relations with other Arab states, as a member of the Gulf Cooperation Council (GCC), as well as with the United States and other Western nations.

The Federal National Council, which has 40 members including eight from Dubai, acts as a consulting body. Until 2006 sheikhs appointed the council members, but the nation is trending toward mass representation and now a group of Emirati, the Electoral College, elects 50% of the chamber. In Dubai, the Dubai Governing Council acts as an advisory body to the sheikh. However, council membership is limited to a small number of Emirati who make up less than 20% of the population. So more than a million people who live and work in Dubai have no political voice.

## BIG DREAMS BECOME REALITY

WORD OF MOUTH. "As a developer it's an incredible place. The stuff they're doing is amazing, they're limited purely by their imagination and the laws of physics." —Donald Trump Jr.

Dubai has experienced astonishing growth and economic success over the past 20 years. In the 1980s, there was nothing here that would attract anyone but oilmen and a few crusty expats. But the Al Maktoums, aware that Dubai's oil reserves will not last forever, had a clear vision of making it a world player in other areas as well.

In the drive for diversification, the government first targeted tourism as a growth industry, which really started paying off in the 1990s. It positioned Dubai as a luxury market, where mass market would never mean down market. First to come were European tourists, and the emirate is now targeting the rapidly growing Indian and Chinese middle classes. Between 2001 and 2006, Dubai's hotels-and-restaurants sector increased in value from AED 2,977 million to AED 5,793 million (about $81 million to $158 million), and room occupancy numbers rose by 228%, much of which is credited to hotel investments and shrewd advertising. Passenger traffic at Dubai International Airport also surged from approximately 5 million in 1990 to almost 29 million in 2006.

As the first phase of diversification succeeded, the emirate unveiled its long-term vision and a range of initiatives aimed at establishing Dubai as one of the world's principal business hubs. An appealing financial package is key to growing business, and Dubai offers many fiscal benefits, including no taxes on corporations and personal income, and 100% repatriation of capital and profit. No foreign exchange controls, trade barriers, or quotas exist, and vast free zones allow importing and exporting with no financial consequences for manufacturing and trade. Dubai acts as a Middle Eastern base for multinational companies—in fact, more than a quarter of Fortune 500 companies have regional offices here. The government forecasts that these and other developments will create more than 800,000 new jobs by 2015 and that growth is drawing people like magnets. According to the government, more than 24,000 people settled in Dubai each month during 2006—that's an astonishing 33 new residents every hour.

For visitors, construction sites are the obvious sign that Dubai's economy is booming. Annual spending on new buildings surged from AED 5,2 billion in 2001 to an amazing AED 21,5 billion in 2006—and most of that money was invested in thought-provoking architecture that got the world's attention. Slated for 2007–2008 are 125,000 residential units, but government projections suggest that

**CLOSE UP**

# Sheikh Mo

Sheikh Mohammed bin Rashid Al Maktoum, known affectionately as "Sheikh Mo," envisioned only the most prosperous future for Dubai. In fact, it was his dream that brought about Burj Dubai, the Palm islands, the tallest tower in the world, and Dubai Marina. But he didn't stop there—nothing seems to faze this man, who officially became Dubai's ruler in 2006.

Born in 1949, Sheikh Mo was the third son of Sheikh Rashid and grew up on the bank of the Bur Dubai. He excelled at the Al-Ahmadiya School and was allowed at an early age to attend the *majlis,* or meetings, where his grandfather Sheikh Saeed dealt with matters of state. When his father, Rashid, became sheikh in 1958, he and his brothers began to take on responsibility within the emirate. Mohammed finished his education at a language school in Britain, after which he enrolled in a six-month officer training program at Aldershot in 1968.

When Mohammed returned to Dubai in 1968, he took control of the emirate's police force. At this time, Britain announced its withdrawal from the region. His father, along with Sheikh Zayed bin Sultan Al-Nahyan of Abu Dhabi, was instrumental in the creation of the United Arab Emirates in 1971, and Mohammed was appointed minister of defense of the new country.

Sheikh Rashid expanded Dubai's horizons as a trading and transport hub for the greater Gulf region. He began offering more challenging roles to his son, who at that time oversaw infrastructure improvements, including the expansion of Dubai International Airport, and the management of Dubai's oil supplies. In 1981, Sheikh Rashid fell ill, so Mohammed and his brothers collectively assumed control and soon became known for their open-minded approach to government. Sheikh Rashid died in 1990 and was succeeded by his eldest son, Sheikh Maktoum, under whose guidance Mohammed broadened his portfolio and grew his reputation as an approachable leader willing to take risks. In 1995 Sheikh Maktoum declared Mohammed Crown Prince of Dubai, paving his way to the sheikhdom.

Throughout his adult life Mohammed's favorite pastime has been horse racing. He and his brothers own the successful Godolphin stables and have invested billions of dirham in fine horses that have been trained at state-of-the-art facilities in Newmarket, UK, and Dubai. The Dubai World Cup, the highest purse in the sport, is both a source of pride and passion for Mohammed.

an additional 500,000 units will be needed by 2017. Office space in the emirate doubled between 2006 and 2008, and growth of the business industry continues. In an emirate awash with petrol dollars, money has never been an object, and Dubai's open real estate market has been a draw for investors from around the world. The first freehold real estate projects were such a success—turning $1 million investments into $3 million returns—that the resulting influx of foreign dollars has kept the property market red-hot.

Several *bourses,* or stock exchanges, and trading platforms have been established, catapulting the Emirate Dubai International Financial Centre (DIFC) onto the radar of world finance. The DIFC's goal is to host 20% of the world's investment funds—its 110-acre free-trade park already includes such companies as Morgan Stanley, JP Morgan, Merrill Lynch, Chase Bank, Ernst & Young, Allianz, Deutsche Bank, State Bank of India (SBI), and HSBC. In addition, a rapidly expanding Financial Exchange, a Diamond Bourse, and a Gold and Commodities Exchange have been set up since the turn of the millennium.

Dubai is a world of superlatives—the world's tallest tower, the world's biggest airport, the world's largest artificial harbor, the world's largest man-made port, the world's biggest man-made island—just to name a few. No one knows how long this prosperity will last, but at the moment there's no end in sight. In January 2008, Nakheel, one of Dubai's largest developers, announced the emirate's sixth offshore project, The Universe, and several other major projects aren't slated to begin for another decade. However, there may be a few bumps in the road ahead. Because of its success, the emirate's economy is strained, with average rent and food price increases far exceeding wage increases. This only pressures the lowest paid workers who keep the wheels of daily life turning. More important, India and China are both experiencing unprecedented growth, and the price of raw materials like steel and cement are skyrocketing. In addition, skilled labor is in such short supply that some developers are delaying project completion dates. If a jittery world market turns bear, it will certainly squeeze investment. Dubai plunged into the fray with gusto and in doing so made itself susceptible to global economic factors that even Sheikh Mohammed can't control.

**DID YOU KNOW?**   Twenty-seven percent of the world's construction cranes can be found in Dubai. More than 70% of the world's sea dredgers work on Dubai's Palm Deira—just one of five offshore projects in the emirate.

Between the Sea and the Desert Sand, sea, and mountain come together to create the important, yet fragile, ecosystem in Dubai. The emirate covers 1,588 square miles, nearly 5% of the UAE total, and occupies the northernmost parts of the Rub' al Khali—the **Arabian Desert** or Empty Quarter, a desert the size of France that runs south through Abu Dhabi and into the Arabian heartland.

The Empty Quarter was first made famous during the mid-20th century in the writings of British explorer and travel writer Wilfred Thesiger. It's one of the least populated places in the world, but it's been a Grand Central Station for geologists in the latter part of the century because of its expansive oil reserves. Although some stretches are devoid of vegetation, the Dubai desert is not the ocean of sand that many envision. In almost every acre a vivid vegetation contrasts with the terra-cotta-colored dunes and flats—a hue that results from the iron-oxide coating of feldspar mixing with the mainly silicate sand. All species living here are adapted to arid conditions, but their existence hints at life-giving moisture in the earth. Wild grasses and low scrub form a thin carpet over much of the area, with acacia trees standing sentinel. The date palm is endemic to the region and has been cultivated for generations, as it's highly nutritious and portable.

In western Dubai, the desert meets the warm waters of the Arabian Gulf. If left to nature, this coastline would offer only sandy beaches, grass-covered dunes, and swaths of mangrove trees, but there's very little virgin landscape left. Only a few square miles at Jebel Ali, close to Abu Dhabi, have escaped the developers' clutches. The **Dubai Creek,** a sheltered tidal inlet, is a rare find around the Gulf and could have been a rich natural environment. However, it's been dredged and managed since the 1950s, resulting in artificial banks flanked by buildings and manicured parks and golf courses. Still, the **Ras al Khor Wildlife Sanctuary** (2.4 square mi) gives visitors a glimpse of the diverse animal and plant life that used to thrive here. Mangroves, mudflats, *sabkha* (salt-encrusted flat that lies above the water), and reed beds are an important last refuge for 266 species of birds and animals, and 47 types of plants. The sanctuary is an important stop on the migratory routes for many bird species, including plovers, sandpipers, sanderlings, snipes, terns, stilts, and a flock of elegant flamingos.

Just offshore, a narrow skirt of shallow coral reefs runs parallel to the coast, which then leads to a continental shelf and a deeper ocean trench. These varied ocean depths offer a wide variety of habitats for fish and other marine life. The warm shallows host small, colorful tropical fish, and the offshore waters support populations of dugong, several species of dolphin and porpoise, and hawksbill and green turtles. The coolest, deepest waters in the Gulf provide a conduit for larger pelagic species, including whales and sharks, but not in regular enough numbers to attract a whale-watching industry.

Perhaps the most surprising geological features in Dubai are the serrated peaks of the **Hajar Mountains,** which form a crescent-shaped collar around the northwestern coast of the Gulf. They are the oldest and highest region in the UAE, and act as a physical boundary between Dubai and neighboring Oman. The Hajar are a rare and archetypal example of *ophiolite* volcanic geology, or rock that lay below sea level and collected a dermis of sedimentary rocks after which they were thrust upward by the movement of the earth's tectonic plates.

Camels are the most common desert animals by far, some wild, some feral. You are unlikely to see any other large creature during your explorations here and may have to search hard for small animal life. Even though it may seem the desert is void of life, it's out there. The Arabian Peninsula has a range of predators found in small numbers. The Arabian leopard, more petite than Asian and African leopards, lives mainly in the Hajar Mountains and hunts antelope and the occasional goat or sheep. The smaller sand cat—approximately the size of a house cat—lives on a smorgasbord of desert creatures, from rodents to insects. The final hunter in the desert is the sand fox, and this species extends its diet to plant life, including carrion, fruit, and berries.

Predators currently are under stress as prey becomes more difficult to find. Numbers of the ibex, a once-common mountain goat known for its magnificent horns, have dropped to only about 500, and the Arabian oryx (a horned antelope) no longer roams in the wild. A bigger selection of smaller mammals exists as more than 40 rodent species, the largest of which is the desert hare, still call Dubai home. Gerbils and mice in a mind-numbing array of genera have been most successful in the sand and in arid rocky environments. They share space with reptiles, including the well-camouflaged desert chameleon and the rare colorful gecko.

Insects vary from huge black-dung beetles to grasshoppers and crickets to mantises. Dubai has far more moths than butterflies. In fact, more than 350 species of moths have been documented, including various types of the striking hawk moth.

Environmental protection has been a low priority during Dubai's drive for development. Very few areas are officially protected, and as vast tracts of desert and marine shallows continue to be transformed for human use, biodiversity declines while land degradation increases. Although the off-shore islands may be engineering marvels, the jury is out on how they affect surrounding coral reefs, turtle-nesting habits, and migrations of larger marine creatures. In addition, 5-star hotel ratings can be quite taxing on the environment, as Dubai's water usage and waste production (per capita) are some of the highest in the world. In 2007, a United Nations report declared the Gulf environment "stressed."

There is some good news, though. The Arabian oryx has been reintroduced in small numbers and is thriving in the sanctuary at the **Al Maha Desert Resort.** Plans for the offshore islands include enrichment of the submarine environment by creating habitats that are conducive to sea life. Once the projects are completed, scientists should see a rise in sea-life numbers again. However, the potential problem is that the scale of the projects may disrupt breeding cycles for such species as turtles for so long that they will not be suitable sites for recolonization. However, some scientists suggest that the artificial reefs are already starting to attract new species and an increasing number of fish.

## PEOPLE

WORD OF MOUTH. "Dubai is a tourist area and therefore very tolerant of Westerners in general. As a female, I'm quite comfortable there and I feel free to do as I wish. —Melnq8

Well over a million people live in Dubai but only 17% are native Emiratis. From the very early days, the country has used foreign workers to oil the wheels of the economy. Traders from India and Iran have been established here for more than a century, many with fathers and grandfathers born in the city. But during the last 20 years, the need for more workers has exploded.

Nowhere else in the world do so many nationalities exist together in harmony. Representatives from about 180 countries bring their disparate religions, diets, and points of view to the Dubai melting pot. The relaxed and convivial atmosphere cultivated by the Dubai royal family filters through the whole population, and these attitudes foster a spirit of understanding and respect for other cultures and individuals. No doubt this is helped along by a lingua franca: English. Most first-time visitors, even when surrounded by the unfamiliar, express surprise at how safe the city feels. Crime barely even registers on the scale. Minds from every continent work here, but the dynamic is a bit more complicated than the simple-happy-people image that's pushed by the tourism authorities.

Most residents of Dubai came here to do one thing—make money. They see the emirate as a land of opportunity where they can benefit, but there are vast differences in the economic status expat workers are able to obtain. Thus their daily lives can differ greatly, as well as their tax-free profits.

Many white-collar positions in business, finance, insurance, real estate, and hotel management are equipped with impressive salaries and more. In addition to earning tax-free wages, most offer generous housing allowances, school placements for kids, country-club memberships, abundant vacation time, and gym memberships for nonworking spouses. These packages, shoo-ins to the glitzy lifestyle for which Dubai is famous, are attracting Brits, Europeans, Australians and New Zealanders, South Africans and North Americans, and increasingly highly educated Indians and Southeast Asians. It is an international resume builder and a stepping-stone to success.

The blue-collar experience is quite different. Salaries are low for store assistants, room maids, and taxi drivers, and most have to leave their families behind in India, Pakistan, or the Philippines. Their employers own their contracts, and some workers have to turn over their passports for the duration of their employ. Blue-collar workers often sleep in small apartments, several to a room, because accommodation is so expensive. Still, for most, their earnings far exceed what they could make in their native countries.

The construction industry in Dubai has been the subject of several press exposés, and critics argue that the city's economic success has been built on exploitation. Hundreds of thousands of mainly Indian and Pakistani laborers are employed at a time on the project sites around the city. Long hours and unenforced safety protocols result in a high percentage of injuries and deaths—880 workers died in 2005. Construction workers also complain about extremely low pay, with salaries rumored to be only 10% of the Dubai average. The government was slow to react but began discussing draft labor laws in early 2007; although its proposals still fall short of accepted international standards, according to Human Rights Watch.

The push for modernization and modernism has been wholeheartedly welcomed by Emiratis, and they embrace the have-it-all lifestyle. Before the 1950s, when the first modern infrastructure arrived in Dubai, Emiratis lived a very different life. Many were nomadic Bedouins who traveled around the desert in extended family groups, eking out a living with their livestock of goats and camels. The Bedouin existed in harmony with the shifting sands. Everything they owned could be carried, including their large tented homes, gold wealth, and foodstuffs such as dates and nuts. Family fealty was and still is paramount in the structure of Emirati society. But one effect of the dramatic economic transformation has been to squeeze the old ways into narrow margins. It's only been during the past few years that the government has started to invest in preserving the heritage of the country, rather than pumping all of its funds into Dubai's new personality. Of all the nationalities that inhabit Dubai, Emiratis are in some ways the most invisible, even though it is their home. They are relatively small in number and guard their home life in hopes of preserving traditional values. The wheeler-and-dealer business types and royal elite can be spotted making deals in Dubai's numerous hotel lounges, but most ordinary Emiratis live quiet lives within family compounds. Don't mistake their reserve for unfriendliness, though; Emiratis simply live a bit apart from the energy that surrounds Dubai.

## DUBAI'S ENGINEERING MIRACLES

The rush of groundbreaking developments in Dubai makes it easy to forget it started less than 15 years ago. Dubai began its first foray into engineering history when Sheikh Mohammed announced plans for the Burj Al-Arab hotel in the late 1990s, and today this dramatic hotel takes its place alongside structures such as the Hoover Dam as icons of the modern age.

## Women in Emirati Society

First, let's clear up one of the most common misconceptions about women in Dubai—they can and do drive. Women have more freedom here than in other Arab states, but the government still is working on initiatives that aim to widen the role of women in society and break down generations of entrenched gender roles.

Dubai women are free to take advantage of education and enter the workplace. You'll see many Emirati women working in administrative positions for the government and banks, and a growing number are now seeking higher education. However, few women have risen to positions of authority in Dubai, as homemaking and child-rearing are the main responsibilities of women at all social levels. Still, change may be on the horizon. Teenagers are often seen in shopping malls, socializing with their friends like girls in the West. Also a large number of Emirati women moving toward adulthood now choose to forego the face veil and instead opt for the long loose *abaya* dress when out in public.

Non-Arab women in Dubai have nearly the same freedoms they do in their native countries, with the understanding that they don't go out drunk or scantily clad in public. The large number of expat women living and/or working in Dubai attests to the relative ease with which they can settle here. Nonworking wives of expat executives often spend their time driving to the mall in powerful SUVs to meet the girls for coffee, just as they might do in the States. Western fashions are well accepted here so long as they don't reveal too much flesh, including the tops of the thighs, lower curve of the buttocks, or even a small expanse of midriff. Harassment isn't an issue for single women or women-only groups, and some say they felt safer in Dubai than in other places they've traveled.

The sheikh wanted the design of the Burj to symbolize the traditions of his lands, and architect Tom Wright was inspired by the shape of a dhow sail when it catches the wind. For the concept to work Wright had to make the hotel look as if it was floating on water, so it was decided the structure would sit on a little artificial island built about 900 feet off the Jumeirah shore. This island posed interesting problems for Atkins Architects, the firm contracted to build the hotel. To secure the offshore location, Atkins had to construct a firm foundation for the hotel by driving 230 concrete piles 40 meters into the substrate. Atop these piles, a surface layer of concrete blocks was added and held in place by a collar of concrete. This breakthrough feat took three years to complete.

The hotel itself is a masterpiece of modern architecture, with two long steel columns visually anchoring the building and acting as the "mast" to its "sail." Steel struts that measure 278-feet long form the structure's skeleton, some of which were lifted 656 feet into the air to be correctly positioned. Over 160,000 square feet of Teflon-coated Dyneon flouropolymer material—a revolutionary membrane that offers high UV resistance and allows 90% of light to pass through—is the sail. It softens the lighting streaming into the hotel's monumental 590-foot interior atrium. Because the floating restaurant sits off from the building's center, it posed a design and construction challenge. But the tiny circular helipad at the summit of the hotel, 725 feet above water, is a simple structure supported by a metal cantilever. While this landmark construction was underway, Sheikh Mohammed also launched the **Palm Jumeirah** project, an artificial island concept so massive in scale that it can be seen from space. It was soon nicknamed the "Eighth Wonder of the World."

True to its name, the Palm Jumeirah was designed in the shape of a palm tree. A 2-mi-long core development of hotels, apartments, and shopping and entertainment complexes in the shape of a trunk will link the palm to the Dubai mainland. At the end of this trunk, a 6.8-mi, 656-foot-wide protective breakwater will surround the palm canopy, which will be made of 17 1.2-mi-long, 820-foot wide "fronds" where exclusive private villas will be built. This project—the most audacious land reclamation project in history—was slated to be built offshore from Jumeirah Beach.

More than 50 engineering and environmental studies were conducted before work commenced to assess everything from traffic flow to water quality. The main challenge was creating a landmass stable enough to support high-rise development. The basic technique involved dredging sand to form the basic shape, driving deep foundations into the sandbanks, covering that core with monumental rocks to anchor the base, and then spraying sand on top of the rocks—a technique called rainbowing—to the final level on which developers could build.

The height of the breakwater canopy was critical as it needed to sit 14.7 feet above normal sea level to account for rising water levels during regular *shamal,* or storm systems, and a once-in-100-year mega-storm scenario. Therefore, the seabed had to be raised nearly 50 feet in some areas. To complete the work, almost 175 million cubic feet of rock had to be strategically placed in the sea to create the curved shapes. This rock was then rainbowed with a staggering amount of sand to soften the landmass.

Despite the vast size of the project and the revolutionary techniques employed, the basic ground works were complete and Palm Jumeirah was ready for development in only two years. There were 20,000 workers on the project at the peak of the infrastructure development.

In the last few years, Nakheel broke ground on two far larger palm projects. Palm Jumeirah's interior diameter is just over 3 mi, while Palm Jebel Ali's interior diameter is 4.6 mi and **Palm Deira** is a pear-shaped 7.5 mi by 5 mi. However, each project will be built using the same principles as Palm Jumeirah—now an industry standard for all such development.

But even then, Nakheel didn't rest on its laurels; the company's next megaproject, **The World,** posed different problems again for the structural engineers. An archipelago of 300 man-made islands (the smallest around 150,000 square feet) in the shape of the continents, with a 16.7-mile breakwater forming the outline of the planet, The World was the first development to have no land link to the Dubai mainland. Everything from fuel to food and water for the construction workers had to be transported on giant barges from the mainland 2.5 mi to the east. Rock and rainbowing were again used to create the 10-foot base island height. Around 3,884,650,000 cubic feet of sand were needed. Logistical problems included freshwater supply and sewage removal, but these have been solved by allocating an island within each cluster of islands as a distribution and service point for utilities.

The World concept was unveiled in 2003 by Sheikh Mohammed, and the substrate was ready by early 2008. This is the ultimate in real estate. Every tropical island is equipped with state-of-the-art utilities and communication systems, and can be "terraformed," or shaped and landscaped, to fit each client's needs. Nakheel won't tell who has purchased the islands, but those who have can get to work building their private villas, pools, and gardens. Several exclusive resort developments have been approved and these will surely become must-see hotels in the next five years. There's a vast amount of work yet to be done on The World, and even more work to be done before Dubai breaks from its construction frenzy.

# DOING BUSINESS IN DUBAI

The entire UAE has a liberal outlook and is committed to free trade. The country has a modern business infrastructure with high-quality, high-tech office space and well-established travel logistics, a beneficial fiscal plan for corporations and individuals, and a confident business atmosphere. Contrary to popular belief, only 30% of the nation's gross domestic product comes from oil revenues—an even smaller percentage in Dubai because of its diverse, robust economy.

The UAE is a major consumer of U.S. goods and services, with $8.4 billion worth of imports. More than 500 U.S. companies have offices in the UAE, and nearly 20,000 Americans live and work here. The UAE and the U.S. are negotiating a future free trade agreement, but nothing has been decided yet.

If you are heading to the emirate for business, you might want to follow a few points of etiquette. Make sure that any brochures or materials you take are high-quality, and carry lots of business cards, printed in English and Arabic. English is widely used in the business world, but a few words of Arabic, a polite phrase or two, will be considered good manners by your Emirati clients.

Many Emirati businesses are family run, and you may be required to meet junior members of the firm to begin building a relationship before you are allowed to meet the real decision-makers.

Arrive for meetings on time, but know that punctuality is not highly valued and you may find yourself waiting to meet the client. Similarly, your meeting may be disrupted by telephone calls and even personal matters.

Business is not conducted in a vacuum here. At the beginning of a meeting it's normal to have a drink with your client (tea, coffee, or a soft drink—no alcohol) and to chat about general topics to build a bond. Oftentimes, business is done over a meal. If you receive an invitation for a meal, it is considered polite to respond in kind even if it prolongs your discussions.

Emirati businesspeople usually put greater emphasis on verbal agreement than most executives in the Western corporate world. In the UAE, your word is binding, so make sure you mean what you say when agreeing to terms, conditions, or prices.

**Other useful information:**

• Make sure any printed materials, such as brochures or pamphlets, don't have pictures of women that could be regarded as sexy or provocative. Don't include images of alcohol, people drinking alcohol, or pigs or pork.

• Pointing is considered rude, so don't use a pointed finger to accentuate your words.

• Be prepared to put a lot of time up-front into building relationships before you start seeing a return.

• Haggling is at the heart of all business transactions, so factor this in to your pricing structure.

• The silent one in the group is often the decision-maker, so address answers to all meeting attendees.

It's important to note that Dubai has a different attitude than other Arab countries toward women in business. For example, Abu Dhabi and Kuwait have much stricter rules regarding dress and behavior. Here are some things to consider:

• At large multinational conventions or smaller meetings with Arab female staff or clients, you may find tables labeled "women only." Women aren't required to use these tables, but men are required to sit elsewhere, allowing women to separate themselves from male company if they choose to do so.

• At formal dinners women and men may be seated at different tables or on different sides of the room.

• Women can wear standard feminine Western business dress—meaning no short skirts, no midriff-baring, and no cleavage on show. Slacks are acceptable. If possible, clothing should be loose-fitting so as not to draw attention to the shape of the body.

• Some Muslim men won't touch women to whom they are not related or married. Take your cue on handshakes from your host. If he offers his hand, shake it; otherwise make eye contact and nod in acknowledgement as you are introduced to each other.

# PERFECT DAYS AND NIGHTS

1

## A PERFECT DAY DOWNTOWN

Dubai has only recently started thinking about highlighting its history, but the handful of attractions it does have give a clear view of what the city once was—before the economic frenzy took hold. They're set close together, making it possible to see them all in one day with plenty of time in between for refreshment stops, shopping, and a good lunch.

Start on the Deira side in the Al Ras district. Tour **Heritage House,** a historic home, for a glimpse into family life during the 1930s and Al-Ahmadiya School, one of Dubai's most renowned educational institutions. From here, it's only a five-minute walk to the **Gold Souk** where you can haggle for one of Dubai's best commodities—jewelry—though the atmosphere is better here in the evening. After visiting the souk, or market, walk to the creek front to the **Spice Souk** where you can buy supplies of frankincense and saffron. Cross the creek by *abra* (boat) to Bur Dubai and follow the route through the **Textile Souk** (left of the abra station) to visit **Dubai Museum** in Al-Fahidi Fort. It's a rendition of the trading center the city used to be.

By this time, it'll be late morning and the old districts of the city will be preparing for a siesta in the heat of the day. Enjoy a leisurely lunch, perhaps at the **Fish Market** at the **Radisson SAS Hotel,** which overlooks the creek on the Deira side. Or better yet, take a taxi to Dubai Creek Golf and Yacht Club where you can dine alfresco at **Boardwalk** restaurant.

In the late afternoon, return to Bur Dubai and visit **Sheikh Saeed Al Maktoum House** for its collection of photographs of the city during the mid-20th century and outstanding views across the lower creek. Have a drink at a creek-front café as you wait for the Heritage and Diving villages to come alive around nightfall. Then make your way to Bastakiya and explore the beautiful old quarter under the gentle light of street lamps. Enjoy dinner at Bastakiya Nights amidst genuine Arabic architecture, decor, and cuisine. Plus, the upstairs terraces have views of the activity on the north and south banks of the creek. At night Emirati and Indian families spend the evenings strolling in the cool air, so relax with an after-dinner walk soaking in the sights and sounds.

# Dubailand: Coming to a Desert Near You

Dubai's pleasure dome is a colossal fun-park. At 3 billion square feet, it's bigger than Disneyland and Disney World combined, more than four times the size of Manhattan, and covers the equivalent of 52,000 football fields. Dubailand will be the king of all themed entertainment complexes, including 26 megaparks and dozens of smaller-scale attractions. An eclectic range of organizations and individuals are investing funds in Dubailand—Tiger Woods, Dreamworks, and the Natural History Museum in London. Each brings expertise to the plate to draw crowds from around the world.

At press time the only completed projects were the Dubai Autodrome, the Ernie Els golf course, and the Dubai Outlet Mall. But this is just the tip of the iceberg. New delights will continue to be unveiled between now and 2018, when the finished project estimates 15 million visitors a year.

In 2007 Universal Studios announced that its fourth park—6.5-million square feet in size and a $2.2 million investment—will be built here. Other investors are less well known but their plans are just as grand. Falcon City of Wonders, designed to look like a bird of prey with outstretched wings, will feature life-size copies of some of the world's most iconic architecture. Visitors will be able to experience the Italian *dolce vita* at the City of Rome or the *joie de vivre* of Paris' Eiffel Tower, which will double as a hotel. At City of Arabia, the Restless Planet Dinosaur Park will immerse you in a Jurassic land with more than 100 life-size animatronic dinosaurs foraging and hunting near active volcanoes while being bombarded by meteors. Meanwhile Legends of the World will offer a sampling of the world's ecosystems in miniature. The Great Dubai Wheel will be the second largest in the world next to the one in Shanghai and will offer exceptional views extending 50 mi out on a clear day. Each park in Dubailand will have its own luxury resort accommodation, and Bawadi—a 6-mi strip running through the core of the complex—will host 51 hotels offering a total of 60,000 rooms. The mall of Arabia, located in Bawadi, will be the largest in the world.

For those who can't wait to see the final product, Dubailand headquarters has produced an impressive, to-scale model of the developing complex, complete with moving parts and neon lights.

CITYSCAPE DUBAI. **Considered the world's largest business-to-business property development and investment exhibition, Cityscape Dubai is where you learn of the emirate's real estate and megaproject plans. Sheikh Mohammed outlines his vision for future flagship developments in Dubai and around the Gulf region in state-of-the-art presentations. In 2007 nearly 52,000 investors, property developers, government agencies, architects, and designers from 136 countries attended the exhibition. Cityscape Dubai takes place in early October.**

## A PERFECT DAY OF RETAIL THERAPY

If you love to shop, Dubai is certainly the place for you. From massive air-conditioned malls, to historic shopping quarters, the city is alive with retail options, and warmly welcomes visitors who have an urge to splurge.

Malls open at 10 AM, so fortify yourself with some caffeine and spend an hour or two at either of the supersized malls, Mall of the Emirates or Ibn Batutta Mall. However, if it's Friday or Saturday morning between October and April, postpone the mall excursion and head first to the art market in Dubai Marina. Vendor kiosks selling handmade art, handicrafts, and clothing line **Marina Walk,** and the setting on the water's edge surrounded by the high-rise towers is amazing. From Dubai Marina, it's an easy taxi ride to both malls.

If you'd rather have lunch at a mall with more pleasant views, take the 30-minute taxi ride to Festival City where you can have a quick snack or light lunch in one of the casual canal-side eateries. Or walk through the mall to the connecting **InterContinental** and **Crowne-Plaza** hotels and take in impressive views of the creek from the restaurant's terrace. After lunch, you can stroll around the mall.

Downtown souks usually close during the afternoon and open again around 4 PM. They really begin to bustle around 7 PM. Visit the Spice Souk for stocks of saffron, cinnamon, and frankincense, then walk a few minutes to the Gold Souk for a dazzling display of precious stones and metals.

If you have energy left to burn, head south to **Madinat Jumeirah** where you can complete your list of souvenirs at the modern souk's shops. Then relax over dinner or a drink at one of the waterside restaurants. **Pierchic** or **Zheng He's** are both highly recommended.

## A PERFECT DAY AT PLAY

Start early in this desert state, where visibility is best in the couple hours after sunrise. Better yet, head out before dawn in a hot-air balloon, where you'll see the sun's first rays break the horizon (only available during winter). You'll witness the whole exciting process—setting up the rig and inflating the huge canopy. Or if the balloons make you nervous, instead try zipping across the water and lifting off in a Cessna seaplane. The tours along the coast offer a bird's-eye view of Dubai's incredible offshore islands.

Later in the morning, hook up with a guide for an hour or two of bashing through the desert along a wadi (dry riverbed) or in the hills around **Hatta** in a gusty 4WD vehicle. It's an adrenaline-packed trip that takes you through some extreme landscapes.

After lunch, book a desert driving course. You'll need your utmost concentration to tackle the loosely packed dunes of the Empty Quarter and triumph over the sand. If you'd rather not get behind the wheel, try the more traditional camel safari. The "ship of the desert" carries you at a sedate pace and provides a perfect perch from which you can watch the sun drop and the desert sand take on a glowing rose hue.

From here, head back to Dubai for an hour on the piste at **Ski Dubai** where the black run will tax even the most experienced skier. Then you can finally relax over an evening cocktail knowing you gave it your all.

**NABATI: PAST AND PRESENT.** Nabati, the traditional poetry of the desert, is a form of prose that uses the everyday language of the Bedouin people rather than elevated Arabic. Used as a type of oral history since the 16th century, Nabati communicates past events to future generations and strengthens family bonds by providing entertainment around the campfires on cold desert evenings. Various themes, including chivalry and wisdom, reach to the heart of the Bedouin character. Sheikh Mohammed loves the art form and writes his own Nabati tales. Examples can be seen on his Web site at ⊕ www.sheikhmohammed.co.ae.

# Exploring
# Dubai

**WORD OF MOUTH**

"My wife and I had a great trip to Dubai in March last year. We had a bit of fun at the beach, got to see the beautiful hotel Burj Al Arab, went shopping in the souks, walked around in town looking at buildings and people and so on. But at the same time it was different from the other western big cities that I have been to . . . and not in a negative way."

—Gard

By Lindsay
Bennett

**SEVERAL DISTINCT ZONES** and quarters, each with its own purpose and atmosphere, make up the city of Dubai. The older districts around the mouth of Dubai Creek—Deira, Al-Rigga, and Bur Dubai—have developed over the last 150 years into a maze of narrow streets and alleyways that are often choked with traffic. However, the museums and attractions here are clustered close together, making this area the most walkable in the city. You'll need to cross the creek on the *abra* (boat) service, about seven or eight minutes long, to get from one bank to the other.

To venture beyond this downtown core you'll need to take transportation. If you have time, buses are very cheap, new, and air-conditioned, and their routes pass by many major attractions. However, taxis are efficient, inexpensive, and metered, making them a more flexible option if you're only in Dubai for a short time and every minute counts.

Sheikh Zayed Road is the multilane road that links old Dubai with the newer Dubai districts to the south—about 15 mi to the southernmost communities. It runs 3 mi inland from the ocean and parallel with the coastline. Every well-marked intersection off Sheikh Zayed Road leads to a different district—including Dubai Marina, Emirates Hills, and Knowledge City—as well as that area's major attractions. This road is the thoroughfare for most of the traffic traveling north and south, so it's always busy. By taxi, the trip from Deira to Dubai Marina takes about 45 minutes.

Dubai doesn't use building numbers in its street addresses. People navigate by referencing major hotels, roads, intersections, or other well-known landmarks. Taxi drivers know how to reach all the main attractions, but if you're looking for something off the beaten path—say, a particular specialty store—find out which hotel, mall, or other geographical marker is close to your destination. Direct your driver to that location, so he knows the general area to which you want to go.

# DEIRA AND THE NORTH BANK

Extending north of Dubai Creek—to the border of neighboring Sharjah—is a patchwork of tightly packed districts known by the name of its oldest area, Deira. The district, the historic core of Dubai, has been a commercial hub for rice, spice, and gold trading for more than a century. The traditional souks here, just as important as the city's

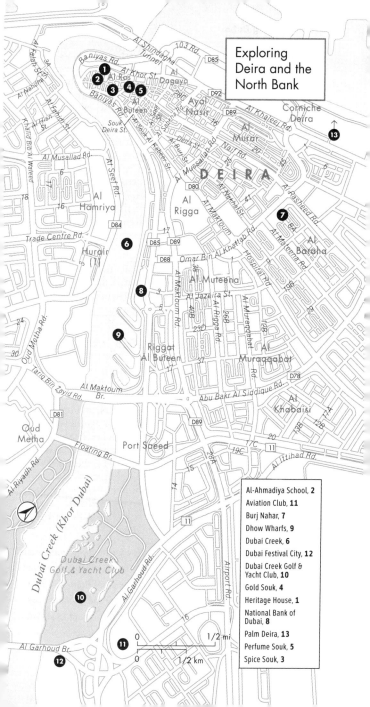

## Exploring Deira and the North Bank

Al-Ahmadiya School, **2**

Aviation Club, **11**

Burj Nahar, **7**

Dhow Wharfs, **9**

Dubai Creek, **6**

Dubai Festival City, **12**

Dubai Creek Golf &
Yacht Club, **10**

Gold Souk, **4**

Heritage House, **1**

National Bank of
Dubai, **8**

Palm Deira, **13**

Perfume Souk, **5**

Spice Souk, **3**

modern malls, make quite the contrast as customers haggle over merchandise and barrow-toting warehousemen weave through the crowds. In the Al Ras region, which abuts Deira to the west, you'll find some of Dubai's oldest historic buildings amongst the shops and commodity warehouses.

In recent years the Deira side has expanded dramatically, spreading to the east and southeast down Dubai Creek. Dubai's first high-rises define Al-Rigga, also known as the financial district, where banks and government buildings are staffed by Emiratis dressed in crisp *dishdashas* (tunics worn by Emirati men). The creek once defined Dubai, and although the city has spread and the modern heartbeat has drifted south, it's still the place to come to watch the last of the old boats doing business and to take a trip on a Dubai abra.

Head up the creek to the Garhoud and Festival City districts near the airport to enjoy central Dubai's first purpose-built community and the closest golf course to downtown.

---

## WHAT TO SEE

❷ **Al-Ahmadiya School.** A window to the past, this school was founded by Sheikh Mohammed bin Ahmed bin Dalmouk in 1912 and operated until 1962. But today it's been renovated and the classrooms have been laid out to look like they would have in the 1920s and 1930s. Some have a formal appearance with twin desks in neat rows, and others feature life-size figures of boys sitting cross-legged on the floor around the Al-Muttawa, or religious teacher. The building's structure, especially the central courtyard, is a fine example of Islamic architecture with delicate fluted arches. One wing has an interesting collection of sepia photographs depicting several generations of the Al Maktoum family and daily scenes from Dubai during the 20th century. ⊠ *Al Ras Rd., Al Ras (behind Heritage House)* ☎ *4/226–0286* ⊞ *AED 3* ☉ *Sat.–Thurs. 8 AM–9:30 PM, Fri. 2 PM–7:30 PM.*

**LESSONS LEARNED.** Until the mid-1930s education was dominated by religious studies and paid for by the family. When government funding was initiated, it became a universal right, and other subjects, including mathematics, astrology and grammar, were introduced. A formal curriculum was established in 1956, with further required topics such as English and science.

⓫ **The Aviation Club.** A social hub for the white-collar ex-pat community, the Aviation Club—complete with sporting facilities, spas, restaurants, and bars—is one of Dubai's leading places to relax and network. *For more information on individual attractions, see also ⇨Chapter 3, Where to Eat; ⇨Chapter 6, Nightlife & the Arts; and ⇨Chapter 7, Sports & The Outdoors. ⊠Off Sheikh Rashid Rd., Garhoud ☎4/282–4122.*

❼ **Burj Nahar.** The last surviving example of a series of inland-facing fortifications that protected Dubai city from attack by hostile desert tribes, this small self-contained mud and coral-stone *burj* (tower) has been swallowed up by modern development. You can drive past the ruins, but they are not open to the public. *⊠Omar bin al Khattab Rd., Naif.*

❾ **Dhow Wharfs.** Cooking oil heading for Somalia, refrigerators for Iran, and used cars for countries around the Gulf—all of these goods and more are piled high on wooden dhows at the commercial wharf. A stroll around the wharfs highlights Dubai's continued importance as a merchant city and offers insights into the low-tech trade that supplies much of the region, from the east coast of Africa to the west coast of the Indian subcontinent. This isn't a primped-up tourist attraction, it's a workaday dock. So be aware of trucks and lifting equipment operating in the area. *⊠Deira Waterfront close to the Bank of Dubai Building, Baniyas Rd., Al-Rigga.*

★ **Fodor'sChoice Dubai Creek and the Abra.** Without the creek,
❻ Dubai would not exist. This safe inlet, one of a few in the Gulf area, was the obvious choice for a commercial port for the sea-trade that funds the region. Dubai port developed into the natural focus for ocean traffic around the Gulf, to the west, and for boats from India and Africa. The waterfront bears little resemblance to its early years, because it's been dredged and widened several times during the 20th century. On the Deira bank near the creek mouth are a series of low-rise merchant districts that include the major souks. Further inland at Al-Rigga and Garhoud, the Deira creek front is home to the first modernist architecture that transformed the city from local hub into worldwide style icon. Dubai's abra, or water taxis, have been transporting people across the creek for as long as anyone can remember. Once powered by oars, tiny engines now push the 20-person wooden craft on the seven- or eight-minute crossing. Abras carried more than 27 million passengers in 2007. *⊠Two*

*stations on the Deira Waterfront (Baniyas Rd.) close to the Spice Souk and at Al Sabkha* ☎4/284–4444, 800–9090 *toll-free* ⊠*Abra fare AED 1* ⊙*Abra 24 hours.*

⑫ **Dubai Festival City.** The first of Dubai's megaprojects to enter
★ development stages, Dubai Festival City would be getting much more press if its more recent plans hadn't been so imaginative. The self-sustaining city—complete with living, shopping, sports, and entertainment quarters—is located on the north bank of Dubai Creek. The plan is to transform acres of natural tidal sahbka into a Mediterranean-style marina with a wide, 1.5-mi-long promenade for lengthy strolls. The city will feature cafés and eateries for alfresco dining, and the Festival Waterfront Centre shopping mall *(see ⇨Chapter 5, Shopping)*, which opened in late 2007. The main hotels that anchor the complex are ready for business and the residential sector is taking shape to the southwest of the mall and marina. ⊠*Festival Blvd., off Al Rebat St., south of Business Bay Bridge* ☎4/232–5444 ⊕*www.dubaifestivalcity.com* ⊙*Festival Waterfront Centre: daily 10–10.*

⑩ **Dubai Creek Golf & Yacht Club.** Designed by UK-based firm Godwin, Austen and Johnson and modeled after the billowing sails of a dhow catching the ocean breeze, the elegant clubhouse here was built around the same time as the headquarters of Ott's National Bank of Dubai—which marked Al Maktoum's first foray into cutting-edge architecture. It was the hit of the inaugural Dubai Desert Classic tournament and gained numerous admirers in the architectural community. The clubhouse has several eateries for all types of dining and is popular with white-collar expats—even those who don't golf—for lunch and dinner. ⊠*Off Baniyas Rd. at the junction with the floating bridge, Garhoud* ☎4/295–6000 ⊕*www.dubaigolf.com.*

★ **Fodor's**Choice **Gold Souk.** Take sunglasses when you visit the
❹ Gold Souk—no matter what time of day. The window displays shine with precious metals and cut stones that are so reflective they nearly strain your eyes. The Gold Souk is one of the world's most important jewelery trading centers, catering to customers from the Gulf region and beyond. Trade in gold reached $5.23 billion in the third quarter of 2007, and it's estimated that 20% of the world's gold stock passes through Dubai. Thirty-five percent of sales go to the domestic market, meaning visitors from all over the world purchase 65% of Dubai's gold. In a region where

the mobile Bedouin lifestyle was the norm until about a generation ago, gold is a precious commodity, with worth far beyond its beauty. Jewelry was a portable method of storing wealth, and gold still makes up part of a woman's wedding dowry in many societies in Africa, the Arabian Gulf, and India. Citizens of these countries flock to Dubai to buy gold because prices are some of the most competitive in the world. Gold is sold by weight here, based on daily rates, and precious stones cut and polished in Antwerp, Belgium, change hands for much less than they do in Europe.

It's fun to shop or browse here, and the souk is also great for people-watching, as it may be one of the world's most international marketplaces. ⊠*A maze of streets around Sikkat al-Khail St., Deira* ☎*4/352–6460 administrative offices* ⊕*www.dubaigoldsouk.com* ⊘*Most stores open daily 10* AM*–1* PM *and 4* PM*–10* PM.

**ALL THAT GLITTERS.** Pure gold is too soft to use for jewelry, so it is hardened by adding base metals to it, including copper (resulting in yellow gold) and palladium or nickel (producing white gold). The gold content of the finished alloy is measured in carats (k) with the purest commercial gold being 24k. The greater the alloy level, the lower the k value, all the way down through 22k, 18k, 14k, 10k, and 9k. Most of the gold sold in the Gold Souk is 22- or 18-carat quality.

**❶ Heritage House.** One of the few old buildings left north of the creek, Heritage House belonged to a wealthy merchant family and has been restored to mimic the local fashions of the mid–20th century. The oldest parts of this former home date from the 1890s, but the original structure was modest. In 1910, Heritage House was purchased by a family in the pearl-diving industry and expanded with profits from its business. Ibrahim al Said Abdullah bought the house in the 1930s, and it remained in his family until the Dubai government bought and renovated it during the 1990s.

Each room has a diorama depicting the traditional activities that would have taken place there, including life-size figures who appear focused on prayer, study, embroidery, or cooking over an open stove. Heritage House has re-created an *al hilja* (bride room), where a bride and her female relatives are staged in ritual wedding preparations. These customs continue today with a bride being bathed and painted in henna before being helped into her ornate trousseau and dowry jewelry. ⊠*Al Ras St.* ☎*4/226–0286* ⊠*AED 3* ⊙*Sat.–Thurs. 8 AM–8:30 PM, Fri. 2:30 PM–7:30 PM.*

**❽ National Bank of Dubai.** One of Dubai Creek's most recognizable buildings, the National Bank of Dubai was designed by Carlos Ott in the 1990s to redefine the financial district Al-Rigga. Ott used the graceful lines of a dhow sail as his inspiration and recreated its curve in a bronze curtain of glass that appears to billow in the breeze. The arched curtain looks as though it is suspended between two towers faced in granite—the masts—and the main banking hall is glazed in green glass representing the waters of the Gulf. ⊠*Baniyas Rd., Al-Rigga* ☎*4/310–0101 general banking* ⊙*Sat.–Thurs. 8 AM–2 PM.*

**CARLOS OTT.** Born in 1946 in Montevideo, Uruguay, Carlos Ott is one of the leading modernist architects of our time. After graduating from the University of Uruguay he received a Fulbright Scholarship and continued his studies in Hawaii and the Washington University School of Architecture in St. Louis. In 1983 he burst onto the international scene when he was chosen to design a Paris opera house on the site of the historic Bastille.

**⓭ Palm Deira.** The second in the trilogy of offshore Palm islands to break ground—or break water—Palm Deira aims to be the biggest man-made island in the world with a city of more than a million people when completed. It is scheduled to be seven times bigger than the original palm, Palm Jumeirah, a mind-boggling feat of engineering and logistics reaching 12.5 kilometers into the Gulf waters that will completely alter the north bank's coastline to the border with Sharjah. Palm Deira will comprise nine discrete but interconnected island districts. Work on raising the land above sea level will take place until 2013, after which the task of building the city will begin. ⊠*Off the Deira Corniche.*

**❺ Perfume Souk.** Scents play a significant role in Arab traditions. Burning herbs and incense fill a room or tent with fragrance, and natural essential oils are mixed to create perfumes for the body. Personal perfumes traditionally were a luxury for the rich and were stored in ornate bottles with tops fashioned from semiprecious stones. Even with today's international fragrance brands, you can still have your own scent mixed at the Perfume Souk. Spend time with the experienced perfumiers, as they can advise you on which oils are most suitable for your skin and lifestyle.

# The 4 C's

The price of diamonds is determined by four factors, also known as the 4 C's—color, cut, clarity, and carat weight.

Diamonds are cut into several styles, with the brilliant cut being the most common. But the "cut" category of the 4 C's doesn't actually deal with shape. Instead, it refers the diamond cutter's skill in working the stone, which allows it to sparkle as the light hits its faces.

"Clarity" relates to the number of flaws, or inclusions as they're called in the trade, a stone has. Very few diamonds have no inclusions, which are graded by size after examining the stone under a 10x magnification device called a loop. Some inclusions can be seen with the naked eye and these stones are considered to be the poorest quality for jewelry.

To the inexperienced eye all diamonds appear to be colorless or clear, but if they are laid side by side they do vary in color. The most prized diamonds are classed as colorless—D, E, and F on the diamond merchant's color scale—whereas V, W, and X have a yellowish hue and are less expensive.

Finally, the weight of a diamond also is fundamental to the price, and the stones are graded in carats (each carat being 0.2 grams). Larger diamonds are more rare than smaller diamonds, so on a simple scale they are more expensive. But when you take all 4 C's into account, you can see why a smaller, flawless, and colorless stone may be pricier than a larger, yellow-toned stone with obvious flaws.

⊠*Sikkat Al Khail Rd., abutting the Gold Souk* ⊙*Most shops daily 10* AM–*1* PM *and 4* PM–*10* PM.

❸ **Spice Souk.** Rare and expensive foodstuffs have been traded
★ in Dubai for well over a century. Today, the Spice Souk is still the most important of its type in the Gulf region, though much of the trade is done on a retail scale and deals are made in air-conditioned offices. The Spice Souk also caters to local domestic use and tourists searching for expensive and exotic ingredients to use in their kitchens back home. It's a small market but a stroll along the narrow alleyways takes you on an olfactory journey through the East, as aromas of pungent chili, cinnamon, and ginger mingle in the air. Saffron is the most prized culinary ingredient in the Spice Souk, but fragrant frankincense is the biggest seller. ⊠*Off Baniyas Rd., Deira* ⊙*Most shops daily 10* AM–*1* PM *and 4* PM–*10* PM.

FRANKINCENSE. Frankincense, or lubban as it's known in Arabic, is an aromatic resin harvested from the Boswellia tree. When the bark of the tree is cut, a sticky resin is secreted as a natural defense against insect infestation or infection. After the resin hardens, it is harvested and when burned gives off a strong aroma (and heavy smoke) that's been used as an air freshener since ancient times. It is particularly important in religious rites in the Christian Orthodox religion.

# BUR DUBAI AND THE SOUTH BANK

This area, a tightly packed residential and trading district, is known by the name of Bur Dubai, so if you hear people talking about the "Bur Dubai side" you'll know they mean the south side of the creek.

Most of Dubai's important historical attractions are located along the south bank, just a stone's throw from the creek. Fortifications, mansions, and the city's last remaining historic quarter are within easy reach of one another, and the largest downtown park is also on the south side. Bur Dubai is home to several busy souks, or markets, and bustling bazaars where you cannot miss the city's multicultural mix.

## WHAT TO SEE

❾ **Al Nasr Leisureland.** These mixed facilities stretch across 48 acres and are part private members club, part public venue, and part dining and entertainment. The sports provision is extensive and varied, with ice-skating, tennis, squash, swimming, bowling, and a fitness station. In the evening there is a program of shows and spectacles, including ice dance spectaculars; check local publications for up-to-date schedules. The Lodge nightclub is one of the city's hot spots. Restaurants are open for breakfast, brunch, lunch, and dinner. ⊠*Off Umm Hurair Rd., Oud Metha* ☎*4/337–1234* ⊕*www.alnasrll.com* ☏*Day admission, AED 10; fees for activities, shows, and spectacles priced individually* ⊗*Daily; all individual venues have different operating hours.*

★ **Fodor'sChoice Bastakia Quarter.** The only surviving historic
❽ district in Dubai, Bastakia (also spelled Bastakiya) almost fell victim to the demolition squads in the 1980s but now is the only place where visitors can get a real feel of what the emirate was like before developers moved in. The area first

2

## A GOOD TOUR

Start your tour at the Bur Dubai *abra* (boat) station with your back to the water. Walk to the north along the creek past several small cafés until the promenade widens for easy strolling. On the west side you'll find the strong stucco walls of **Sheikh Saeed Al Maktoum House,** the grandest of Dubai's historic houses, where you can explore traditional architecture and photographs of Dubai from the 1950s. Carry on along the creek-front promenade and you'll next reach the Heritage and Diving Villages with their folkloric displays.

Retrace your steps back along the creek front to take in the views upstream, and from the abra station walk half a block inland where you'll find the entrance to the **Textile Souk** to the west. Stroll along the alleyways that parallel the creek, peeking into the tourist stalls and textile shops until you reach the **Grand Mosque.** To the south of the mosque is Al Fahidi Fort, now the **Dubai Museum** where you will find life-size dioramas of traditional life. After leaving the fort, walk to the south to Al Fahidi Street and turn west along here for a couple of hundred feet to find the entrance to the **Bastakia Quarter,** where you can wander through the restored 19th-century district.

Take this tour at night if you like to see streets bustling with activity. Or, if you prefer a quieter environment, come in the afternoon when businesses are closed because of the heat.

If you want to take a break, **Basta Art Café** (✉*Bastakia Quarter, Bur Dubai* ☎*4/353-5071*) is the place to have a fresh juice or lunch. There's an open courtyard with shady trees and comfy Arabian sofas.

was settled in the early 19th century by a group of traders from Bastak in Persia, or today's Iran. The traders thrived here and built fine mansions for their families that flanked the lanes and alleyways. Today, these mansions and the connecting thoroughfares have been renovated to house attractions, galleries, souvenir shops, and cultural organizations. Look out for *barjeels,* traditional towers that top the plain stucco walls. If you visit Bastakia in the evening, there will be more going on. During the afternoons, most shops and attractions are closed, creating a much sleepier atmosphere. ✉*Bastakia, off Al Fahidi S.*

# Exploring Bur Dubai and the South Bank

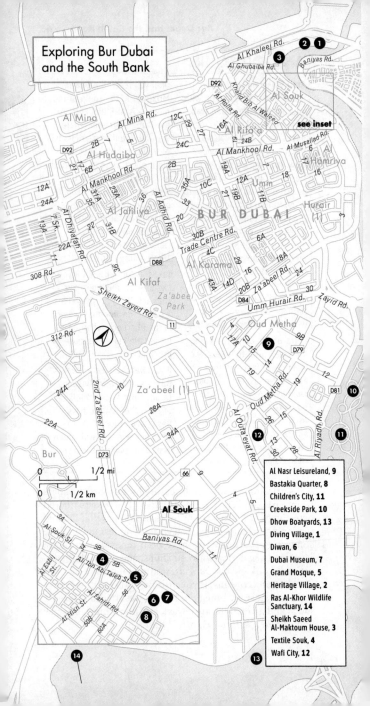

**Al Nasr Leisureland, 9**

**Bastakia Quarter, 8**

**Children's City, 11**

**Creekside Park, 10**

**Dhow Boatyards, 13**

**Diving Village, 1**

**Diwan, 6**

**Dubai Museum, 7**

**Grand Mosque, 5**

**Heritage Village, 2**

**Ras Al-Khor Wildlife Sanctuary, 14**

**Sheikh Saeed Al-Maktoum House, 3**

**Textile Souk, 4**

**Wafi City, 12**

**KEEPING COOL.** Barjeels are elegant, square towers that protrude from the top of traditional Emirati buildings, but they are not simply architectural elements—historically, they were used as a form of air-conditioning. The open-sided towers were designed to catch air movements and direct the cooler air into the ground-floor rooms of people's homes.

**⑪ Children's City.** As the first interactive educational discovery center in the United Arab Emirates, Children's City was opened in 2002 and offers fun activities for all ages. It's a great place for children to let off steam in air-conditioned comfort, especially when the summer heat is overwhelming. Many activities and displays are linked to school curriculum, focusing on science and nature—for example, some show the workings of the human body or explore the solar system. For young children, play and learning are intertwined with building bricks, sand pits, and water pools for tactile experiences. Children's City hosts special activity days and competitions throughout the year. ✉*Creekside Park (Gate 1 is closest to the Children's City entrance), Umm Hurair* ☎*4/334–0808* ⊕*www.children city.ae* 💲*Adults AED 15, children (ages 2 to 15) AED 10, family (2 adults and 2 children) AED 40* ⊙*Sat.–Thurs. 9 AM–8:30 PM, Fri. 3 PM–8:30 PM.*

**⑩ Creekside Park.** For high-rise views of the north bank's dramatic architecture, the cable car at Creekside Park (also known as Creek Park) is hard to beat. It's a stately 20-minute one-way journey that gives you a bird's-eye view of the park. This 221-acre green space is the largest in the downtown area and offers a 1.6-mi walk along Bur Dubai's creekside, a botanical garden, manicured flower beds, and stretches of shady lawns where families gather on weekends for fresh air and a picnic (barbecue cooking pits are located in certain areas throughout the park). Almost 300 plant species flourish here, and you can tour on foot or by minitrain. ✉*Several entrances off Riyadh Road, Umm Hurair* ☎*4/336–7633* 💲*AED 5* ⊙*Daily 8 AM–11 PM; Wed. only women admitted.*

**⑬ Dhow Boatyards.** The graceful wooden dhow is the staple craft of the Gulf region and has been for centuries—and Dubai has always been a center of construction for the vessel. Today most goods are imported in containers on large modern ships, but a few dhows still are created by hand along the banks of Dubai Creek. Each dhow builder eyes the length and width of wooden planks needed to create the curving shape of the bow, then produces it with no plans and few modern tools. Dubai's dhow-building yards occupy a valuable stretch of creek waterfront, so it remains to be seen how long the trade will continue here. Be sure to watch your step if you visit the yards. They aren't common tourist attractions and wood, tools, and other items are often left lying around. ⊠*Off Sheikh Rashid Road, Jaddaf* ☉*Daily dawn–dusk.*

❶ **The Diving Village.** Pearl diving was the driving force behind Dubai's first economic boom at the start of the 20th century. The dangerous but lucrative business is explored here, along with other sea-related activities, including boatbuilding and ship repair. Call ahead and visit the village when net mending and boat repairs are going on (they aren't well publicized), as there may be little in the permanent displays to hold your attention apart from photographs of old fishermen. ⊠*Shindagha waterfront* ☎*4/393–7151* ⊠*Free* ☉*Sat.–Thu. 8 AM–10 PM, Fri. 8 AM–11 AM and 4 PM–10 PM.*

**ANATOMY OF A PEARL.** When a grain of sand or some small piece of detritus becomes trapped inside the shell of an oyster, the oyster has a unique way of dealing with the invader. It coats the offending grain with layers of nacre (or mother-of-pearl), and as the layers increase it becomes a pearl. Cultured pearls are produced in exactly the same way as natural pearls, but the grain at the heart of the pearl is deliberately placed in the oyster rather than letting the process occur naturally.

❻ **Diwan.** A low-rise, traditional-style modern complex that abuts Dubai Creek and the Bastakia Quarter, the Diwan (or Ruler's Court) is the main meeting place for several government bodies. The architecture dates back to the Mamluk Islamic period, found across North Africa and the Arabian Gulf, from the 13th to the 16th century. This building is not open to the public. ⊠*Shindagha waterfront* ☎*4/353–1060.*

★ **Fodor'sChoice Dubai Museum.** The tiny Al Fahidi fort was built ❼ in 1787 to protect the port from marauding landward tribes and seafaring pirates. During the 20th century the fort fell into disrepair, but the coral stone and stucco walls were restored, and today it hosts Dubai's national museum. Upon entering the museum, you step back in time to before the discovery of oil and the arrival of container ships. A series of cleverly designed subterranean spaces take you through the daily life of Dubai's past. For instance, you can stroll through a life-size re-creation of the creekside wharfs and souks, where lifelike figures include fishermen, pearl traders, spice merchants, and metal workers. The sights and sounds of different trades come to life in original sound tracks that play in the background, and with the help of projected images, life-size figures appear as though they're performing tasks. Here, you can feel the excitement and energy of what was once one of the Arab world's most exciting port towns. The final series of galleries, before the gift shop and museum exit, holds cases of artifacts found on archaeological digs around the emirate. The earliest ones date from the 3rd millennium BC, and include human remains from ritual burials and such grave goods as spearheads. ⊠*Al Fahidi Fort, Al Fahidi St., Bur Dubai* ☎*4/353–1862* ⊟*AED 3* ☽*Sat.–Thurs. 8:30–8:30, Fri. 2:30 PM–8:30 PM.*

❺ **Grand Mosque.** Dubai's largest mosque bustles with local traders taking time out from their work to make the call to prayer. Located on the boundary of the Textile Souk, the unadorned sandstone walls don't advertise the building's purpose. It's only the line of shoes left outside by worshippers that indicate it is a mosque. However, the minaret is a better marker—it's the tallest in downtown Dubai. Unfortunately, only Mulims may enter. ⊠*In front of Dubai Museum, Bur Dubai.*

❷ **Heritage Village.** This government-funded attraction mimics daily life from a generation or two ago by re-creating a number of traditional Arab Bedouin activities. One of the more vibrant atmospheres you'll encounter here is the desert camp, where numerous sounds and smells will assail you. Watch as the ladies do embroidery and the men work metal while you eat skewers of meat that were cooked over coals and sip from cups of sweet mint tea. Shepherds watch over their flocks of desert sheep, and others in traditional dishdasha tend camels or prepare falcons for a hunt. On Arabic feast days and each night during Ramadan, the Heritage Village puts on a feast fit for the sheikhs with traditional dancing and fine foods. However, visit at the wrong time—particularly during the afternoon any time of year— and you may see only a tacky tourist souk. ⊠*Shindagha waterfront* ☎*4/393–7151* ⊟*Free* ☽*Sat.–Thurs. 8 AM–10 PM, Fri. 8 AM–11 AM, 4 PM–10 PM.*

**⓮ Ras al-Khor Wildlife Sanctuary.** As the only remaining expanse of natural creekside landscape in the emirate, Ras al-Khor (meaning "head of the creek") is an important desert wetland habitat. The sanctuary (also called Ras al Khawr) covers only 2.4 square miles, and its tidal wetlands, mudflats, mangroves, reed beds, and stretches of *sabkha* (salt-encrusted flats common to the coastline) are the last refuge for many native plants and animals. Most important, Ras al-Khor is an important over-wintering ground more than 250 bird species, several of which can be found here in "important numbers," or more than 1% of the global population according to scientists. Overall bird numbers can reach 30,000 between December and March. The small year-round population of flamingos found here is often shown on publicity images touting Dubai's eco-credentials, but the sanctuary boundaries are under strain from surrounding development—particularly The Lagoons project, which includes a city set on natural waterways. In 2007, the Ras al-Khor Wildlife Sanctuary was added to the list of important wetland areas that should be preserved. Three hides, or camouflaged shelters, have been erected at points around the park, and a visitor center is on the way. To visit the site now you need a permit from the Environmental Department of Dubai Municipality. ✉*Oud Metha Road, Ras al-Khor district* ☎*4/206–3631 Dubai Municipality, 4/800–900 toll-free* ✆*Free* ☉*Daily dawn–dusk.*

**RAMSAR.** Wetlands are some of the world's most vulnerable ecosystems, as coastal landscapes are swallowed up for development and inland flood plains are drained for farming. The Convention on Wetlands of International Importance especially as Waterfowl Habitat, better known as the Ramsar Convention, was signed in Ramsar in Iran in 1971 to protect rare habitats and raise awareness of global good practices in wetland protection. Today more than 1,700 separate sites totaling 58 million square miles are protected, and 157 countries have signed a commitment to the Ramsar protocol.

**❸ Sheikh Saeed Al Maktoum House.** This late-19th-century palace
★ overlooks Dubai Creek and was the epicenter of power until the mid–20th century, as the former home of Sheikh Saeed Al Maktoum, grandfather of the present sheikh, who ruled the emirate from 1912 until his death in 1958. The house was a *majlis*, or meeting place, where all major court decisions were made. Sheikh Saeed Al Maktoum House was

## National Dress

Dress codes in Dubai are the most liberal in the Gulf region, but Emiratis still maintain a modest appearance in public. Women wear the *abaya*, a full-length loose-fitting dress or light coat (traditionally black in color) and cover their hair with a *hajab*, a scarf that wraps around the neck and leaves the face exposed. The *niqab* (face veil) is not required in the UAE, but some women do choose to wear it, including females visiting from more conservative Arab countries. Traditional male dress is the *kandura* (known locally as a *dishdasha*), an ankle-length, long-sleeved garment usually made of white cotton. Completing the ensemble is a *kaffiyeh* (white headdress of cotton fabric) held in place by a rope (*agal*). Traditionally the agal was used during the night to hobble a camel and during the day to keep the kaffiyeh secured to the head.

restored in 1986 and offers Dubai's last example of traditional large-scale, high-quality domestic architecture. All the rooms open off a large courtyard and each is decorated with fine carpets, furniture, and life-size figures performing what were common tasks. The upper galleries offer excellent views down the creek, where you can imagine the sheikh surveying the land and waterfront quays.

Aside from its noteworthy architectural elements, Sheikh Saeed Al Maktoum House also holds several interesting collections. Two wings of the house have been converted into galleries that display photographs of Dubai taken throughout the 20th century. The Al Maktoum Wing holds mainly images from the late 1940s and early 1950s, many of which chart projects that brought Dubai into the technological age. In contrast, those in the Marine Wing document the final era of the old ways, including the last of Dubai's pearl divers. Sheikh Saeed Al Maktoum House also displays a coin, stamp, and document collection. Examples date back to the early Trucial States and Dubai's first-issued postage stamps. ⊠*Shindagha waterfront* ☎*4/393–7139* ⊠*AED 3* ☉*Sat.–Thurs. 8 AM–8:30 PM, Fri. 3 PM–8:30 PM.*

❹ **Textile Souk.** No matter what you need material for—curtains, a business suit, or a fancy ball gown—this souk has it all. Hundreds of tiny neighboring shops with thick wooden shutters showcase samples of their speciality materials in doorways and on walls. Most of the fabric comes from India and China, and includes quality cottons for the Emirati dishdasha and sheer bejewelled fabrics for the colorful saris worn by Hindu women. You can order a full skein of cloth to take home. Or if there's a favorite garment you'd like to duplicate, you can have one made from your chosen fabric within a couple of days. Numerous stalls on the fringes of the souk sell kitschy souvenirs, from sequined slippers to belly-dancing outfits, and colorful imports from India add to the allure. ☎No phone ☉Most shops daily 10 AM –1 PM and 4 PM –10 PM.

**⑫ Wafi City.** Dubai's first self-contained city within a city, Wafi City is a small-scale urban development known for its shopping and entertainment offerings for tourists. The complex draws inspiration from ancient Egypt, with decorative duplicates of monumental statues of Pharaoh Ramses II, papyrus-themed columns, and hieroglyphs, the most dramatic of which is the colossal glass-sided pyramid housing the Raffles Dubai hotel. The Wafi City Mall (*for more information, see the listing under Bur Dubai & the South Bank in Chapter 5, Shopping*) is the main attraction with the entire third floor dedicated to the Encounter Zone, a children's entertainment complex with specific areas for kids 9 years old or under and for those over 10. In addition, there's a spot for video games and a rollerblading arena. The Fort, a neighboring development, has more restaurants and a number of nightclubs, and is popular with expats after dark. ☒*Sheikh Rashid Rd., Umm Hurair* ☎*4/324–4426.*

# JUMEIRAH BEACH

Dubai's beach strip runs 11 mi south from Bur Dubai to the new developments around Dubai Marina. For years this stretch of sand was an unappreciated treasure used only by fishermen, but it became a major weapon in Dubai's arsenal when the emirate started luring tourists. The first sun worshippers—mostly northern Europeans escaping cold winter months—soon began to flock here.

Commonly known in the brochures as Jumeirah (also Jumeira) because of its northernmost district, the strip has lengthened over time to include neighboring Umm Suqeim and Al Sufouh to the south, and the newest and largest hotels are located at the southern end, farthest away from downtown.

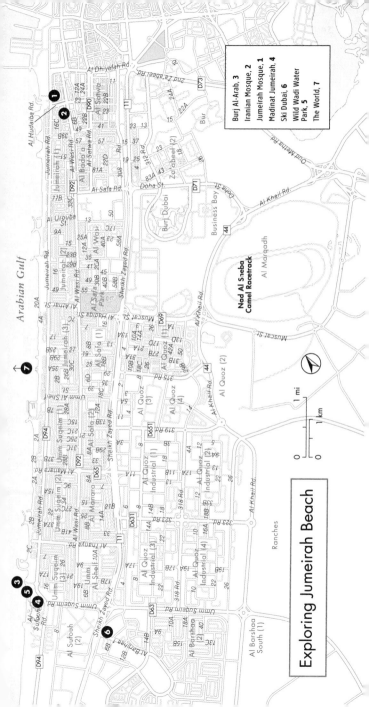

# Exploring Jumeirah Beach

**Burj Al-Arab, 3**
**Iranian Mosque, 2**
**Jumeirah Mosque, 1**
**Madinat Jumeirah, 4**
**Ski Dubai, 6**
**Wild Wadi Water Park, 5**
**The World, 7**

Arabian Gulf

Nad Al Sheba Camel Racetrack

Al Marqadh

Business Bay

Burj Dubai

Al Quoz (2)

Al Quoz (3)

Al Quoz (4)

Al Quoz Industrial (1)

Al Quoz Industrial (2)

Al Quoz Industrial (3)

Al Quoz Industrial (4)

Al Barshaa (2)

Al Barshaa South (1)

Al Sufouh (2)

Ranches

0   1 mi
0   1 km

Jumeirah's large resort hotels are a huge tourist draw, with high-quality restaurants, exciting nightlife, and private beach clubs that have first-rate sports facilities on and off the water. The low-rise residential districts that back the beach are popular with Western expats, and you'll find a range of smaller malls, independent spas, boutiques, and restaurants here.

## WHAT TO SEE

★ Fodor'sChoice **Burj Al-Arab.** The building of Burj Al-Arab put
❸ Dubai on the map. The hotel has triumphed since its opening in 1999, and its curved exterior has been featured on the covers of numerous design magazines. Sheikh Mohammed wasted no time in exploiting the furor created by Burj Al-Arab, with well-funded advertising campaigns intended to woo the world. Designed by Thomas Wills Wright of Atkins Group, the metal and glass structure that is perched on a small, artificial offshore island posed several engineering conundrums for its constructors.

The graceful curves, designed to mimic wind caught in the sails of a dhow, are beautiful and unique, but it's the interior of Burj Al-Arab that's caught the notice of travelers. It is said to be the world's first 7-star hotel, but its owner (Jumeirah Hotels) insists that it's only 5-Star Luxe—the highest possible quality under the current rating system.

Inside the hotel is one of the world's tallest atriums at 590 feet. A sumptuous decor designed by Kuan Chew of KCA International blends rich blues, reds, and greens with acres of gilt. Head to the Skyview Bar for exceptional views of the coastline, including Palm Jumeirah and The World. Even if you don't stay here, come for lunch, tea, cocktails, or dinner; however, you must have proof of a confirmed reservation at a restaurant or bar in order to gain admittance (no exceptions). ✉*Jumeirah Rd., Jumeirah 2* ☎*4/301–7777.*

❷ **Iranian Mosque.** Although not open to the public, this mosque is worth visiting to see the exquisite enamel and ceramic decoration blanketing the dome and facade. The Islamic style is displayed in Persian influences of flower motifs and an onion-shaped dome, constrasting with the Jumeirah Mosque (*see below*), which is only a few blocks to the west. ✉*Top of Al Wasl Rd., Jumeirah 1.*

★ FodorśChoice **Jumeirah Mosque.** The finest *masjid* (mosque)
❶ in Dubai, Jumeirah Mosque pays homage to the classical architectural style favored by Cairo's Egyptian rulers during Islam's first Golden Age at the end of the first millennium. The sandstone dome and minarets feature detailed carvings, while the interior is covered with ornately painted panels on robin's-egg blue backgrounds. Jumeirah Mosque is the only one in Dubai open to non-Muslims, but to gain entrance you must take a guided tour organized by the Sheikh Mohammed Centre for Cultural Understanding in Bastakia. Wear conservative clothing that covers the shoulders, midriff, and upper thighs. ⊠*Jumeirah Road, Jumeirah 1* ☎*4/353–6666 Sheikh Mohammed Centre for Cultural Understanding* ⊒*Free* ⊙*Guided tours Sat., Sun., Tues. and Thurs. 10* AM.

★ FodorśChoice **Madinat Jumeirah.** Translating to Jumeirah City
❹ in Arabic, Madinat Jumeirah is a vast resort that pays homage to the best of classical Islamic architecture and art. It comprises three hotels, a mall, and an entertainment district—all of which are set amongst a series of artificial canals and lush greenery.

Souk Madinat, a beautifully designed bazaar of narrow alleyways, takes the best aspects of a traditional souk with lots of small stalls piled high with tempting souvenirs, and adds an extra element of comfort—air-conditioning. Art, carpets, and furniture are high quality here, but the prices reflect this and are rarely negotiable.

Madinat Jumeirah's waterfront is a great stopover for a lazy lunch or long dinner. Restaurants and bars line both sides of the canal promenade and many have liquor licenses, so you can enjoy a glass of wine or a cocktail as you relax in the balmy air and watch the social set stroll by. The complex looks especially appealing after dark when soft lighting illuminates the pastel stucco, barjeels, and cobbled courtyards. ⊠*Top of Al Sufouh Rd., Al Sufouh* ☎*4/366–8888 Souk* ⊕*www.madinatjumeirah.com* ⊒*Free* ⊙*Souk open daily 10* AM *–10* PM.

❻ **Ski Dubai.** As the third-largest covered ski park in the world
⟳ (22,500 square feet), Ski Dubai caused a wave of excitement to spread through the Gulf region when it opened in 2005. The hill is a mountain resort in miniature with five runs of varying difficulty, including the first indoor black-diamond slope and a snow park for kids and nonskiers. If you aren't up for playing in the snow, relax at one of

the two cafés in the complex. Ski Dubai does not allow inexperienced skiers on the slopes, so if you have trouble stopping, controlling your speed, or using a chairlift, you'll have to take a lesson. ⊠*Mall of the Emirates, Sheikh Zayed Rd.* ☎*4/409–4000* ⊕*www.skidxb.com* ⊠*Snow park: all ages AED 70; ski slope 2-hour pass: adult (13+) AED 150, child AED 130; ski slope day pass: all ages AED 270; prices include equipment and clothing rental* ⊙*Sun.–Wed. 10 AM–11 PM (last ticket 9:30 PM), Thurs.–Sat. 10 AM–midnight (last ticket 10:30 PM).*

**❺ Wild Wadi Water Park.** Dubai's premier water park, Wild Wadi covers 12 acres and abuts Jumeirah Beach in the shadow of the Burj Al-Arab hotel. There are 30 rides and other watery attractions here, including Jumeirah Scierah (a 50-mph, high-adrenaline chute) and artificial wave rides (Riptide Flowrider and The Wipeout) that were designed by industry leader Thomas Lochtefel. Wild Wadi Water Park has its own artificial beach at Breakers Bay, and the whole family can ride a huge rubber ring down Rushdown Ravine. ⊠*Jumeirah Rd., Jumeirah 2* ☎*4/348–4444* ⊠*AED 180 (over 3.6 feet), AED 150 (under 3.6 feet)* ⊙*June–Aug., daily 11 AM–9 PM; Sept.–Oct. and Mar.–May, 11 AM–7 PM; Nov.–Feb., 11 AM–6 PM.*

**❼ The World.** Riding out his success with real estate sales on Palm Jumeirah, Nakheel (the developer) launched The World, a series of 300 artificial offshore islands shaped like various continents, countries, and cities, each surrounded by its own pristine beach. The project targets the super-rich, offering them ownership of a private island where they can create their dream home. Several luxury island resorts are included among the private domains, but with no road linking them to the mainland they're as exclusive as you can get.

The skeleton structures of The World islands were completed in January 2008 and about half of the real estate has now been sold. In addition, Nakheel has announced it will invest in Coral Island—a residential and resort community surrounding a tropical marina and beach—and an Irish consortium is building an "emerald isle"–themed development. However, details about the purchasers of private islands remain a closely guarded secret. ⊠*Offshore, Jumeirah Beach.*

# WORLD TRADE CENTRE AND BURJ DUBAI

Dubai's newly developed business district stretches along a few miles of Sheikh Zayed Road, from Za'abeel Roundabout south to Interchange 1. Cutting-edge towers flank both sides of the multilane highway. These architectural triumphs, pictured in numerous media, have come to symbolize modern Dubai. The view is especially impressive after dark when the towers are lit up—some, including the Fairmont Hotel, have light shows that play across their facades.

Luxury hotels line the strip, making it a hot spot for entertainment and nightlife. The Dubai International Convention and Exhibition Centre (often called simply the Dubai World Trade Centre) is the heartbeat of the district, and it often teams with people. Work continues on Dubai's latest construction phenomenon, Burj Dubai, just south of Interchange 1, which is set to redefine high-rise living and rewrite the record books.

## WHAT TO SEE

★ **Fodor's**Choice **Burj Dubai.** The world's newest tallest building
❷ dominates the Dubai skyline like a scimitar pointing skyward. Emaar Properties has vowed to keep the final height of its latest development a secret, but the structure had reached an astonishing 2064 feet, or 629 meters, by April 2008. Designed by Adrian Smith of Skidmore, Owings and Merrill, Burj Dubai will house a mixture of commercial and residential spaces, as well as the first Armani Hotel, which will occupy the first 37 floors of the building. The building (not open to the public at this writing) will be the focus of the new 500-acre Downtown Burj Dubai community. The urban business, residential, and entertainment district will house the soon-to-open Dubai Mall—the largest in the world at more than 12 million square feet—and several low-rise, Arabic-styled residential communities. ⌂*Downtown Burj Dubai, off Sheikh Zayed Road* ☎4/362–7600 ⏣*www.burjdubai.com.*

DID YOU KNOW? The tip of the spire that sits atop Burj Dubai can be seen from 60 mi away.

❸ **Emirates Towers.** These twin skyscrapers, located in Dubai's
★ business district, added an extra dimension to the city's

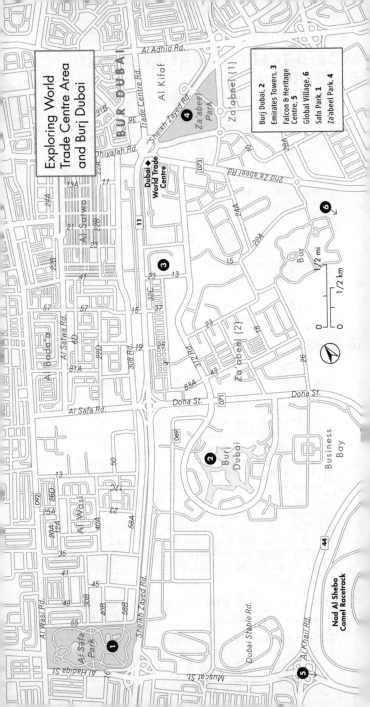

**Exploring World Trade Centre Area and Burj Dubai**

Burj Dubai, **2**
Emirates Towers, **3**
Falcon & Heritage Centre, **5**
Global Village, **6**
Safa Park, **1**
Za'abeel Park, **4**

dynamic architecture when they opened at the turn of the millennium. Architect Hazel Wong of the Norr Group drew her inspiration from the triangle—as a structure and also a repeating shape in Islamic astronomy that reflects the relative positions of the earth, moon, and sun. One tower is dedicated to office space—Sheikh Mohammed had a personal office here before his appointment—and the other hosts the luxurious Emirates Towers Hotel, where the bar on the 51st floor has dramatic long-distance views. The towers are anchored by an upscale mall and entertainment area called Boulevard, a see-and-be-seen spot for the city's movers and shakers. ⊠*Sheikh Zayed Road, Trade Centre district* ☎*Emirates Towers Hotel: 4/330–0000.*

❺ **Falcon & Heritage Centre.** Hunting with falcons and keeping birds of prey is a common pastime in Arabic desert culture. This center is the only place in Dubai where birds may be legally sold. It's also a one-stop shop for all a falconer's needs, including dietary supplements, books, hoods, and lures. Most of the 20 or so stores in the center also have a range of birds on show, and you can learn about them from the knowledgeable store owners. ⊠*Muscat Street, Nad al-Sheba* ☎*4/338-0201* ⊙*Sat.–Thurs. 9–1 and 4–10.*

**DIVING DETERRENT.** You may be surprised to hear this, but falcons aren't only used for hunting. They also play a vital role in keeping construction sites safe in Dubai. Trained falcons are often allowed to fly through high-rise building projects, as they are being erected, to deter pigeons and other birds from dropping their waste—as corrosive and slippery droppings may pose a danger to the workers on-site.

❻ **Global Village.** Winter in Dubai brings about many events, but none are more colorful than those at the Global Village. Every year, delegates from more than 30 countries and regions come together in this vast venue southeast of downtown for the largest cultural festival in the emirate. Each country hosts a pavilion that's full of local handicrafts and stalls offering traditional foodstuffs. Folkloric and fireworks displays take place every night, and a huge amusement park is on-site. ⊠*Emirates Road, Dubailand* ☎*4/362–4114* ⊕*www.globalvillage.ae* ⊒*AED 5* ⊙*Dec.–late Feb. (dates change slightly each year) Sat.–Wed. 4 PM–midnight, Thurs.–Fri. 4 PM–1 AM (Mon. admission restricted to families with children).*

**❶ Safa Park.** Encompassing nearly 160 acres of parkland in one of Dubai's well-to-do residential neighborhoods, this park provides city dwellers with an open green space. First opened in 1975, the facilities have been upgraded to include basic amenities, including restrooms and cafés. Arabic, European-style, and Oriental gardens are scattered around three generous lakes. Clusters of mature trees and grassy lawns invite visitors to relax on blankets or folding chairs, an indoor fair has a selection of rides, and a section of the park is reserved for ladies and children only. Check out the park on the jogging track or sit back and take the minitrain around. ✉*Access from Al Wasi Road, Al Hadiqa Street* ☎*4/349–2111* 💲*AED 3* ⊙*Daily 8 AM–11PM.*

**❹ Za'abeel Park.** This technology-themed park, also known as Zabeel Park, is located between the Trade Centre district and the highly populated Kerama district. It opened in 2005 and spans 116 acres of the northernmost part of Sheikh Zayed Road. Various sections of the park are linked together by footbridges and a minitrain. Final touches to the Stargate Entertainment Centre and Alternate Energy Zone are still in progress, but most people come to enjoy the standard park attractions—including walking and cycling paths, tennis courts, cricket pitches, and other ballparks. Other visitors just sit and enjoy the ornamental gardens and ponds, or have lunch at the lakeside restaurant. Some of the park's vegetation is still immature, but the trees are growing and the increasing shade is sure to attract more people as time goes on. ✉*Access roads off Za'abeel Roundabout or Sheikh Khalifa bin Zayed Street* ☎*4/398–6888* 💲*AED 5* ⊙*Thurs.–Sat. 8 AM–11:30 PM, Sun.–Wed. 8 AM–11 PM.*

**TALLEST OF THE BUNCH.** There's no hard and fast rule that differentiates a tall building from a really tall one. However, the Council on Tall Buildings and Urban Habitat measures buildings based on the following criteria: 1) height to the architectural top; 2) height to the highest occupied floor; 3) height to the top of the roof; 4) height to the top of any appendage (for example, an antenna). Of course, Burj Dubai currently holds the record in all categories.

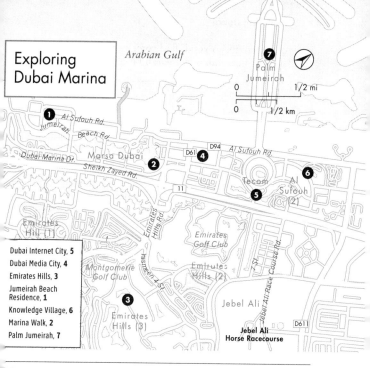

### Exploring Dubai Marina

*Arabian Gulf*

Palm Jumeirah

Al Sufouh Rd.
Jumeirah Beach Rd.
Dubai Marina Dr. Marsa Dubai
Sheikh Zayed Rd.

Tecom
Al Sufouh [2]

Emirates Hill [1]

Emirates Golf Club

Dubai Internet City, **5**
Dubai Media City, **4**
Emirates Hills, **3**
Jumeirah Beach Residence, **1**
Knowledge Village, **6**
Marina Walk, **2**
Palm Jumeirah, **7**

Montgomerie Golf Club

Emirates Hills [2]

Emirates Hills [3]

Jebel Ali

Jebel Ali Horse Racecourse

Jebel Ali Race Course Rd.

0    1/2 mi
0    1/2 km

# DUBAI MARINA

The world's largest man-made marina and waterfront development, Dubai Marina's 50 million square feet changed the face of the southern end of Jumeirah Beach and started a real-estate boom that has yet to peak. It was the first venture in which freehold real estate could be bought by anyone from anywhere around the globe. The Marina is home to 200 high-rise towers that have become an entertainment, leisure, and business hub, which locals call "new Dubai."

In addition, a series of specialized free-zone "cities" and "villages" have sprung up around the Marina since the turn of the millennium, as part of Dubai's long-term plan to become one of the world's foremost investment, research, and enterprise zones. An impressive selection of Fortune 500 companies have their Middle East, Africa, and India headquarters here, and many more are sure to follow.

Be aware that the man-made inlets to Dubai Marina have separated the southern tip of Jumeirah Beach from the main coastal strip, so you'll find some of the older hotels here still use Jumeirah or Jumeirah Beach in their titles.

## WHAT TO SEE

**❺ Dubai Internet City.** A center for software development, e-commerce, consulting, and sales, Dubai Internet City offers a top-of-the-line business platform. Microsoft, Cisco Systems, IBM, Dell, and Siemens all have office suites here surrounding the complex's pristine lawns and fountains. ✉*Off Sheikh Zayed Rd., Interchange 55* ☎*4/391–1111.*

**❹ Dubai Media City.** A regional hub for businesses of all types, Dubai Media City is a one-stop shop for projects in printing, publishing, broadcast, advertising, film, music, and new media. CNN and Reuters are present here, along with hundreds of smaller companies. ✉*Off Al Sufouh Rd., Al Sufouh 1* ☎*4/391–4555.*

**❸ Emirates Hills.** To the east of Sheikh Zayed Road, inland from the Marina area, is Emirates Hills, a spacious residential area favored by families looking for fresh air and a slower pace. The verdant districts are well planned with ample lakes, canals, and fine single-family homes. Emirates Hills is known for its golf courses, which include the eponymous Emirates Golf Club and The Montgomerie, designed by golf professional Colin Montgomerie. ✉*Off Interchange 5, Sheikh Zayed Rd.*

**❶ Jumeirah Beach Residence.** The largest single-building project on the seaward side of Dubai Marina and, according to the developer, the biggest single-phase construction project in the world, this residence offers 6,500 apartments in 36 high-rise blocks. At the base of the rather dour-looking towers, lies The Walk at Jumeirah Beach Residence, a 770,000-square-foot mall and entertainment complex that will hold such community facilities as gyms, movie theaters, and spas. The Walk at Jumeirah Beach Residence will be the social heart of Dubai Marina island. ✉*Al Sufouh Rd., Dubai Marina* ☎*4/391–1114 sales center.*

**❻ Knowledge Village.** This development, opened in 2003, is a self-contained community designed to promote high academic and research opportunities for the Gulf region. More than 350 learning institutions have set up facilities here, including India's Mahatma Gandhi University, Britain's Manchester Business School, and the University of Wollongong in Australia. They recognize the work of local students and provide cross-cultural programs in a variety of academic subjects. The complex also includes research-and-development organizations, "e-learning" companies, conference amenities, and residential districts with cafés and shops. ⊠*The Wide Rd., Off Al Sufouh Rd., Al Sufouh 1* ☎*4/391–0000 help desk.*

❷ **Marina Walk.** The landward side of Dubai Marina has a
★ 7-mi-long waterside promenade that brings outdoor living to the area. European-style boutiques, cafés, and restaurants—great for daytime browsing—become a see-and-be-seen atmosphere at dusk. Think the passeggiata in Italy or the paseo in Spain. The Dubai Marina community holds regular events such as weekly craft markets on Friday and Saturday mornings throughout the winter (October–April). Further attractions are sure to draw more people when the southern end of Marina Walk is completed near the end of 2008. ⊠*Dubai Marina.*

❼ **Palm Jumeirah.** Dubai's first foray into large-scale coastline
★ extension, Palm Jumeirah caught the world's attention when plans were announced in 2001. The development was Sheikh Mohammed Al Maktoum's solution to the area's shortage of beachfront and was created by taking land from the seabed to build new communities. Shaped as a date palm tree for its role as a provider of shelter and food, the 1.2-mi-long trunk protrudes from the mainland and its 17 palm fronds sit in a shallow lagoon surrounded by a protective outer edge or canopy. Palm Jumeirah is a self-contained residential district that combines private villas and apartments with luxury hotels, shopping, and entertainment districts. The first owners took possession of their Palm Jumeirah properties in the summer of 2006 and in September 2007 more than 1,000 "frond" villas were given to clients. The entire project will be completed by 2009. ⊠*Off Al Sufouh Rd., Al Sufouh 1.*

# Where to Eat

**WORD OF MOUTH**

"I visited Dubai last November, and had dinner at Al Mahara [in the Burj al-Arab] – I arrived a little early and had a cocktail at the SkyBar. The food was excellent, and they will give you a fish guide – so you can identify what's swimming in the very large tank."

—thit_cho

By Lindsay
Bennett

**THE DUBAI FOOD SCENE** is one of the world's most diverse. Approximately 180 nationalities live in the emirate, so you can munch your way around the world during your trip. With the exception of maybe Antarctica, every other continent has several restaurants that represent its fare, and eateries run the gamut from refined cuisine by the world's most renowned chefs to mouthwatering snacks from street vendors.

The upper end of the market measures up against the New York and San Francisco dining scenes, as top-tier hotels vie to create authentic cuisine in beautifully styled restaurants. No half measures here. The finest ingredients wing their way around the world to be transformed into culinary tours de force. These restaurants cater to a regular clientele of discerning Western expats with fat tax-free salaries. For them, eating out and entertaining is a natural part of everyday life. Power lunches and dinners are big business and often big budget, meaning prices are high by American standards.

However, you can eat well and quite cheaply if you follow the blue-collar expat workers—hundreds of thousands of Filipinos, Indians, and Pakistanis—to basic, clean, and always friendly eateries for plates full of curry, rice, or noodles.

The restaurant scene here changes almost daily, and it's as image-conscious as a Hollywood starlet posing for the paparazzi. The latest favorites are open kitchens and cooking stations, multicuisine eateries where you can graze on, say, Japanese, Italian, and Lebanese dishes. Also a big hit are tapas-style meals where several small dishes arrive at one time rather than the standard appetizer and entrée.

### ABOUT THE RESTAURANTS

Even though Dubai is a Muslim country, you'll be able to find pork products and alcohol. Alcohol is only available at licensed restaurants and bars, which usually are found in international hotels. But be prepared to hand over a pile of cash, as wine list prices start at about $40 a bottle, beer at $7 a glass, and cocktails at about $12. Fresh fruit juices are a less-expensive and delicious option.

High-class dining spots are scattered throughout the city near international hotels, with a concentration in and around the World Trade Centre and southern Jumeirah Beach. For lower-priced meals, you'll find good options close to the major shopping malls. For low-budget eateries, the districts of Deira and Bur Dubai offer the best range.

| WHAT IT COSTS IN UNITED ARAB EMIRATES DIRHAMS (AED) | | | | |
|---|---|---|---|---|
| ¢ | $ | $$ | $$$ | $$$$ |
| RESTAURANTS | | | | |
| Under AED 35 | AED 36– AED 60 | AED 61– AED 90 | AED 91– AED 130 | Over AED 130 |

All prices are per person in UAE dirhams for a main course at dinner excluding 10% tax.

# DEIRA & THE NORTH BANK

## AMERICAN

$$ ✕**Boardwalk.** For a long alfresco lunch, this location is hard to beat. Tables sit on a large, rustic, wooden deck over the creek, with views across to Festival City and the high-rise towers of Al-Rigga. It's a popular stop-off for golfers between rounds, families on weekends, and expats showing their relatives the sites on weekdays. The menu isn't too adventurous—a selection of salads and burgers and diner-style food—but you can enjoy a beer or glass of wine with whatever you choose. Service is relaxed, but it suits the mood as you settle into your seat. ✉*Dubai Creek Golf Club, Baniyas Rd., Garhoud* ☎*4/295–6000* ▭*AE, MC, V.*

## ECLECTIC

$$$ ✕**The Cellar.** A contemporary take on the medieval banquet hall, including huge stained-glass windows, the style here is a matter of taste. You'll either love the look or hate it, but you won't feel that way about the high-quality food. You can dine inside or outdoors at this popular restaurant, which serves well-cooked and -presented food in elegant surroundings. The reasonably priced menu is a real mix, with signature dishes such as a duck leg marinated in Asian spices and served with bok choy or a succulent lamb pie. Think European heartiness meets Asian subtlety. It may sound odd, but it works. The wine selection here is one of the largest in Dubai, hence the restaurant's name, and you're always welcome to come for a glass or two and skip

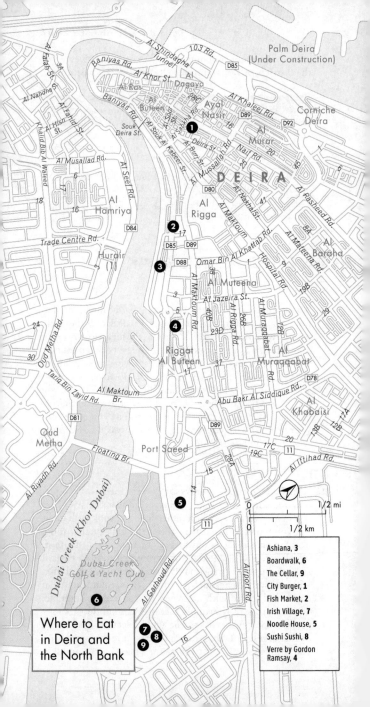

Al Shindagha Tunnel
10.3 Rd.
Palm Deira (Under Construction)
Corniche Deira
Banyias Rd.
Al Khor St.
Al Dagayo
D85
Al Khaleej Rd.
D89
D92
Al Ras
Ayal Nasir
Al Buteen
Souk Deira St.
Al Souk Al Kabeer St.
Banyias Rd.
Al Murar
20
Deira St.
Al Mussallah Rd.
Al Baniyas St.
❶
Nakheel Rd.
Al Mussallah Rd.
23
45
6
DEIRA
Al Rasheed Rd.
Al Musallad Rd.
Khalid Bib Al Waleed
Al Hisn St.
Al Nahda
Al Falah St.
3A
D80
Al Nakhal St.
41
8A
Al Seef Rd.
6
18
16
Al Hamriya
❷
17
D84
D85
D89
Trade Centre Rd.
Hurair (1)
❸
D88
Omar Bin Al Khattab Rd.
Hospital Rd.
Al Mateena Rd.
Al Baraha
38
Al Muteena
9
1
3
Al Jazeira St.
19B
Al Maktoum Rd.
5
40B
Al Rigga Rd.
26B
23D
12B
39
❹
Al Muraqqabat
Riggat Al Buteen
37
Al Muraqqabat Rd.
Al Khabaisi
D78
Oud Metha Rd.
24
30
Tariq Bin Zayid Rd.
Al Maktoum Br.
Abu Bakr Al Siddique Rd.
17
7A
D81
D89
Port Saeed
17C
19C
13B
12B
20
11
Floating Br.
Oud Metha
Al Riyadh Rd.
15
28A
Al Ittihad Rd.
14
Airport Rd.
Dubai Creek (Khor Dubai)
❺
11
0        1/2 mi
0        1/2 km
Dubai Creek Golf & Yacht Club
Al Gaathoud Rd.
❻
Where to Eat in Deira and the North Bank
❼ ❽
❾
16

Ashiana, **3**
Boardwalk, **6**
The Cellar, **9**
City Burger, **1**
Fish Market, **2**
Irish Village, **7**
Noodle House, **5**
Sushi Sushi, **8**
Verre by Gordon Ramsay, **4**

the meal. Wine tastings take place evenings throughout the year. ⊠*The Aviation Club, off Al Garhoud Rd., Garhoud* ☎*4/282–9333* ☐*AE, MC, V.*

## INDIAN

★ Fodor'sChoice ✕ **Ashiana.** Step over the threshold into a cor-
$$ ner of the Raj and dine on what may be the tastiest Indian food in Dubai. Consistently rated the best of its kind in the city, dishes here cultivate a fine balance of spiciness and full flavor, and come complete with dips, chutneys, and breads. Signature entrées include lentils and chickpeas, great options for vegetarians, as well as tandoori lamb chops for meat lovers. The dining area contains discrete spaces separated by ornate handcrafted wooden fretwork, painted to invoke India's glorious architectural traditions. Service is attentive but discreet. ⊠*Sheraton Deira Creek, Baniyas Rd., Deira* ☎*4/228–1111* ☐*AE, DC, MC, V* ⊗*No lunch Fri.*

## IRISH

$$ ✕ **Irish Village.** For some *craic,* or a good time, and a visit to the Emerald Isle, take a seat in this busy Irish pub. The menu comes straight from Grandma's kitchen with stews, pies, and roasted meat platters topped with meaty gravy. Enjoy a pint of tasty Irish stout with your meal and finish up with an Irish coffee. Then stay for the music or indulge in a little barroom philosophy with the expat regulars who make this place a home away from home. Irish Village has a large shady terrace that makes it an excellent choice for a lunch break and it's popular with families on weekends. ⊠*The Aviation Club, Off Sheikh Rashid Rd., Garhoud* ☎*4/282–4750* ☐*AE, MC, V.*

## JAPANESE

$-$$ ✕ **Sushi Sushi.** The name says it all. This unpretentious con-
temporary eatery takes the pomp out of Japanese cuisine by serving fresh and delicious food at reasonable prices. The balance of flavors, from each fresh delicate cut of fish to the pungent wasabi, is excellent. Every item is presented on a series of colored plates, which indicate the price for each dish, with a flair that matches the upscale 5-star hotels. The clientele is a mixture of ages and nationalities—some linger over their meal, others drop in for a quick bite after shopping or before heading out to a nightclub. Sushi Sushi also has a range of hot dishes for those who haven't fallen

under the raw-fish spell. ⊠*Century Village, The Aviation Club, off Sheikh Rashid Rd., Garhoud* ☎4/282–9908 ▤*AE, MC, V.*

## MEDITERRANEAN

★ Fodor'sChoice ✕**Verre by Gordon Ramsay.** Gordon Ramsay is
$$$$ one of Britain's most successful and colorful recent exports. Verre, the celebrity chef's first restaurant outside the UK, continues to receive accolades from Dubai's locals. Ramsay's prodigy, Matthew Pickop, oversees the kitchen and manages the staff, many of whom trained in Ramsay's London eatery. The 70-seat space sits in a glass box (which opens into the hotel), so there's nothing to detract from the food, which is just as it should be. The French- and Italian-influenced menu changes regularly and has a choice of five or so items for each course, allowing each dish to be prepared and cooked to perfection. An extensive, fine-wine list is available for pairing with your meal. ⊠*Hilton Deira Creek, Baniyas Rd., Al-Rigga* ☎4/227–1111 ▤*AE, DC, MC, V* ⊘*Closed Sat. No lunch.*

## MIDDLE EASTERN

¢ ✕**City Burger.** This eatery is located on a noisy intersection but serves quite possibly the best *shwarma* in Dubai—the meat is fresh, the salad is crisp, the pickles are extra tart, the whole thing is moist but not soggy. Backpacking world travelers, Emirati businessmen, and hordes of Pakistani and Indian expat workers will join you at the melamine tables. ⊠*Deira Rd., Deira (at Sabkha Rd.)* ☎4/222–7171 ▤*No credit cards.*

## PAN-ASIAN

$ ✕**Noodle House.** Large quantities of freshly cooked pan-
★ Asian food served by knowledgeable friendly staff at reasonable prices attracts crowds of expats from all over the world. This casual eatery has a flexible menu where you don't need to stay with the appetizer, entrée, dessert formula—order several appetizers if you prefer. Curries and soups are cooked in the open kitchen and arrive as hot and spicy as you desire, and the hot-and-sour soup hits the right note. Usually entrées consist of rice and noodle dishes from Thailand, China, and Malaysia. The open seating area, framed by glass walls with a view into the mall, has cozy booths and long contemporary wood-veneer tables

for groups. Noodle House has other locations at Madinat Jumeirah and Boulevard at Emirates Towers. ⊠*Bin Hendi Ave., Deira City Centre Mall* ☎*4/294–0885* ▭*MC, V.*

## SEAFOOD

$$$  ✕**Fish Market.** Imagine sauntering along a harbor in Maine just after the catch has been landed. What would you choose for lunch? You've got a similar host of options at Fish Market, laid out in a sumptuous spread of tuna steaks, fillet of Nile perch, prawns, crayfish, and oysters. If none of these options tempts your taste buds, check out the impressive live tanks of crab and lobster. Choose your favorite, tell the server how you'd like it cooked, and a few minutes later it will arrive at your table. Book a table by the window for views of the creek. ⊠*Radisson SAS Hotel* ☎*4/222–7171* ⚟*Reservations not accepted* ▭*AE, MC, V.*

# BUR DUBAI & THE SOUTH BANK

## CAFÉS

$   ✕**Basta Art Café.** Located in an enclosed courtyard with the sound of water splashing from an ornate fountain, the menu here caters to Western expats looking for something familiar. Bistro tables are scattered around the center of the space, and long tables with sofas line the walls—but be sure to check your seat for occasional bird droppings, as this spot is a favorite of the local birds. A small, interior, air-conditioned space is available if the shady trees don't provide enough coolness. Juices here are delicious and come in a range of uncommon flavors, though they are pricier than the ones from casual juice bars around town. The lunch menu has crisp salads, soups and sandwiches, and jacket potatoes with a range of fillings. As the name suggests, the café also sells the art that decorates the walls and hosts occasional exhibitions. ⊠*Bastakia Quarter, Bur Dubai* ☎*4/353–5071* ▭*DC, V, MC* ☾*Closed Sun.*

$   ✕**Elements Café.** If you like dramatic modern environments, you'll love this café. Brushed steel walls and light wooden floors contrast with white furnishings. The space is broken up by bay tree and basil topiary, as well as accent lighting—all designed to enhance well-being. From light refreshment to light meals, Elements is a perfect stopover for a small bite to recharge your energy or have lunch. The pastries and Viennoiserie (sweet breads) are delicious and

## Arabian Tidbits

Modern Emirati cuisine is a mixture of dishes found around the Middle East, leaning heavily on dishes that originated in Lebanon and the Levant. The traditional Bedouin diet was very simple, consisting of roasted meat—usually kid or camel—unleavened bread, bulgur wheat, and whatever greens were at hand. This meal was often followed by a dessert of dried fruits or pastries and sweet tea or coffee. Arabian restaurants in Dubai more often serve Lebanese-style food, concentrating on a range of small starter dishes known as *mezze*, which may include any of the following:

■ **Bourek or Burek:** pastries with spinach or cheese stuffing.

■ **Tahini:** sesame seed paste.

■ **Kibbeh:** minced meat, bulgur wheat, and spices in torpedo-shaped fried balls.

■ **Baba ghanoush:** eggplant salad with tahini, olive oil, lemon juice, and garlic.

■ **Dolma or Mahshi:** stuffed vine leaves.

■ **Falafel:** fried balls of crushed chickpeas.

■ **Fattoush:** a salad of seasonal vegetables.

■ **Fuul:** slow-cooked fava beans served as a cold salad.

■ **Kofta:** ground meat, spices, and onions mixed with bulgur wheat, then cooked in sauce, steamed, or fried.

■ **Man'oushi:** miniature pizzas with a range of traditional toppings.

■ **Mujaddara:** cooked lentils with wheat and onions.

■ **Pastirma:** pressed dried meat.

■ **Tabbouleh:** bulgur wheat with finely chopped mint, parsley, tomato, and spring onion.

varied, and come accompanied by tea or coffee in Arabic or Western style. More substantial fare includes salads and pastas, and many of the ingredients are organic. While the air-conditioned interior space is striking, the café also has a large outdoor air-conditioned terrace. ⊠ *Wafi City Mall, Umm Hurair* ☎*4/324–4252* ▤*AE, MC, V.*

## ECLECTIC

★ **Fodor'sChoice** ✕ **Fire and Ice–Raffles Grill.** As much a performance
**$$$$** as an eating experience, the contrasting stations at Fire and Ice promise a night to remember. Open hot kitchens are ringed with flames and chilled cabinets radiate electric blue neon, giving a hint of Arctic atmosphere. The menu is provocative, with choices from the ice counter and the

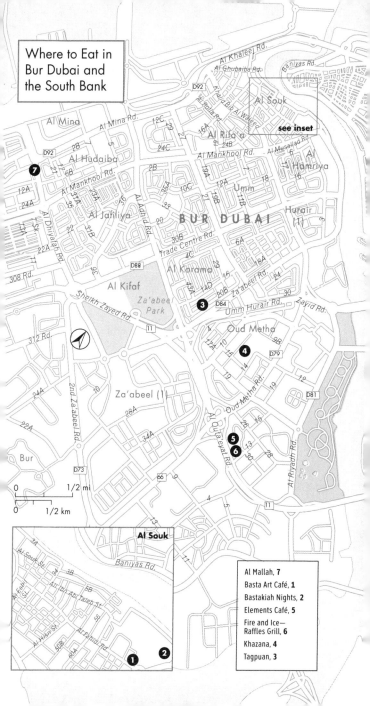

# Where to Eat in Bur Dubai and the South Bank

**Al Souk**

Al Mallah, **7**

Basta Art Café, **1**

Bastakiah Nights, **2**

Elements Café, **5**

Fire and Ice—
Raffles Grill, **6**

Khazana, **4**

Tagpuan, **3**

flame station, but the food doesn't need gimmicks to get by. The tastes are well thought out and fresh ingredients are backed up by a seemingly endless wine list. One wall of the restaurant holds a vast glass-sided cave where hundreds of bottles await. The steaks are the specialties here, including Wagyu beef from Japan and Aberdeen Angus from Scotland. The terra-cotta brick floors provide a strong visual contrast from the ebony and burgundy furniture. Lofted ceilings and mezzanine areas add to the drama of the space. The bill will be a weighty one, but the expertly prepared food is well worth the cost. ⊠*Raffles Dubai, Sheikh Rashid Rd., Wafi City, Umm Hurair* ☎4/324–8888 ☐*AE, DC, MC, V* ⊙*No lunch.*

## INDIAN

**$$$** ✕ **Khazana.** Celebrity chef Sanjeev Kapoor's restaurant is a favorite with European expats for its refined Indian cuisine. This isn't the kind of place where curries come hot, hotter, or fiery. Instead Kapoor complements his dishes with the perfect blend of spices. Prices are steep compared with what you'll pay for Indian street food, but it's worth splurging to savor a plate created by the Indian equivalent of Emeril Lagasse. ⊠*Al Nasr Leisureland, Oud Metha* ☎4/336–0061 ☐*AE, MC, V.*

## MIDDLE EASTERN

**¢** ✕ **Al Mallah.** Tasty, inexpensive Lebanese staples make this simple eatery consistently busy with Emiratis and expat Indians, Pakistanis, and Afghanis. Shwarmas and falafel are a must here. Mezze is also served, but it's better to pop in than to linger here. Come in the evenings when you can watch the street life of the city in full swing. No alcohol license. ⊠*Al Dhiyafha Rd., Satwa* ☎4/398–4723 ☐*No credit cards.*

**$$** ✕ **Bastakiah Nights.** This is a historic patrician mansion that's ★ been transformed into a traditional Arabic restaurant in the heart of downtown. When dining here, you'll enjoy authentic surroundings (if a bit staged) and local dishes served by costumed staff. Tables on the rooftop terrace have fantastic views across the creek and the quarter. If you'd rather eat indoors, the first floor has several small rooms decorated in the same style as a welcoming *majlis* (traditional Arabic seating areas) with tables for dining. Come at night when the restaurant glows with stained-glass lamps and candles. Opt for the set menu if you want to sample a full range of mezze and entrées, or dine à la carte. Generously sized dishes are served on colorful Arabian platters or in ornate dishes. No alcohol license. ⊠*Bastakia Quarter* ☎*4/353–7772* ▤*AE, MC, V.*

## PHILIPPINE

¢ ✕**Tagpuan.** A favorite with the Filipino expat community who come here to find a taste of home, this friendly café sells platefuls of Pinoy staples. Not one of the world's better known cuisines, Pinoy fare usually consists of a mixture of meat and noodles (or rice), and is less spicy than Thai or Indonesian food. If you're on a budget this is a good choice for an inexpensive, tasty meal. Try the *pancit palabok,* noodles smothered in fish sauce topped with boiled egg; *guisado,* beef stewed with tomatoes; or the local favorite *tapa,* stir-fried strips of marinated beef. No alcohol license. ⊠*Omar bin Khatab Rd., Kerama* ☎*4/337–3959* ⚘*Reservations not accepted* ▤*No credit cards.*

# JUMEIRAH BEACH

## AMERICAN

$ ✕**Johnny Rockets.** Ever think there would be a '50s style ☺ diner in Dubai? The cute uniformed staff here hand you a menu of American staples, including a dozen different burgers you can watch them cook at the counter. This is no fast-food joint, though. Everything is prepared to order, and the thick juicy patties come with whatever trimmings you want—dill pickles, chili, or fries. Wash it all down with one of the best shakes in the emirate. Or if a burger and a shake is too much for your appetite, choose a salad or a kid's portion. Johnny Rockets locations are modeled after the bobby-soxer era, but you don't need to have lived through those days to enjoy the fun. Other outlets are at Marina Walk, Dubai Marina, and Mall of the Emirates. No alcohol. ⊠*Jumeirah Rd., opposite Jumeirah Centre* ☎*4/344–7859* ▤*AE, V, MC.*

## CAFÉS

$ ✕**Café Ceramique.** Sure, you'll find tasty light fare here, ☺ including salads, sandwiches, and pastries—but there's more to Café Ceramique than meets the eye. This is a café-cum–pottery shop where people of all ages can grab a plain

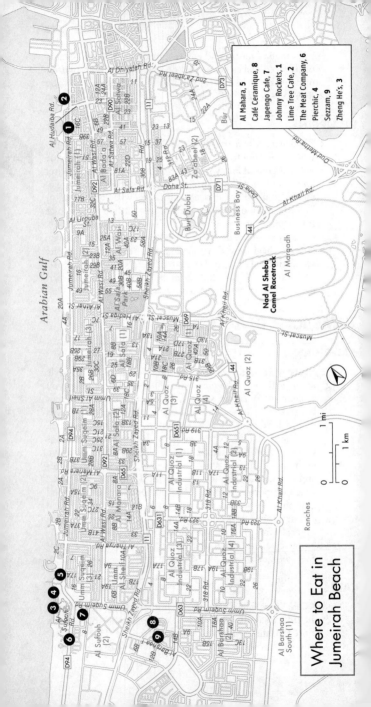

**Where to Eat in Jumeirah Beach**

Al Mahara, 5
Café Ceramique, 8
Japengo Cafe, 7
Johnny Rockets, 1
Lime Tree Cafe, 2
The Meat Company, 6
Pierchic, 4
Sezzam, 9
Zheng He's, 3

Arabian Gulf

Nad Al Sheba Camel Racetrack

porcelain bowl, cup, or mug and some ceramic colors to produce their very own work of art. The amiable staff will have your masterpiece fired (this may take a few days), so you can take home a one-of-a-kind souvenir. On busy shopping days and during hot summer months, this is a popular indoor retreat for families. There's another location on Jumeirah Road. ⊠*Mall of the Emirates, Sheikh Zayed Rd.* ☎*4/341–0144* ▤*AE, MC, V.*

★ Fodor'sChoice ✕**Lime Tree Cafe.** Known throughout the Emirate
$ for its succulent carrot cake, this eatery has many delicious accompaniments for your coffee, including cheesecake and chocolate brownies. Lime Tree also serves such healthy lunch options as salads, wraps, omelettes, and juices in generous portions. The shady terrace is a great place to chill out and listen to the running water of the nearby fountain. There's also a branch at Ibn Battuta Mall. ⊠*Jumeirah Rd., Jumeirah 1* ☎*4/349–8498* ▤*AE, MC, V* ☽*No dinner.*

## CHINESE

★ Fodor'sChoice ✕**Zheng He's.** This is Chinese cuisine with a
$$$$ contemporary international twist. An innovative menu, impressive interior design, and a colorful kitchen on view through glass panes all combine to deliver one of the best dining experiences in Dubai. Dishes marry such ingredients as truffles and asparagus with more traditional items, and signature dishes include sautéed seafood with cashew nuts and chili vinegar, and roast pineapple with mango, ginger, and chili sorbet for dessert. Book a table on the quayside terrace, which overlooks the canals of Madinat Jumeirah and is shaded by date palms, and watch the *abras* (boats) come and go. It's especially romantic at night when the waterside of Madinat Jumeirah is softened by clever lighting. ⊠*Mina A'Salam, Madinat Jumeirah, Al Sufouh Rd., Al Sufouh 1* ☎*4/366–6730* ▤*AE, CD, MC, V.*

## ECLECTIC

$ ✕**Japengo Cafe.** At this pretty canal-side location, you can enjoy light world cuisine, including sushi, noodles, salads, and sandwiches. Japengo is a chain, but the food is fresh, tasty, well-priced, and served throughout the day. The bright tropical decor and rattan sofas add a touch of fun to the Dubai dining scene but don't cross the line into kitsch. There are other outlets at Ibn Battuta Mall, Mall of the Emirates, Sheikh Zayed Road, and Wafi City Mall.

No alcohol license. ⊠*Souk Madinat Jumeirah, Al Sufouh Rd., Al Sufouh* ☎*4/368–6575* ⊟*AE, MC, V.*

$$ ✕**Sezzam.** One could say Sezzam is a glorified mall food court, but that would be a glass-half-empty attitude. Although the eatery is located in the Mall of the Emirates, it is overseen by the 5-star Kempinski Hotel, which is also on-site. It features three open kitchens that have freshly cooked dishes from around the world, allowing diners to venture from continent to continent with each course. A flame station, bake station, and steam station produce Lebanese grilled meats, Italian pastas, and Oriental noodles, while the dessert choices shimmy from baklava to banoffee pie: banana and thickened condensed milk atop crumbled biscuits and butter. Find a seat that overlooks the slopes of Ski Dubai. ⊠*Mall of the Emirates* ☎*4/341–3600* ⊟*AE, MC, V.*

## SEAFOOD

$$$$ ✕**Al Mahara.** At Al Mahara the tables surround an impressive aquarium with a varied population of fish, and they also arrive in delicious sauces for your consumption. This establishment is the signature restaurant of the Burj Al-Arab, which means spending a lot of dirham—the jury is out on whether the food's worth the cost, but for many the atmosphere is the real draw. A prix fixe for AED 890 may be a good deal if you plan to order several courses. ⊠*Burj Al-Arab Hotel, Jumeirah Rd., Jumeirah 2* ☎*4/301–7600* ⌂*Reservations essential* ⊟*AE, DC, MC, V* ⊙*No lunch*.

★ **Fodor's**Choice ✕**Pierchic.** This rustic wooden shack set on a
$$$$ wooden walkway brings to mind a Gulf of Mexico fishing pier—though it lacks the fishermen snoozing in deck chairs as their lines bob in the water. Instead, Pierchic is one of the most romantic settings in the emirate. The ultracontemporary decor complements silver-finished timbers, and glass walls allow diners to sit in air-conditioned comfort while enjoying views of the Burj Al-Arab and Madinat complex. Or, if you prefer, sit on the deck and catch the breeze coming off the ocean. The menu concentrates on seafood and can be accompanied by a fine wine. This is a wonderful place for a leisurely lunch or long dinner—take your pick. ⊠*Al Qasr, Madinat Jumeirah, Al Sufouh Rd., Al Sufouh 1* ☎*4/366–8888* ⌂*Reservations essential* ⊟*AE, DC, MC, V.*

**DESERT DESSERTS.** Emiratis have a serious sweet tooth, and traditional desserts are very saccharine, usually made with some combination of sugar, honey, dates, pistachios, or almonds. Hotels often serve baklava—consisting of multiple layers of paper-thin phyllo pastry, nuts, and honey or sugar syrup—or other similar pastries at the end of a meal. If you order tea or coffee in a hotel, a selection of bite-size sweets generally will arrive with your drink.

## STEAK

$$$ ✕ **The Meat Company.** As the name suggests, this restaurant concentrates on steak, and the attention given to its source shows in the finished product. You can choose aged beefs from the United States, Australia, Japan, and South Africa that are flame-grilled to your exact specification. The menu covers a few chicken and lamb dishes, juicy 100% beef burgers, and there's even fish. But meat is king here. The interior decor is reminiscent of a steak house, with black leather and dark wood. If you sit outside on the terrace, you'll have views of Madinat Jumeirah. In addition, a few outside tables have canal-side seating alongside the main walkway—great for people-watching. There's also an outlet at Souk Al Bahar, Burj Dubai. ⊠*Souk Madinat Jumeirah, Al Sufouh Rd., Al Sufouh 1* ☎*4/368–6040* ▤*AE, MC, V.*

# WORLD TRADE CENTRE AREA & BURJ DUBAI

## CHINESE

$$$$ ✕ **Shang Palace.** Tucked into the mezzanine of the Shangri-La's soaring foyer, you'll find some of Dubai's most refined Cantonese cuisine. Contemporary Chinese decor is apparent in the use of colors—lucky red contrasts with burnished gold tones that don't overwhelm the space. During the daytime, business discussions take place over plates of succulent meats and crisp vegetables in delicate sauces, producing an excellent balance of flavors and textures. The dim sum is also excellent. ⊠*Shangri-La Hotel, Sheikh Zayed Rd.* ☎*4/405–2703* ▤*AE, DC, MC, V.*

**THE DUBAI SNACK.** It doesn't matter how you spell it—shawarma, chawarma, shuarma, or shoarma—the shwarma is the king of Dubai snacks. Thin slices of meat are shaved from a rotisserie-roasted stack of marinated meat, usually lamb or chicken. These

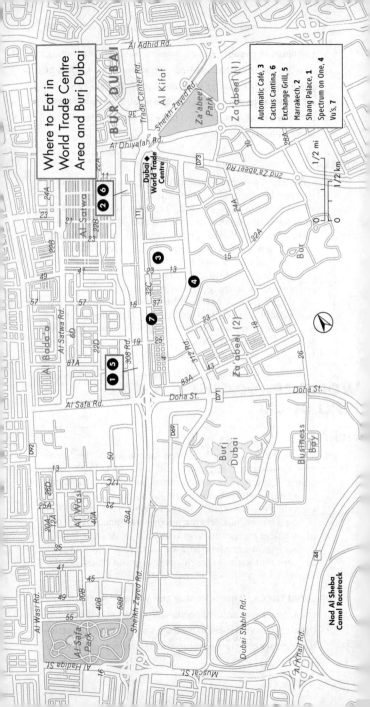

Where to Eat in
World Trade Centre
Area and Burj Dubai

BUR DUBAI

Automatic Café, 3
Cactus Cantina, 6
Exchange Grill, 5
Marrakech, 2
Shang Palace, 1
Spectrum on One, 4
Vu's, 7

Al Adhid Rd.
Al Kifaf
Za'abeel Park
Za'abeel (1)
Trade Center Rd.
Sheikh Zayed Rd.
Al Dhiyafah Rd.
Al Satwa
Dubai ◆
World Trade
Centre
2nd Za'abeel Rd.
D73
1/2 mi
1/2 km
24A
22A
Bur
15
Za'abeel (2)
18
26
Doha St.
D71
Doha St.
D69
Burj
Dubai
Business
Bay
Al Safa Rd.
Al Bada'a
Al Satwa Rd.
308 Rd.
312 Rd.
83A
43
23
25
37
32C
13
23
19
15
22D
87A
6D
57
41
49
57
23
22B
21
23
24A
11
Al Wasl
Al Wasl Rd.
50
13
26D
25A
20A
22A
40A
58A
17C
D92
35
41
45
49
38B
40B
68B
55
Sheikh Zayed Rd.
Al Safa Park
Al Hadiqa St.
16
D44
Nad Al Sheba
Camel Racetrack
Dubai Stable Rd.
Muscat St.
Al Khail Rd.
Muscat St.

are placed on a round of flat bread with such accompaniments as salad, hummus, and tahini; then the whole thing is tightly rolled and wrapped in paper. Shwarmas are frequently served with a side of pickled vegetables for a salty accent, but that's optional.

## ECLECTIC

$$ ╳**Spectrum on One.** With eight open kitchens and a sizeable à la carte menu, this restaurant does a decent job of being all things to all people. The diversity in no way dilutes its quality, with genuine Chinese, European, Japanese, Indian, Middle Eastern, and Thai dishes prepared by a well-oiled team of chefs. The large space is creatively designed, and each station is styled to resemble the location from which its fare comes, including such sites as an Italian piazza and an Asian pagoda. Your culinary journey here may include a plate of Lebanese mezze to start, followed by a curry entrée, and finishing with a sweet Italian gelato—or pick your own combination. ⊠*Fairmont Hotel, Sheikh Zayed Rd.* ☎*4/311–8251* ⊟*AE, DC, MC, V* ⊗*No lunch Sat.–Thurs.*

$$$$ ╳**Vu's.** Come here for incomparable bird's-eye views of Dubai through sheer glass walls that seem to float on a monumental metal skeleton—and the food is something special too. Chef James Viles brings his Australian fusion expertise to the impeccable menu. Fresh seafood meets delicate Thai spices, and Mediterranean classics take a New World twist in dishes such as snow-crab ice cream. These adventurous dishes have been well received by the discerning clientele. But even though the food is excellent, it's still difficult to take your eyes off the scenery. ⊠*Emirate's Towers Hotel, Sheikh Zayed Rd., World Trade Centre 2* ☎*4/319–8088* ⊟*AE, DC, MC, V* ⊗*No lunch Fri.*

## MEXICAN

$ ╳**Cactus Cantina.** For piles of tasty Tex-Mex food in a friendly, fun atmosphere, head to this informal eatery just off Sheikh Zayed Road. Cactus Cantina is popular with families for early evening dinners, as well as expat singles who gather here later in the night. Opt for a huge portion of standard Tex-Mex fare—including chimichangas, enchiladas, fajitas, and tortillas—or go for nachos and chicken wings if you're in the mood for finger food. Wash it all down with a glass or two of sangria while enjoying the colorful painted decor of native scenes of Mexican life.

⊠*Rydges Plaza Hotel, Al Diyafah St., Satwa* ☎4/398–2274
▭*AE, MC, V.*

## MIDDLE EASTERN

¢ ✕ **Automatic Cafe.** This popular chain serves local Lebanese food at excellent prices and is a favorite with families from the Indian subcontinent in the evenings and on weekends. The atmosphere can be boisterous, so it's definitely not the place for a romantic meal, but it's certainly worth an hour of your time. The ample portions are tasty, affordable, and healthy. There's another location in Bur Dubai. No alcohol license. ⊠*Sheikh Zayed Rd., World Trade Centre 2* ☎4/321–4465 ▭*AE, MC, V.*

## MOROCCAN

$$ ✕ **Marrakech.** Walking through the door here is like teleporting yourself to the casbah. There are open tables in the center of the restaurant, but it's better to choose one of the booths that line the walls. Here you can settle into a cozy sofa while examining the menu over a complimentary serving of black olives, olive oil, and warm bread. Everyone who works here is from Morocco—the chef, musicians, and serving staff—so ask for their expert advice on menu options. The superb food includes slow-cooked tender lamb and beef dishes. ⊠*Shangri La Hotel* ☎4/343–8888 ▭*AE, DC, MC, V* ⊗*Closed Fri. No lunch.*

## STEAK

★ Fodor'sChoice ✕ **Exchange Grill.** From the moment the wait
$$$$ staff settles you in a comfy leather seat, you'll notice the elegant place setting (complete with glassware from a château tasting room) and realize you're in for a treat. As you peruse the menu in the sleekly designed restaurant, gaze out the fish-tank-like window to the urban soap opera that is Sheikh Zayed Road. The chefs here concentrate on meat, particularly high-quality steaks, and these arrive cooked to perfection. The wine list is excellent and the service attentive but not fawning. ⊠*The Fairmont Dubai, Sheikh Zayed Rd.* ☎4/332–5555 ▭*AE, DC, MC, V.*

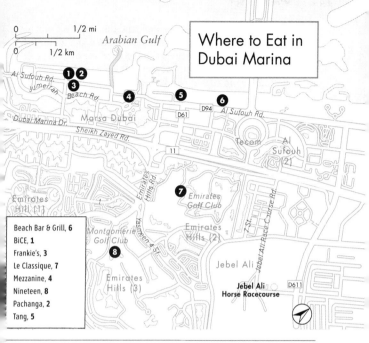

Beach Bar & Grill, **6**
BiCE, **1**
Frankie's, **3**
Le Classique, **7**
Mezzanine, **4**
Nineteen, **8**
Pachanga, **2**
Tang, **5**

# DUBAI MARINA

## ECLECTIC

**$$$$** ✕**Mezzanine.** Celebrity chef Gary Rhodes extends his empire to Dubai with this temple to gastronomy at Grosvenor House. Chef Paul Lupton wowed diners at Rhodes' London eatery and is building a loyal following here too, with cuisine that in turn delights and satisfies. The menu combines delicious English classics, such as jam roly-poly and slow-stewed oxtails, with such fine French staples as *confit de canard* (preserved duck leg). The restaurant decor resembles an ice palace with acres of glass accented by hot patches of red and orange. ⊠*Grosvenor House Hotel, Al Sufouh Rd., Dubai Marina* ☎*4/398–8888* ▤*AE, DC, MC, V* ⊘*No lunch*.

★ **Fodor's**Choice ✕**Nineteen.** The 19th hole at a golf club nor-
**$$$$** mally refers to the bar where below-par rounds are celebrated, but The Montgomerie hotel hit a hole in one when it changed the format. Subtle Asian flavors mingle with European ingredients at this award-winning fusion restaurant. The suave, urban atmosphere contrasts with

the acres of greens right outside, and the major decorative feature is the open kitchen where you can watch your dish come to life. Eat on the terrace and gaze out over the rolling landscape at lunchtime, and perhaps even finish with a tee (pun intended). ⊠*The Montgomerie, off Interchange 5, Sheikh Zayed Rd.* ☎*4/390–5600* ⊟*AE, DC, MC, V* ⊙*No lunch Sun.–Wed.*

$$$$ ✕**Tang.** Although the name sounds Chinese, this European fusion restaurant has some of the most adventurous taste mixtures in Dubai. Dishes come in two sizes, tapas or entrées, so you can mix and share as you wish. The whole point is to try as many combinations as your appetite will allow. The chef uses such innovative techniques as liquid nitrogen, and pairs such classic ingredients as virgin olive oil with ice cream. The decor here is no less inventive. Like a newspaper—black, white, and red all over—the restaurant melds French boudoir with Japanese minimalist style. ⊠*Le Méridien Mina Seyahi Hotel, Al Sufouh Rd., Al Sufouh 2* ☎*4/399–3333* ⊟*AE, DC, MC, V* ⊙*No lunch.*

## FRENCH

$$$$ ✕**Le Classique.** Georges Escoffier, a renowned chef and food writer during the late 18th century, would have been right at home with the menu here. The timeless dishes have been served on the boulevards of Paris for generations. Dubai's twentysomethings may balk at the staid surroundings and house piano playing modern classics, but the lack of neon lights and burnished steel shouldn't be taken as a sign of a jaded menu—wake up and taste the foie gras. This is certainly grand dining, but the set menus are a surprisingly good value. ⊠*Emirates Golf Club, Emirates Hills* ☎*4/380–2222* Jacket and tie ⊟*AE, DC, MC, V.*

## ITALIAN

$$$$ ✕**BiCE.** With outlets in major cities around the world, this Italian chain has authentic fare, and despite its location in one of the less-fashionable hotels here, it still attracts regular crowds. The restaurant's success surely comes from its attention to detail: the finest virgin olive oil, the most mature balsamic vinegars, and herb-infused meat and fish, as well as standard pizzas and pastas. ⊠*Hilton Dubai Jumeirah, Al Sufouh Rd., Dubai Marina* ☎*4/399–1111* ⊟*AE, DC, MC, V.*

**FORGET LUNCH, GO BRUNCH.** In Islam, Friday is the holiest day of the week, so Friday and Saturday are the Dubai weekend and Thursday is a major party night. It's common on Fridays to have a leisurely lunch after the main prayer service, which takes place at about 1 PM, and many hotels have lavish fixed-price buffets that start around 11 AM and last well into the afternoon. Start with a champagne cocktail and finish with a spectacular dessert tray.

**3**

$$$ ✕**Frankie's.** A culinary partnership between a champion jockey and an enfant terrible chef, Marco Pierre White, sounds like a recipe for fun. At horseman Frankie Dettori's Dubai restaurant, Las Vegas crooning comes from the speakers while diners dig into innovative Italian fare. Crystal chandeliers and velvet-covered furnishings give the bar area the feel of a Louisiana brothel, while the sleek dining room is much more contemporary with its mirrored walls and stainless steel fittings. Trattoria fare—pizzas and pastas—don't quite do justice to the surroundings, so try some of chef Marco Pierre White's more complex entrées, including grilled sea bass with citrus or duck confit with olives. ⊠*Al Fattan Marine Tower, Al Sufouh Rd., Dubai Marina* ☎4/399–4311 ⊟*AE, MC, V.*

## LATIN AMERICAN

$$$ ✕**Pachanga.** The heavily themed decor is a bit over the top, but the high quality food at this South American restaurant is the draw. You can dine in corners styled like various streets in Argentina, Brazil, Cuba, or Mexico and order specialties from each country. The steaks are particularly good, with imported aged meats, and portions are generous. Enjoy a range of cocktails, including various tequilas, Cuban rums, and a passable mojito—as well as a Cuban cigar if that's your thing. Nightly music from south of the border encourages everyone to get up and dance. Or better yet, come on one of the regularly scheduled theme nights and shake it to some salsa music. ⊠*Hilton Dubai Jumeirah, Al Sufouh Rd., Dubai Marina* ☎4/399–1111 ⊟*AE, DC, MC, V* ☺*No lunch.*

## SEAFOOD

$$$ ✕**Beach Bar & Grill.** You can almost reach your toes far enough to dip them in the water at this beachfront grill, a popular spot for locals and visitors alike. Swaying palms shade the wooden deck—making it a good location for a leisurely lunch or casual candlelit dinner. Grilled seafood dominates the daytime menu, but flame-grilled steaks and meat skewers put in an appearance during the evening. Portuguese *cataplana* is the restaurant's signature dish, and this is the only place in Dubai where you can find this clam and spicy sausage stew. ⊠*The Palace, One&Only Royal Mirage, Al Sufouh Rd., Al Sufouh 2* ☎4/399–9999 ▤*AE, DC, MC, V.*

CAFÉ SOCIETY. Socializing in cafés is common in Dubai, and shisha (water pipe) cafés are an institution in the Gulf. Traditionally, these coffee shops were a place where Arab men got together to chat and relax over a coffee and a smoke. However, modern coffeehouses have hit it big here, and stopping in for a latte is as much a ritual in Dubai as it is in Seattle.

# Where to Stay

**WORD OF MOUTH**

"I have stayed at the Burj [Al-Arab] and it was an amazing experience. I felt the staff and service was very warm and genuine. I never felt like it was too over the top. I have walked around the Jumeirah Beach Hotel. This is definitely where I will stay next time."

—patsy120

By Lindsay Bennett

**THE WORLD'S MOST EXCITING HOSPITALITY INDUSTRY** is in Dubai, and the emirate's decision to aim at the top end of the market has made it synonymous with luxury. More than a hundred 4- and 5-star hotels have opened their doors since 2000, and 150 new hotels are projected to open by 2010—creating a sort of gold-rush fever as every hotel group rushes to stake its claim.

Now for the downside. In 2007 research showed that Dubai was the third most expensive place to stay in the world after New York and Moscow. Budget accommodations are next to impossible to find, as anything rated lower than 4 stars doesn't fit into Dubai's marketing strategy.

Understanding hotel rates in Dubai is like trying to unravel the Da Vinci code. They change by the day, depending on occupancy, and hotels keep their rack rates a closely guarded secret. Even in hotels with a large number of beds, their average occupancy hovers at around 85% (one of the highest in the world) and is buoyed by vast numbers of business travelers, giving them little incentive to discount. Many companies prefer to leave rooms empty rather than attract guests who don't fit their demographics.

Peak tourist season is from November to April, but instead of lowering rates during off-peak times, resort hotels often ramp up their offerings with special value-added packages. These incentives usually include extras, such as meals in signature restaurants and spa treatments, and business hotels give preferential rates on weekends when demand drops. Prices also drop during Ramadan, but services are curtailed at this time. Only one restaurant per hotel will be open during daylight hours, and visitors are asked to refrain from eating, drinking, or smoking in public during the day.

Now that you know you'll be handing over a wad of cash for your lodging, and location, location, location is the prime consideration after checking your budget—what's the main reason for your visit to Dubai? If sunning and water sports are your prime objective, book a beach resort. If old Dubai is the enticement, look for a hotel downtown. By determining your interests before you come, you'll spend much less time traveling and much more time doing.

**ABOUT THE HOTELS**

Rack (or walk-in) rates and Internet rates don't usually include a 10% municipality tax and 10% service charge, so prices may be 20% higher than indicated.

Most 4- and 5-star hotels in Dubai have an executive floor. An airport transfer, buffet breakfast, and evening cocktails and canapés often are looped into the package, and, considering the sky-high price of alcohol, those benefits may make it worthwhile to pay a higher rate.

| WHAT IT COSTS IN UNITED ARAB EMIRATES DIRHAMS (AED) | | | |
|---|---|---|---|
| $ | $$ | $$$ | $$$$ |
| HOTELS | | | |
| Under AED 800 | AED 800– AED 1,200 | AED 1,200– AED 1,800 | Over AED 1,800 |

All prices are per person in UAE dirhams for a double room in high season excluding 10% tax and 10% service charge.

**5-STAR PLANS** Dubai has a seemingly endless number of soft openings and grand openings for hotels that stretch out to 2015 and beyond, as Palm Jumeirah, The World, Palm Deira, Dubailand, Palm Jebel Ali, and Dubai Waterfront come onstream. Bawadi, the hotel strip of Dubailand, will have 50 5-star properties, and each Dubailand park has at least one 5-star hotel on the blueprint. You'll have a choice of more than 100 places to stay when the complex is complete.

## DEIRA & THE NORTH BANK

$ ⛺ **Al Hajiz Heritage Motel.** In a residential and merchant district at the heart of the heritage quarter beside Heritage House and Al-Ahmadiya School, Al Hajiz is a modern version of a traditional Bedouin or Arabian resting house. It has clean basic rooms that are a good value for travelers from around the globe. Rooms surround an interior courtyard and come in various sizes suitable to everyone from single travelers to families or groups. All rooms have whitewashed walls and substantial hardwood furniture carved in local style. Bathrooms are simple with a tiled shower, sink, and toilet. The communal courtyard has a relaxation area where locals stop for tea or Arabic coffee, and it stays open

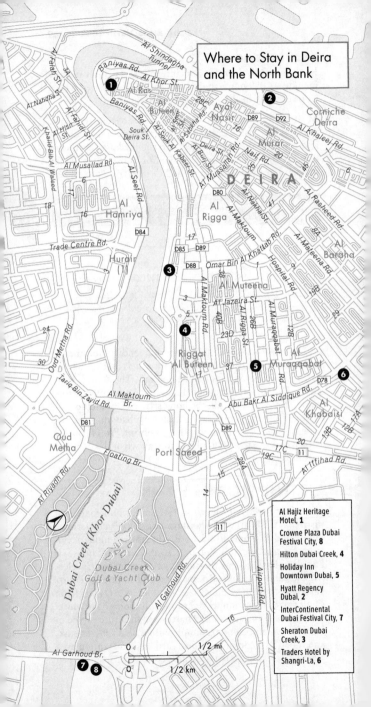

Where to Stay in Deira
and the North Bank

Al Hajiz Heritage
Motel, **1**

Crowne Plaza Dubai
Festival City, **8**

Hilton Dubai Creek, **4**

Holiday Inn
Downtown Dubai, **5**

Hyatt Regency
Dubai, **2**

InterContinental
Dubai Festival City, **7**

Sheraton Dubai
Creek, **3**

Traders Hotel by
Shangri-La, **6**

until late if clients linger. **Pros:** genuine Arab hospitality. **Cons:** muezzin calls for several minutes from the minaret next door at 5 AM every day; interior courtyard allows little natural light; noisy coffee shop occasionally stays open late. ⊠*Al Ras Rd., Al Ras, behind Heritage House* ☎*4/225–0085* ⊕*www.alhajizmotel.com* ➾*21 rooms* ⌂*In-hotel: restaurant* ⊟*No credit cards* ⦿*EP.*

★ **Fodor'sChoice** 🛇**Crowne Plaza Dubai Festival City.** The minimalist
**$$–$$$$** Asian-inspired decor and upscale facilities, including high-tech electronics, make the standard rooms at the Crowne Plaza some of the best options in the city. Though spacious and modern, the lobby is no more than functional compared with other parts of the hotel. The pool and sundeck area are laid out in a comfortable manner, making it a great place to relax and check out the views across Dubai Creek. Neutral walls and carpeting make the rooms (only about 120 square feet) seem more expansive than they are, and glass screens between the bedroom and bathroom keep the areas light. MP3 consoles are in every room. Although the hotel does not have its own spa, guests may use the facilities at the spa in the neighboring InterContinental hotel. **Pros:** on-site shops, eateries, and entertainment. **Cons:** transport needed to all other attractions in the city. ⊠*Dubai Festival City* ☎*4/701–2222* ⊕*www.ichotelsgroup.com* ➾*316 rooms, 18 suites* ⌂*In-room: DVD, Ethernet. In-hotel: 2 restaurants, room service, bars, pool, gym, laundry service, concierge, executive floor, public Wi-Fi, parking (no fee), no-smoking rooms* ⊟*AE, DC, MC, V* ⦿*EP.*

**$$$** 🛇**Hilton Dubai Creek.** This building, designed by Carlos
★ Ott, was originally commissioned by one of the sheikh's relatives as a grand 21st-century home, but they never took possession and Hilton stepped in to create one of the most up-to-date properties in the city. A boutique hotel by Dubai standards, the foyer makes a bold statement with twin steel staircases that reflect against the black marble walls. Rooms have clean lines, full-length windows that fill at least one wall, and warm wood veneers with a Scandinavian feel. The striking bathrooms are decked out in marble and clear glass. You can charge your laptop while storing it in the safe, and clocks are MP3 compatible. The renowned Verre restaurant (*see* ⇨*Chapter 3, Where to Eat*) is located here, and there are two intimate rooms that seat up to 25 people for small business meetings. There's a daily shuttle to the sister property on Jumeirah Beach. **Pros:** intimate size; contemporary style; within strolling distance of downtown attractions. **Cons:** lack of on-site facilities

won't suit families. ⊠*Baniyas Rd., Al-Rigga* ☎*4/212–7510* ⊕*www.hilton.com* ➾*154 rooms* ⚘*In-room: safe, DVD, Ethernet. In-hotel: 3 restaurants, room service, pool, gym, laundry service, concierge, executive floor, parking (no fee), no-smoking rooms* ⊟*AE, DC, MC, V* ⊙*EP.*

$$ ▣ **Holiday Inn Downtown Dubai.** The sexy, gray-blue glass facade of this downtown hotel, a welcome property in this price range, is a dramatic sight. The Holiday Inn is within walking distance of the Deira and Bur Dubai creekside attractions and souks, as well as downtown's bustling streets. On-site amenities add value. The rooftop pool isn't huge, but it's good for cooling off and has a deck for relaxing and sunbathing. The bar and restaurant are serviceable, but there are better ones within walking distance. Rooms are comfortable but not large, with enough space for a small table and chairs in addition to the TV stand. Decor is American classic, with stripes of strong blues and golds set against neutral walls. **Pros:** modern facilities; good budget option; close to downtown attractions. **Cons:** busy street location; few facilities for leisure travelers. ⊠*Al-Rigga Rd., Al-Rigga* ☎*4/228–8889* ⊕*www.ichotels.com* ➾*138 rooms, 1 suite* ⚘*In-room: VCR, Ethernet. In-hotel: Restaurant, bar, pool, gym, laundry service, concierge, executive floor, airport shuttle, parking (no fee), no-smoking rooms* ⊟*AE, MC, V* ⊙*EP.*

$$$ ▣ **Hyatt Regency Dubai.** This high-rise tower rises above the seafront north of the creek mouth, overlooking the coast and the growing Palm Deira offshore. Although the exterior seems a bit somber, the interior makes a dramatic first impression, with a sea of cool ivory marble that spreads across the vast lobby. Dark wood veneers, cool neutrals, and marble baths add contemporary touches to rooms, which are reflected throughout the property. The Hyatt Regency is more than just a hotel, with the Galleria shopping mall and an ice-skating rink on-site. Or enjoy nine holes at the golf course. The Al Dawar restaurant atop the tower rotates slowly so while you dine you get a 360-degree panorama of the northern section of the city. **Pros:** contemporary look; range of eateries and facilities on-site. **Cons:** the hotel is on the coast, but there's no beach; site may get dust, noise, and increased traffic from the Palm Deira construction site just offshore. ⊠*Waterfront, Corniche Deira* ☎*4/209–1234* ⊕*www.hyatt.com* ➾*414 rooms and suites* ⚘*In-room: safe, Ethernet. In-hotel: restaurant, room service, bars, golf course, pool, gym, spa, laundry*

service, concierge, executive floor, parking (no fee), no-smoking rooms. ⊟AE, DC, MC, V ⦿EP.

★ Fodor'sChoice ⚯**InterContinental Dubai Festival City.** Fashioned
$$$$ along the lines of a sailing yacht, the hotel cuts a striking silhouette rising from the south bank of Dubai Creek. The sweeping marble foyer is a triumph of less-is-more modernism. The Intercontinental, opened in the beginning of 2008, has been designed for discerning travelers with MP3 docks and large flat-screen TVs standard furnishings. The pale contemporary rooms also have dressing areas and marble island baths for relaxing. The hotel caters to businesspeople with well-planned convention and meeting spaces and also to vacationers with its expansive free-form pool and sundecks, top-notch spa, and proximity to Festival City's shopping and dining. **Pros:** contemporary style; excellent leisure facilities in hotel and at Festival City; city views from creek-facing rooms. **Cons:** transportation required to reach downtown and beach areas; atmosphere is cool and crisp but not cozy. ⊠*Dubai Festival City, Festival Blvd., off Rabat St.* ☎4/701–1111 ⊕*www.ichotelsgroup. com* ⌕*376 rooms, 121 suites* ♿*In-room: safe, DVD. In-hotel: 2 restaurants, room service, bars, pools, gym, spa, concierge, executive floor, laundry service, parking (no fee), no-smoking rooms* ⊟AE, DC, MC, V ⦿EP.

$$$ ⚯**Sheraton Dubai Creek.** As the oldest hotel on the creek, the Sheraton opened to great fanfare in the early 1970s, but it's showing its age. The atrium is dated with clay-colored wrought-iron balustrades in art-deco style. Public areas and rooms have been updated, so comfort levels are higher than the design might suggest. Bathrooms are compact with older style shower-tub combos. There are no tea/coffee facilities in the rooms, but a quick call to room service is all that's needed. During the last 30 years, the Sheraton has been a social gathering spot in the Deira area, and it's still popular in the evenings despite increased competition from newer properties. You'll also have the use of the beach club at Sheraton Jumeirah Beach at 50% of normal day rates. **Pros:** creekside location; within walking distance of downtown attractions; good range of eateries on-site. **Cons:** dated appearance. ⊠*Baniyas Rd., Al-Rigga* ☎4/228–1111 ⊕*www.sheraton.com* ⌕*262 rooms, 30 suites* ♿*In-room: safe, DVD, Ethernet. In-hotel: 3 restaurants, room service, bar, tennis court, pool, spa, laundry service, concierge, executive floor, public Wi-Fi (fee), parking (no fee), no-smoking rooms* ⊟AE, DC, MC, V ⦿EP.

**$$$** ⌂**Traders Hotel by Shangri-La.** This hotel, part of the Shangri-
★ La group, is one of the few hotels in Dubai in the 4-star
category. It's not too expansive in terms of size or range
of facilities, but the accommodation is high quality with
luxurious up-to-date design and beige marble dominating
the public areas. The rooms are designed with Eastern-
influences—earthy accents of chocolate and amber mingle
in the drapes and soft furnishings and dark wood furniture
adds to the warm feel. Some rooms look over the verdant
interior courtyard. The hotel's public Wi-Fi is located in
the restaurant. **Pros:** good quality for the price. **Cons:** taxis
are tough to get on this busy intersection (but a metro
stop will be nearby when completed); small interior pool.
⊠*Corner of Abu Baker Al Siddique Rd. and Salah Al Din
Rd.* ☎*4/265–9888* ⊕*www.shangri-la.com* ⌁*240 rooms, 10
suites* ⌂*In-room: safe, Ethernet. In-hotel: restaurant, room
service, 2 bars, pool, gym, spa, laundry service, executive
floor, public Wi-Fi, parking (no fee), no-smoking rooms.*
⊟*AE, DC, MC, V* ⍾*EP.*

# BUR DUBAI & THE SOUTH BANK

**$$–$$$** ⌂**Arabian Courtyard Hotel & Spa.** With an ideal city loca-
tion overlooking Al Fahidi Fort and the Bastakia Quar-
ter and Creek, it's a shame more thought wasn't put into
the exterior design of the hotel, as it spoils the historic
surroundings. The interior has an Arabian style, and the
rooms are pleasing to the eye with ornate fretwork, wooden
headboards, mirrors, tables and chairs, and wooden floors.
However, they are not the biggest in the city. The hotel is
located in the middle of the action, and there's a shuttle
to Jumeirah Beach Park. **Pros:** close to downtown Dubai;
pretty rooms with local design. **Cons:** dated lobby and
public areas; rooms are smaller than those in modern build-
ings; street noise from people and traffic. ⊠*Al Fahidi Street,
Bur Dubai* ☎*4/351–9111* ⊕*www.arabiancourtyard.com*
⌁*150 rooms, 4 suites* ⌂*In-room: safe, Ethernet. In-hotel:
4 restaurants, room service, bar, pool, gym, spa, laundry
facilities, concierge, executive floor, no-smoking rooms*
⊟*AE, MC, V* ⍾*EP.*

**$–$$** ⌂**Arabian Park Hotel.** This simple, modern seven-story hotel,
which displays IKEA furnishings throughout, caters to busi-
ness clients and leisure travelers looking for a good value
in pleasant surroundings. Eateries are available on-site and
include a 24-hour deli for post-clubbing snacks. The hotel
has shuttles to Wafi City and Jumeirah Beach Park. Rooms

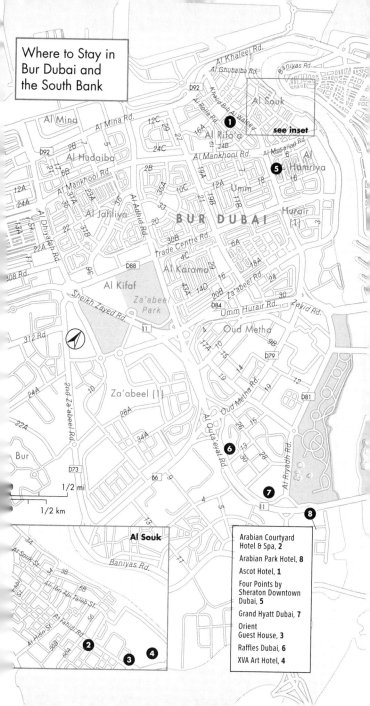

# Where to Stay in Bur Dubai and the South Bank

Al Khaleej Rd.
Al Ghubaiba Rd.
Baniyas Rd.
Al Souk
see inset
D92
Al Mina
Al Mina Rd.
12C
29
2J
16A
Khalid Bin Al Waleed
Al Raffa Rd.
2B
Al Rifa'a
24B
Al Musallad Rd.
D92
24C
Al Mankhool Rd.
Al
Al Hudaiba
Hamriya
6B
2B
19A
5
16
12A
Al Mankhool Rd.
23A
38A
10C
12A
18
24A
36
37A
33
21
19B
11B
Umm
Al Jahliya
90
Hurair
Al Adhid Rd.
30B
(1)
3
22
37B
BUR DUBAI
6A
Al Dhiyafah Rd.
22A
96
Trade Centre Rd.
18A
308 Rd.
4C
29
Al Karama
16
24
D88
43A
14D
20B
Za'abeel Rd.
30
Al Kifaf
Za'abeel
D84
Umm Hurair Rd.
Zayed Rd.
Park
11
4
Oud Metha
312 Rd.
17A
10
9B
24A
15
D79
19
14
2nd Za'abeel Rd.
10
Za'abeel (1)
19
72
D81
22A
28A
26
15
34A
Al Qutaeyat Rd.
6
13
Bur
3C
28
D73
66
9
7
11
1/2 mi
4
8
1/2 km
13
71

## Al Souk
34
Al Souk St.
34
3B
Baniyas Rd.
Al Fahidi St.
56
Al Hisn St.
56A
56B
2
60A
3
4

Arabian Courtyard Hotel & Spa, **2**

Arabian Park Hotel, **8**

Ascot Hotel, **1**

Four Points by Sheraton Downtown Dubai, **5**

Grand Hyatt Dubai, **7**

Orient Guest House, **3**

Raffles Dubai, **6**

XVA Art Hotel, **4**

are spacious with marble floors and minimal furniture in pale veneers with an accent of earthy terra-cotta and burnt umber in the soft furnishings. **Pros:** clean, modern style; bright rooms, range of eateries. **Cons:** just a street or two out of the way; it's not easy to pick up taxis; saltwater pool. ⊠*Off Sheikh Rashid Rd., Jaddaf* ☎*4/324–5999* ⊕*www. arabianpark.com* ⇨*318 rooms* ⌂*In-room: safe, Ethernet (some). In-hotel: 4 restaurants, room service, bar, pool, gym, laundry service, executive floor, concierge, airport shuttle, parking (no fee), no-smoking rooms* ⊟*AE, MV, V* ⎟◎⎟*EP.*

$   ⊞ **Ascot Hotel.** One of the least expensive hotels in Bur Dubai, this is also the oldest, built in the 1970s. The ornate Edwardian architrave decoration and overly festooned drapes in the spacious rooms and public spaces shows its maturity, and wear and tear is apparent in some places. There are several well-known bars and restaurants on-site, including Waxy O'Connor's Irish Pub, making it a hot spot for expats on weekends. Its 5-star sister property, the Royal Ascot, is just next door, which widens your dining and entertainment choices. Plus, it has a pool that Ascot Hotel guests can use. **Pros:** social center of Bur Dubai; beach shuttle available. **Cons:** some rooms need updating; nightclub can be noisy into the early hours. ⊠*Khalid bin Waleed Rd., Bur Dubai* ☎*4/352–0900* ⊕*www.ascot hoteldubai.com* ⇨*71 rooms, 9 suites* ⌂*In room: Ethernet. In-hotel: 5 restaurants, bar, laundry service, parking (fee)* ⊟*AE, MC, V* ⎟◎⎟*EP, MP.*

$$   ⊞ **Four Points by Sheraton Downtown Dubai.** A city hotel is a good option for smart, current accommodations (no resort frills) at reasonable rates. Four Points is a hit with business clients, and it's in walking distance of downtown attractions for vacationers. Rooms are well proportioned and have warm decor, with deep terra-cotta carpets and walls complemented by dark wood furniture. The rooftop pool area is a real bonus, with a nice, free-form pool and an area for relaxing and sunbathing. Suites have kitchenettes with washing machines. There's a restaurant on site and many inexpensive eateries are within walking distance. **Pros:** well-furnished rooms; nice pool. **Cons:** busy, sometimes noisy district; limited restaurant facilities. ⊠*Street 4C off Manhkool Rd., Bur Dubai* ☎*4/354–3333* ⊕*www.sheraton. com* ⇨*224 rooms, 28 suites* ⌂*In-room: safe, kitchen (some), refrigerator (some), Ethernet. In-hotel: restaurant, room service, pool, gym, laundry facilities (some), laundry*

service, concierge, public Wi-Fi, no-smoking rooms ⊟AE,
MC, V ⌑EP.

**$$$–$$$$** ⊡**Grand Hyatt Dubai.** As Bur Dubai's largest hotel, with
a colossal 600 rooms and almost 200 serviced apart-
ments, this property makes a real statement. The building
is designed in two sweeping sensuous curves and is sur-
rounded by 37 acres of beautifully manicured grounds on
Dubai Creek. On-site amenities are extensive, including an
ample choice of eateries, a popular nightclub, golf course,
and a large sports club. Big free-form pools sit among tropi-
cal gardens. Public areas are on a grand scale, decorated
with flourishes and flounces popular in the '80s. More
modern rooms are spacious with a classic international
design, including pale stone, and tan and brown hues.
The Hyatt Grand has excellent conference facilities and
often holds large conventions. **Pros:** wide range of quality
activities on-site; excellent pools and gardens. **Cons:** very
large hotel that risks being impersonal. ⊠*Sheikh Rashid
Rd., Umm Hurair* ☎*4/317–1234* ⊕*www.hyatt.com* ⌑*632
rooms, 42 suites* ⌑*In-room: safe, Ethernet. In-hotel: 10
restaurants, room service, bars, golf course, tennis courts,
pools, gym, spa, laundry service, concierge, executive floor,
public Wi-Fi, parking (no fee), no-smoking rooms* ⊟*AE,
DC, MC, V* ⌑*EP.*

**$$** ⊡**Orient Guest House.** The restored Bastakia quarter wouldn't
be complete without a traditional hotel, and this intimate
courtyard-style property is it. The building has been renovated with high-quality hardwood beams, doors, and
window frames. The interior decor takes cues from the
region with plain whitewashed walls complemented by
locally produced hardwood furniture, sumptuous Persian
carpets, and local handicrafts. The communal lounge acts
as a modern-day *majlis,* where guests often sit and chat
about their day. Courtyards and a roof terrace are good
spots for quiet relaxation. Guests can use the facilities
of the Arabian Courtyard Hotel & Spa just 200 meters
away. **Pros:** in the heart of old Dubai, old-world style in
an intimate setting. **Cons:** limited services on site; other
services at nearby sister establishment. ⊠*Bastakia Quarter*
☎*4/351–9111* ⊕*www.orientguesthouse.com* ⌑*10 rooms*
⌑*In-room: safe. In-hotel: room service, public Wi-Fi* ⊟*AE,
MC, V* ⌑*BP.*

★ **Fodor'sChoice** ⊡**Raffles Dubai.** The crowning glory of Wafi
**$$$$** City's ancient Egyptian design theme, this majestic glass
pyramid houses a classy 5-star hotel. It's a beautiful
property—the theme goes overboard only in the huge lobby

where Egyptian columns overwhelm the space. The rest of the hotel, including the suites, displays current Arabic and Asian design themes, with deeply colored drapes and carpets that contrast with cool wood and marble. Suites are a generous size, each with a floor-to-ceiling glass window leading to a wide balcony with twin sun beds and a table. There's a great pool, a large spa, and a rooftop garden (unique to downtown Dubai). Come to Fire and Ice for a meal, even if you aren't staying at Raffles. **Pros:** one-of-a-kind style; great restaurants and bars on-site; access through the hotel to Wafi City Mall and The Fort entertainment area. **Cons:** check-in desk nearly hidden behind Egyptian columns; entrance difficult to reach on turnoff from Sheikh Rashid road, causing taxi drivers some concern. ⊠*Sheikh Rashid Rd., Wafi City, Umm Hurair* ☎*4/234–8888, 800/768–9009 toll free in U.S. and Canada* ⊕*www.dubai.raffles.com* ⇖*248* rooms ⚐*In room: safe, Wi-Fi. In hotel: 5 restaurants, room service, 5 bars, pool, gym, spa, laundry services, concierge, executive floor, public Wi-Fi, parking (fee), no-smoking rooms* ⊟*AE, DC, MC, V* ⦾*EP.*

★ Fodor'sChoice ⊠**XVA Art Hotel.** Dubai's first boutique hotel still
$  has a faithful following of trendy guests, and it's easy to see why. Housed in a century-old mansion, the property has stylish rooms set around two intimate courtyards. Each room is individually designed by local professionals and personalized by local art. Alongside the hotel is one of the hippest galleries in the city, which hosts prestigious exhibitions of avant-garde arts, film festivals, and product launches throughout the year. XVA also has a courtyard café that serves fresh snacks, including tasty soups and salads. **Pros:** room rates are affordable; in center of art scene. **Cons:** standard room services are limited; few extra facilities on site. ⊠*Bastakia Quarter Bur Dubai* ☎*4/353–5383* ⊕*www.xvagallery.com* ⇖*6 rooms* ⚐*In-room: no TV. In-hotel: restaurant* ⊟*AE, MC, V* ⦾*BP.*

## JUMEIRAH BEACH

★ Fodor'sChoice ⊠**Al Qasr.** Arabian Nights meets Ali Baba and
$$$$  the Forty Thieves here at Al Qasr. The name translates to "The Palace," and from the moment you pull into the drive with its fountain of life-size prancing horses, you'll know that it fits the description. The property epitomizes the traditional architecture of the Arabian Gulf. No expense has been spared in any area of the resort, with acres of marble,

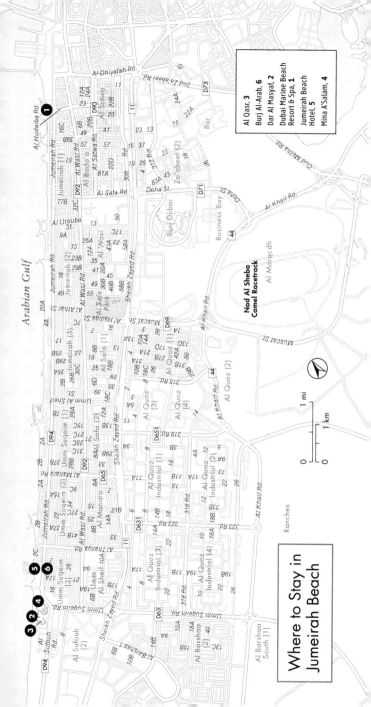

# Where to Stay in Jumeirah Beach

**Arabian Gulf**

Al Qasr, **3**
Burj Al-Arab, **6**
Dar Al Masyaf, **2**
Dubai Marine Beach
Resort & Spa, **1**
Jumeirah Beach
Hotel, **5**
Mina A'Salam, **4**

Nad Al Sheba
Camel Racetrack

Al Maraq.dh

Ranches

0   1 km
0   1 mi

ornate wooden patterns, and flourishes of Arabic lettering on the floors and walls. Exterior facades are a riot of elaborate stucco topped by a forest of barjeels. Al Qasr's lobby lounge is a wonderful place where businessmen can meet or guests can have afternoon tea, like a luxurious majlis with comfy chairs and views across the whole Madinat complex. Guests are an international mix of vacationers and business people. The beach, 2 km long, is the finest in Dubai and is shared with other Jumeirah guests in neighboring hotels. **Pros:** exceptional Arabian style; wide range of activities and eateries in the complex. **Cons:** complicated layout of room corridors. ✉*Madinat Jumeirah* ☎*4/366–8888* ⊕*www.madinatjumeirah.com* ➾*292 rooms* △*In-room: safe, Ethernet. In-hotel: 4 restaurants, room service, bars, pools, gym, spa, beachfront, diving, water sports, children's programs (ages 4–11), laundry service, concierge, parking (no fee)* ▤*AE, DC, MC, V* ⊙*EP.*

**$$$$** ☎**Burj Al-Arab.** The style icon that put Dubai on the tourist map, the Burj Al-Arab has to be one of the most famous hotels in the world, and its graceful lines have been featured in numerous design magazines. The press has christened it the world's first 7-star property, though that accolade is played down by its owners, Jumeirah Hotels. The decor throughout is sumptuous Arabian with deep pile carpets and acres of gold plate. The suites-only property has set new standards of service in the region. There's a check-in desk on each floor and every suite has a butler for personal service. You can also book helicopter transfer or arrange a Rolls-Royce to pick you up from the airport. The hotel prides itself on its ability to satisfy even the pickiest guest, and so has many services in addition to its standard leisure programs. The public can't gain access to the hotel (except with a restaurant or bar reservation) because it sits on a man-made islet just offshore, so you'll have a ton of privacy, but you'll be paying for the privilege. **Pros:** incredible architectural elements; luxurious, expansive suites; very private. **Cons:** room rates are sky-high. ✉*Jumeirah Beach* ☎*4/301–7777* ⊕*www.burj-al-arab.com* ➾*202 rooms* △*In-room: safe, refrigerator, DVD, Ethernet. In-hotel: 6 restaurants, room service, 2 bars, pool, gym, spa, water sports, children's programs (ages 1–12), laundry service, concierge, parking (no-fee), no-smoking rooms* ▤*AE, DC, MC, V* ⊙*EP.*

**$$$$** ☎**Dar Al Masyaf.** Like the summer houses preferred by the Arabian sheikhs, Dar Al Masyaf offers an intimate hideaway for those who want to be secluded. Each two-story courtyard house, complete with barjeel, comprises a number of spacious rooms and suites that surround a private pool. Although the attractions of Madinat Jumeirah are nearby, Dar Al Masyaf can only be reached by taking a hotel *abra* (boat) across the waterway that links the hotels with the surrounding properties. So guests can luxuriate here, tucked away from the hustle and bustle, while their private butlers serve them cooling drinks. Some villas have direct beach access, others are in verdant gardens. Guests have access to all the Madinat Jumeirah facilities. **Pros:** more private than other hotels; attention to detail; close to more than 45 restaurants, bars, other hotels, and nightclubs. **Cons:** interconnecting suites ideal for families but can spoil the ambience for lovers; most hotel facilities are not on-property. ✉*Madinat Jumeirah* ☎*4/366–8888* ⊕*www.madinatjumeirah.com* ⇲*283 rooms in 29 houses* ⌂*In-room: safe, Ethernet. In-hotel: 2 restaurants, room service, tennis courts, pools, gym, spa, beachfront, diving, water sports, no elevator, children's programs (ages 4–12), laundry service, concierge, parking (no fee), no-smoking rooms* ▭*AE, DC, MC, V* ⏿*EP.*

$$$$ ⛱**Dubai Marine Beach Resort & Spa.** The least expensive lodging option in Jumeirah Beach, this holiday village of two-story whitewashed Andalucian-style buildings is an interesting contrast to the high-rise blocks and mega-resorts dominating the emirate. One of the first resort properties in Dubai, the hotel sits on a small sandy bay at the northern end of Jumeirah Beach. It's kept pace with developments in the hospitality industry, adding a small spa and some hip eateries and entertainment options, but room decor is dated and some resort frills (like Ethernet) have yet to be installed—making it more suitable for leisure travelers than for business visitors. **Pros:** low-rise accommodation; palm-fringed gardens; rates include breakfast. **Cons:** dated appearance; limited Internet access. ✉*Jumeirah Rd., Jumeirah 1* ☎*4/346–1111* ⊕*www.dxbmarine.com* ⇲*96 rooms, 97 suites* ⌂*In-room: safe. In-hotel: 11 restaurants, room service, bars, tennis court, pools, gym, spa, beachfront, water sports, no elevator, laundry service, executive floor, parking (no fee), no-smoking rooms* ▭*AE, DC, MC, V* ⏿*MP.*

$$$$ ⛱**Jumeirah Beach Hotel.** This resort property combines intimate accommodation for lovers or honeymooners with facilities that satisfy kids and parents—a tough job to pull off. One of Jumeirah Beach's most recognizable landmarks, the lines of the building rise and fall in the shape of a giant wave, and the interior is designed so that each room and

suite has an ocean view and a glimpse of the graceful outline
of the Burj Al-Arab Hotel (*see above*). A long stretch of
beach, multiple pools, and a range of sports facilities ele-
vates the hotel above its neighbors and 5-star peers. Guests
have free use of the Wild Wadi Water Park and can charge
meals at other Jumeirah hotels to their room. There are
numerous activities for kids. Clients who want a secluded
stay should enquire about private villas. **Pros:** wide range
of activities, eateries, and sports available. **Cons:** too big
for some people's taste. ⊠*Jumeirah Beach* ☎*4/348–0000*
⊕*www.jumeirahbeachhotel.com* ⊷*598 rooms* ⚷*In-room:
safe, refrigerator, Ethernet. In-hotel: 14 restaurants, room
service, bars, tennis courts, pools, gym, spa, beachfront,
diving, water sports, children's programs (ages 2–12), laundry service, concierge, executive floor, parking (no fee),
no-smoking rooms* ▤*AE, DC, MC, V* ⓘ*EP.*

**$$$$** ▧**Mina A'Salam.** Jumeirah calls Mina A'Salam a boutique
hotel, but it may be stretching the definition to say a property with nearly 300 rooms truly fits into that category. Part
of the vast Madinat Jumeirah complex, it is the simplest,
least opulent option of the three (*see also* ⇨*Al Qasr and
Dar Al Masyaf, above*) in its decor but still offers stylish Arabian touches with deep golds, greens, and blues
accenting the neutral walls, dome-shaped archways, and
carved warm wood furniture (produced locally). Many
rooms interconnect, making it a good option for families.
In addition, dining and leisure activities are excellent with
the other Jumeirah hotels close by and at your disposal.
**Pros:** wide range of activities, eateries, and sports available.
**Cons:** not as much bling for your buck as at Al Qasr. ⊠*Madinat Jumeirah* ☎*4/366–8888* ⊕*www.madinatjumeirah.
com* ⊷*280 rooms, 12 suites* ⚷*In-room: safe, refrigerator.
In-hotel: 4 restaurants, room service, bars, tennis courts,
pool, gym, spa, beachfront, water sports, laundry service,
concierge, executive floor, parking (no fee), no-smoking
rooms.* ▤*AE, D, DC, MC, V* ⓘ*EP.*

# WORLD TRADE CENTRE AREA & BURJ DUBAI

**$$-$$$** ▧**Chelsea Towers.** This futuristic 49-story high-rise block
in the heart of the business district has an excellent selection of hotel apartments that cater to long- and short-stay
visitors, the majority of which are on business. The quality is evident as soon as you walk into the contemporary

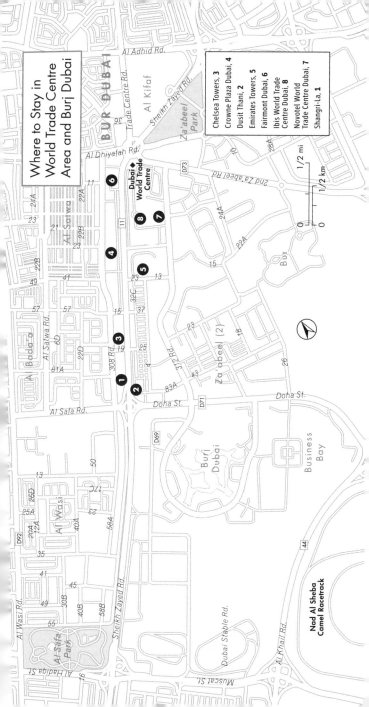

Where to Stay in World Trade Centre Area and Burj Dubai

Chelsea Towers, **3**
Crowne Plaza Dubai, **4**
Dusit Thani, **2**
Emirates Towers, **5**
Fairmont Dubai, **6**
Ibis World Trade Centre Dubai, **8**
Novotel World Trade Centre Dubai, **7**
Shangri-la, **1**

BUR DUBAI

Al Adhid Rd.

Al Kifaf

Za'abeel Park

Trade Centre Rd.

Sheikh Zayed Rd.

Al Dhiyafa Rd.

Dubai ◆ World Trade Centre

D73

2nd Za'abeel Rd.

24A

22A

Bur

Za'abeel (2)

18

26

Doha St.

Business Bay

Burj Dubai

Dubai Stable Rd.

Al Khail Rd.

Muscat St.

Al Safa Park

Al Hadiq St.

Sheikh Zayed Rd.

Al Wasi Rd.

Al Satwa

Bada

Al Satwa Rd.

6D

Al Wasi

Al Safa Rd.

D69

D71

D92

Nad Al Sheba Camel Racetrack

1/2 mi

1/2 km

0

marble lobby. You can choose from one to three bedrooms, each with a cozy living area (and a sofa bed for extra guests) and a full kitchen. Rooms are bright and modern with full-length windows in bedrooms offering great long-distance views. The tower has a good 82-foot lap pool with a surrounding sundeck and gym. **Pros:** access to some of the best eateries and entertainment on your doorstep; spacious accommodation for price range. **Cons:** limited on-site facilities; taxis not always available; one-bedroom units are on lower floors with less interesting vistas. ⊠*Sheikh Zayed Rd.* ☎*4/343–4347* ⊕*www.chelseatowerdubai.com* ↪*80 apartments* ♿*In-room: safe. In-hotel: restaurant, 2 pools, gym, room service, laundry facilities, laundry services, concierge, parking (no fee), no-smoking rooms* ▤*AE, MC, V* ⍟*EP.*

$$$$ ⍟**Crowne Plaza Dubai.** This is the oldest hotel along the Sheikh Zayed strip, and it shows. The recent addition of Zen pebble pools didn't succeed in disguising the multi-colored art-deco theme of the original design. Still, the hotel has many loyal clients, and its varied restaurants and small attached shopping mall make it a popular stop on the Dubai social scene for visitors and residents. Upgrades in 2007 gave the rooms a more contemporary feel, with part-parquet and part-carpet flooring and space for a small seating area in every room. Bathrooms are smallish, with tub-shower combos. **Pros:** lots of dining and entertainment on site. **Cons:** dated-looking public areas; ordinary rooms. ⊠*Sheikh Zayed Rd.* ☎*4/331–1111* ⊕*www.ichotelsgroup. com* ↪*568 rooms, 19 suites* ♿*In-room: safe, ethernet. In-hotel: bars, pool, gym, laundry service, concierge, executive floor, public Wi-Fi (fee), airport shuttle, no-smoking rooms* ▤*AE, DC, MC, V* ⍟*EP.*

$$$–$$$$ ⍟**Dusit Thani.** This Thai hotel group brings more than a touch of its homeland to this 5-star property. The avant-garde building—which resembles an upside-down tuning fork—is one of the most recognizable on the strip. Upon entering, its dramatic exterior gives way to a gentle bow of welcome from the Thai-silk-enrobed reception staff. Interior decor takes its cues from Thailand, with acres of dark wood in the public areas and rooms, in which an ornately detailed shutter separates the living area from the bathroom. Deep-colored carpets add to the warm tones. The second-floor coffee lounge is the most contemporary space in the hotel and has large flat-screen TVs. The roof-top pool area has a stylish European feel with a modern adjoining gym. There's an excellent Thai restaurant on-

site. **Pros:** warm Thai welcome. **Cons:** dark decor is not ultrafashionable; no flat-screen TVs in rooms. ⊠*Sheikh Zayed Rd.* ☎*4/317–4210* ⊕*www.dusit.com* ⤴*321 rooms* ⌂*In-room: DVD (some), ethernet. In-hotel: 4 restaurants, room service, bars, pool, gym, laundry service, concierge, executive floor, parking (no fee), no-smoking rooms* ⊟*AE, DC, MC, V* ⊧*EP.*

$$$$ ⊞**Emirates Towers.** The in-house magazine here, *Etalks*, epitomizes the hotel's atmosphere of cool sophistication, quality, and money. Emirates Towers is an icon and a favorite of wealthy business travelers who consistently vote it one of the world's best. The triangular building displays acres of structural metal, with transparent walls rising up through soaring cathedral-like proportions, and gray and black marble accenting the natural light. The furnishings have sensuous curves, contrasting with the sharp angles of the structure itself. If you don't stay here, you'll get a sense of the place at the Vu's bar on the 51st floor with fantastic views and stunning design. The dozen or so on-site reputable eateries are a magnet for resident expats. The rooms take a "less is more" approach, which can be disappointing when compared with the public spaces. The style is Scandinavian with touches of art nouveau. One floor is dedicated to women guests, with all female staff, in-room cosmetics fridges, and yoga mat and yoga DVDs. **Pros:** one of the most fashionable addresses in Dubai, great bars and restaurants on site. **Cons:** minimalist decor can seem cold. ⊠*Zabeel Rd. 2, off Sheikh Zayed Rd.* ☎*4/330–0000* ⊕*www.jumeirah. com* ⤴*360 rooms, 40 suites* ⌂*In-room: DVD, Ethernet. In-hotel: 11 restaurants, room service, bars, pool, gym, spa, laundry service, concierge, executive floor, parking (no fee), no-smoking rooms.* ⊟*AE, DC, MC, V* ⊧*EP.*

$$$$ ⊞**Fairmont Dubai.** Famed for its portfolio of historic hotels in North America, the Fairmont here is a modern glass tower—a late-20th-century take on the traditional Arab *barjeel*. The hotel chain's ethos of professional service and quality accommodation, honed over the last 150 years, is very much in evidence when you step through the door. The hotel's handful of top-class restaurants and bars are leaders in Dubai's dining and social scenes. Each has a unique decor—from an urban stainless steel neon theme to an ultrachic minimalist vibe. There's a great 40,000-square-foot spa on site with two noteworthy mosaic pools on the sunrise and sunset sides of the hotel. For business travelers, the Fairmont has excellent meeting facilities and is within walking distance of the Dubai Convention Centre. **Pros:**

4

high-class on-site facilities. **Cons:** slow elevators; cluttered lobby. ⊠*Off Trade Centre Roundabout, Sheikh Zayed Rd.* ☎*4/332–5555* ⊕*www.fairmont.com* ⮡*274 rooms, 120 suites* ⚒*In-room: safe, Ethernet. In-hotel: 10 restaurants, room service, bars, pools, gym, spa, laundry service, concierge, executive floor, public Wi-Fi, some pets allowed, no-smoking rooms* ⊟*AE, D, DC, MC, V* ⦿*EP.*

$ ⊞**Ibis World Trade Centre Dubai.** If you are looking for a clean budget room backed by an international hotel chain, this property is a great choice. Because it's attached to the Dubai Convention Centre, the hotel has a split personality and is very busy when conventions are in town and quiet when they're not. Daily rates reflect this changing atmosphere but weekend rates are an excellent value. Don't look for fancy frills like corridors filled with artwork and seating areas on every floor that no one ever uses. Rooms are some of the smallest in Dubai though they have decent-sized beds. Bathrooms, however, are tiny. The hotel is one of the few in Dubai to offer a free, around-the-clock airport shuttle. **Pros:** free airport shuttle; budget room rates; shuttle buses to beaches and shopping malls. **Cons:** mini-bathrooms; taxis can be tough to get when convention center is busy. ⊠*Dubai Convention Centre, Sheikh Zayed Rd.* ☎*4/332–4444* ⊕*www.ibishotel.com* ⮡*210* ⚒*In-room: safe, refrigerator. In-hotel: restaurant, bar, public Wi-Fi, parking (no fee), no-smoking rooms* ⊟*AE, DC, MC, V* ⦿*EP.*

$$–$$$ ⊞**Novotel World Trade Centre Dubai.** Novotel's reputation across Europe for dependable mid-range accommodation is carried on here in Dubai. It's a favorite with budget business travelers, as it is a good value in the center of the business district. It also appeals to leisure travelers on a budget with good on-site amenities and close proximity to clubs, restaurants, and bars on Sheikh Zayed Road. Rooms are decorated in somewhat forgettable neutral tones, but the beds are an ample size. Bathrooms too are adequate though not spectacular in style. The hotel tends to be packed during convention meetings but quiet otherwise. **Pros:** good value for location; airport shuttle. **Cons:** unexciting decor. ⊠*Zabeel Rd. 2, Dubai Convention Centre* ☎*4/332–0000* ⊕*www.novotel.com* ⮡*412 rooms, 13 suites* ⚒*In-room: safe, Ethernet, Wi-Fi. In-hotel: 2 restaurants, room service, bars, pool, gym, airport shuttle (no fee), parking (no fee), no-smoking rooms* ⊟*D, DC, MC, V* ⦿*EP.*

★ Fodor'sChoice ⊞**Shangri-La.** This award-winning property
$$$$ makes a striking 43-story statement at the heart of the Sheikh Zayed business district, and its cool contemporary

interiors are a great place for meetings—work during the day and play when evening comes around. The Lobby Lounge attracts movers and shakers for informal meetings, and expansive facilities back up its credentials as the best business hotel of the year 2006 (DEPA). The property also caters to leisure visitors, with a range of excellent restaurants that are high on the list of expat spots to see and be seen. The Health Club & Spa offers total relaxation, and there's a private free-form pool for sunning. **Pros:** contemporary design; high-quality restaurants on-site. **Cons:** small pool. ⊠*Sheikh Zayed Rd.* ☎*4/343–8888* ⊕*www.shangri-la. com* ⤳*271 rooms, 30 suites* ⚷*In-room: safe, Ethernet. In hotel: 5 restaurants, room service, 3 bars, pool, gym, spa, laundry service, concierge, executive floor, public Wi-Fi, no-smoking rooms* ⊟*AE, DC, MC, V* ⍥*EP.*

# DUBAI MARINA

**$$** ☒**Express by Holiday Inn Dubai–Internet City.** This low-rise hotel, which resembles a mammoth stucco brick from the outside, has a sleek contemporary feel on the inside. Opened in 2007 in the middle of Knowledge Village, Express appeals mainly to business travelers and leisure visitors who want smart accommodations without the resort extras that raise the room rates. Rooms are simply furnished with dark wood pieces and stylish bedding and drapes. Each room has a work area, and the standard-issue bed is a plush, high-quality king-size model. **Pros:** good value in this area, modern decor. **Cons:** few activities, entertainment options nearby and in hotel. ⊠*Tecom Zone, Knowledge City* ☎*4/427–5555* ⊕*www.ichotels group.com* ⤳*244 rooms* ⚷*In-room: safe, Ethernet. In-hotel: restaurant, bar, gym, laundry service, public Wi-Fi, airport shuttle, parking (no fee), no-smoking rooms* ⊟*AE, DC, MC, V* ⍥*EP.*

★ **Fodor's**Choice ☒**Grosvenor House.** The first marina hotel to open **$$$–$$$$** its doors, this is one of the most fashionable addresses in Dubai. The conservative exterior of this high-rise building, where uniformed bellhops eagerly await you, gives way to a neon-lit *pharos* (lighthouse) by night. This hotel is a hit with the twenty- and thirtysomething fashionistas and young wealthy Arabs. Public areas are expansive and tastefully decorated to create a sense of modern timelessness, with acres of marble, rich wooden veneers, and supple leather. The geometric designs on the carpets are striking scenes of ivory, red, and gold hues. Grosvenor House is

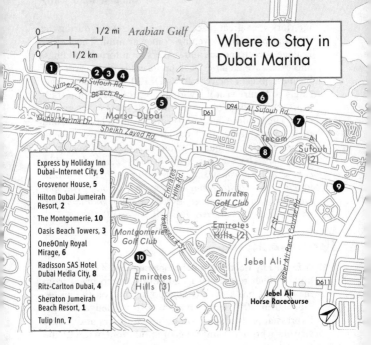

**Where to Stay in Dubai Marina**

Arabian Gulf

0 — 1/2 mi
0 — 1/2 km

Al Sufouh Rd.
Jumeirah Beach Rd.
Dubai Marina Dr.
Marsa Dubai
Sheikh Zayed Rd.
Al Sufouh Rd.
D94
D61
Tecom
Al Sufouh (2)
Emirates Hills Rd.
Emirates Golf Club
Emirates Hills (2)
Montgomerie Golf Club
Yasmeen St.
Emirates Hills (3)
Jebel Ali
Jumeirah Beach Rd.
Jebel Ali Race Course Rd.
Jebel Ali Horse Racecourse
D611

Express by Holiday Inn Dubai–Internet City, **9**

Grosvenor House, **5**

Hilton Dubai Jumeirah Resort, **2**

The Montgomerie, **10**

Oasis Beach Towers, **3**

One&Only Royal Mirage, **6**

Radisson SAS Hotel Dubai Media City, **8**

Ritz-Carlton Dubai, **4**

Sheraton Jumeirah Beach Resort, **1**

Tulip Inn, **7**

one of Dubai's social hot spots, so if you're a guest here you'll only need to leave your room to be at the center of it all. Beachfront and water sports are accessible through its sister hotel, Le Royal Meridien Beach Resort and Spa. **Pros:** one of the coolest spots in Dubai; great people-watching, excellent modern style. **Cons:** property construction will continue until mid-2009; beach is located across construction site. ⊠*Al Sufouh Rd., Dubai Marina* ☎*4/399–8888* ⊕*www.starwoodhotels.com* ⌕*217 rooms* △*In-room: safe, DVD, Ethernet. In-hotel: 10 restaurants, room service, bars, pool, gym, spa, laundry service, concierge, executive floor, parking (fee), no-smoking rooms* ☰*AE, DC, MC, V* ⊙*EP.*

**$$$–$$$$** ☷**Hilton Dubai Jumeirah Resort.** An ancient hotel by Dubai standards, this resort was located in what was once considered Jumeirah Beach but is now part of the elaborate Dubai Marina. Needless to say, the dour low-rise Hilton looks a little out of place surrounded by glossy high-rise towers, but guests who stay here will be in the center of one of Dubai's hot spots. Facilities are comprehensive, including BiCE, an Italian restaurant that's one of the best in the city. Rooms are simply furnished in neutral tones, enlivened by a colorful quilt on the bed. Most rooms have a balcony. **Pros:** good price point for location. **Cons:** dated appearance; small resort footprint. ⊠*Al Sufouh Rd., Dubai Marina* ☎*4/399–1111* ⊕*www.hilton.com* ⤶*389 rooms* ⌂*In-room: safe, DVD, Ethernet. In-hotel: 10 restaurants, room service, bars, pool, gym, beachfront, water sports, children's programs (ages 4–12), laundry service, concierge, executive floor, public Wi-Fi, parking (no fee), no-smoking rooms* ⊟*AE, DC, MC, V* ⊺⊙*EP.*

$$ ⊡**The Montgomerie.** A truly bijou property that combines
★ country-house chic with a high level of service—on 200 acres with the renowned Montgomerie Golf course on-site. This hotel suits couples looking for a retreat or some pampering after a full day of sightseeing or shopping. The sleek decor is complemented by modern geometric art and cool neutral backgrounds. Each room has a private balcony and butler service, and there is a good range of facilities considering the modest size of the resort. The award-winning Nineteen restaurant is worth a visit whether you are staying here or not. **Pros:** personal service; excellent quality for price; airport transfers are included in room rates. **Cons:** distant from mainstream attractions. ⊠*Off Interchange 5, Sheikh Zayed Rd.* ☎*4/390–5600* ⊕*www. themontgomerie.com* ⤶*21 rooms* ⌂*In-room: safe, refrigerator, DVD, Ethernet. In-hotel: 4 restaurants, room service, bar, golf course, pool, gym, spa, laundry service, concierge, airport shuttle (fee), parking (no fee), no-smoking rooms* ⊟*AE, DC, MC, V* ⊺⊙*EP.*

$$$$ ⊡**Oasis Beach Towers.** Self-catering accommodations are becoming ever more popular in Dubai, and this high-rise hotel and apartment tower is an excellent example. Large bedrooms, ample living space, and a well-appointed kitchen allows guests the freedom to relax and make a snack on their own or order a meal from room service—they'll even stock your fridge, and all you have to pick up is the cost of the food. In addition, the apartments have access to beach and water-sports activities on south Jumeirah Beach. The property is well suited to leisure travelers looking for a flexible itinerary, business travelers who want a home away from home, and families who need more space and their own schedule. The towers offer exceptional views over Jumeirah Beach and the burgeoning Palm Jumeirah. **Pros:** spacious accommodation with living area and kitchen; some hotel services. **Cons:** beach access is across the street; no on-site restaurant. ⊠*Al Sufouh Rd., Dubai*

Marina ☎4/399–4444 ⊕www.oasisbeachtower.com ➷180 apartments ⚿In room: safe, DVD. In hotel: room service, pool, beachfront, water sports, laundry facilities, concierge, executive floor, public Wi-Fi, parking (no fee), no-smoking rooms ⊟AE, DC, MC, V ⱺEP.

$$$$ ▣**One&Only Royal Mirage.** Your eyes aren't playing tricks on
★ you—this beautiful Arabian-style resort keeps stacking up the awards for quality. This grand resort hotel has exquisite design throughout that attracts honeymooners and couples. Located on a long stretch of fine sand, it has all the amusements you'll need for long lazy days of R&R. The Royal Mirage is divided into three discreet properties, each of which has its own pool and restaurants. At the Palace, the oldest property, standard rooms are nicely proportioned with soft chintz furnishings that add cozy colorful accents to the neutral beige walls and drapes. Rooms are homey but still classic and simple, especially when compared with the riot of Arabian detail in the resort's public spaces. The Arabian Court and the Residence and Spa offer greater luxury and an even higher level of service. **Pros:** incredible attention to detail; lush grounds; excellent beach; great bars and restaurants. **Cons:** rooms lack a contemporary feel. ⊠Al Sufouh Rd., Al Sufouh 1 ☎4/399–9999 ⊕www. oneandonlyresorts.com ➷420 rooms, 47 suites ⚿In room: safe, dial-up. In-hotel: 8 restaurants, room service, bars, tennis courts, pools, gym, spa, beachfront, diving, water sports, children's programs (ages 4–11), laundry service, concierge, executive floor, parking (no fee) ⊟AE, DC, MC, V ⱺEP.

$$$ ▣**Radisson SAS Hotel Dubai Media City.** A trendy curved glass edifice reminiscent of a 1950s movie theater, the 4-star Radisson SAS is in the heart of Media City and attracts a hip, electronically savvy business clientele. The decor throughout the property is up-to-the-minute, with glass walls in the public areas and glass showers in the bathrooms. Warm wood veneers and deep terra-cotta colors add natural accents. The hotel's popular bars and restaurants attract Dubai's young crowd, so there's a vibrant buzz about the place even though it's off the usual tourist route. **Pros:** contemporary decor; trendy bars on-site. **Cons:** not near any tourist attractions. ⊠Dubai Media City, Al Sufouh 1 ☎4/366–9111 ⊕www.radisson.com ➷241 rooms, 5 suites ⚿In-room: Ethernet. In-hotel: 5 restaurants, room service, bar, pools, gym, spa, laundry service, concierge, executive floor ⊟AE, DC, MC, V ⱺEP.

$$$$   ⊞**Ritz-Carlton Dubai.** This hotel's international reputation for high quality and exquisite service continue at its beachfront property in Dubai. Rather than using local design themes, The Ritz-Carlton Dubai is decked out in Mediterranean style, with muted stucco, Italian marble, and draped windows inspired by the French Riviera. The classic European room decor features polished French wooden furniture, and patterned cushions and drapes with touches of gold that add an exotic element. The resort is a refined location for honeymooning or romantic vacations, and also attracts discerning business travelers. **Pros:** good beach; nice beachfront gardens and pools; excellent spa. **Cons:** compact grounds feel a little snug; dull exterior design. ⊠*Al Sufouh Rd., Dubai Marina* ☎*4/399–4000* ⊕*www.ritzcarlton.com* ⇴*138 rooms* ♿*In-room: safe, DVD. In-hotel: restaurants, room service, bars, 4 tennis courts, golf course, 3 pools, gym, spa, beachfront, diving, water sports, children's programs (ages 4–12), laundry service, concierge, executive floor, parking (no fee)* ▭*AE, DC, MC, V* ⭗*EP.*

$$$–$$$$   ⊞**Sheraton Jumeirah Beach Resort.** One of the older properties on the seaward side of Dubai Marina, the Sheraton has become more attractive as new properties continue to crop up around it. The outside of the structure screams "passé" and the room decor could be at a Sheraton anywhere. But this may work to your advantage, as its dated fashion makes it a good bet for more affordable room rates. The hotel has lush trees but not expansive gardens and a good stretch of beach. **Pros:** good location; close to the growing Dubai Marina. **Cons:** mediocre style; set on a small patch of real estate; expensive rack rates for the pricey. ⊠*Al Sufouh Road, Dubai Marina* ☎*4/399–5533* ⊕*www. sheraton.com* ⇴*256 rooms and suites* ♿*In-room: kitchen (some), Ethernet. In-hotel: 6 restaurants, room service, bars, pool, gym, spa, beachfront, water sports, children's programs (ages 4–12), laundry service, concierge, executive floor, parking (no fee), no-smoking rooms* ▭*AE, DC, MC, V* ⭗*EP.*

$$   ⊞**Tulip Inn.** In the heart of Knowledge Village, this well-priced (for Dubai) modern hotel attracts a mixed clientele of budget-conscious businesspeople, students, and academics from various school campuses—giving the area a young international feel. Rooms are a bit bland, but are bright and clean. It's only 10 minutes by taxi or bus to Dubai Marina or Madinat Jumeirah, but the immediate surroundings are more professional neighborhoods. **Pros:** good price point,

modern structure. **Cons:** surrounded by school campuses so feels a bit academic; few facilities in immediate area. ⊠*Knowledge Village* ☎*4/367–1222* ⊕*www.tulipinnfzllc. com* ⇨*40 rooms* ☝*In-room: Wi-Fi. In-hotel: restaurant, room service, bar, gym, laundry service, no-smoking rooms* ⊟*AE, MC, V* ⊙*EP.*

# Shopping

**WORD OF MOUTH**

"Visit the souks! It is fun to barter."
— the4canadians

"If you are up for retail therapy then you are in the right place."
— Losttime

By Lindsay
Bennett
**DUBAI IS A MECCA OF SHOPPING,** and if it's sheer volume that gets you to part with your dollars there are few spots on earth that can beat it. With tax-free prices and billions of dollars' worth of giveaways for customers, the emirate has gained a reputation as the place for bargains.

Dubai produces next to no products, but it never mattered because historically goods came flooding in from around the Gulf, the Indian subcontinent, and the horn of Africa. Now they stream in from around the globe, as designers hunger to establish a presence in this red-hot town.

The top buys start with gold and precious stones—Dubai is one of the cheapest places in the world to buy quality jewelry. It's also the largest marketplace, outside of Iran, for handmade Persian rugs, and prices are much more affordable than in the United States and Europe. Indian and Chinese silks and satins occupy an important sector of the market, while spices and incense are must-buy items. The city has what might be the best range of up-market goods outside of New York Fashion Week. It's rare to find such a saturation of French, Italian, American, and British designers together in one city.

The alleyways of the old downtown souks still have the bustling atmosphere of a traditional Arab trading port, and you can get down to some serious haggling here. But Dubai has fallen in love with the air-conditioned mall, and these modern retail temples range over millions of square feet.

Although Dubai certainly appears to be shopping heaven, it's worthwhile keeping in mind the Latin phrase *caveat emptor,* or "buyer beware." Large electronics producers use Dubai to offload last year's stock, so many computers, electronics, and cameras are not current models. And even though the shopping is tax free, it doesn't necessarily mean that prices for international goods will be cheaper than in your hometown. Numerous shoppers come to Dubai from countries where luxury goods and designer labels are hard to get, so price is less important than availability. If getting a bargain is the main reason for traveling to Dubai, make sure to research prices of similar goods at home before you come.

# SHOPPING DISTRICTS & MALLS

## BUR DUBAI & THE SOUTH BANK

**BurJuman Centre** (⊠*Sheikh Khalifa bin Zayed St., Al Mankool* ☎*4/352–0222*), an 800,000-square-foot boxy building, houses a some of downtown's finest designer names and a smattering of top-label street brands. There are more than 300 stores in total, including Christian Lacroix, Cartier, Dior, Donna Karan, Hermès, Valentino, and a Saks Fifth Avenue department store.

At **Karama Market** (⊠*Off Za'abeel Rd., Karama* ☎*No phone*), Dubai's largest general souk, products span the gamut from mundane essentials to mass-produced souvenirs to the latest designer copies and fakes—all in huge quantities. Goods spill onto the walkways of this small commercial quarter of shops and kiosks, and all the activity makes for an electric environment. Karama is popular with expat workers who aren't on big tax-free salaries, including thousands of shop assistants, taxi drivers, and construction workers on the lookout for bargain clothing or gifts to take home to their families. There's a range of cheap eateries around the market—tasty Indian and Pakistani fare, and Filipino and Sri Lankan cuisine—making it a great place for budget travelers.

THE NIGHT SOUK. From mid-December to early February, this nightly souk is open on Al Seef Road, alongside the creek in Bur Dubai. Hundreds of stalls sell inexpensive handicrafts and local snacks, and there's a small amusement park. This spot is a favorite of expat Filipinos, Indians, Pakistanis, and Sri Lankans, as well as local Emirati families. It's a great place to spend a few hours and immerse yourself in the colorful multicultural landscape that is Dubai.

**Lamcy Plaza** (⊠*Off Umm Hurair Rd., Oud Metha* ☎*4/335–9999*) is a useful all-purpose mall. Lamcy Plaza caters not only to shoppers but aims to be more of a community facility than other shopping centers in the city. Here, you'll find driving centers, shoe repairs, key cutting services, and a post office among the many stores. Lamcy Plaza is strong on main street names, including well-known brands Guess, Van Heusen, Next from the UK, and Giordano from Southeast Asia. It is also the only mall in Dubai that opens at 9 every morning.

At **Wafi City Mall** (⊠*Sheikh Rashid Rd., Umm Hurair* ☎*4/324–4426*) style is a watchword, though the Egyptian theme of the mall comes across a bit kitschy. Wafi isn't the largest mall in the city—with just more than 100 stores—but it provides niche retailing you can't find elsewhere. Renowned names such as Chanel, Pierre Cardin, and Cerruti are joined by Marks and Spencer, independent boutiques, and the largest department store in Dubai, Salem.

## DEIRA & THE NORTH BANK

**Al Ghurair City** (⊠*Al-Rigga Rd., Al-Rigga* ☎*4/222–5222*), Dubai's first mall, still draws shoppers in droves with its well-known labels, including Adidas, French Connection, La Senza, Liz Claiborne, Naturalizer, Nine West, and Timberland. It is especially popular with Emirati women as it has an excellent selection of abaya shops. The mall is anchored by a BHS department store. **Deira City Centre Mall** (⊠*Baniyas Rd., Al Saeed* ☎*4/295–1010*), the most popular shopping center on the Deira side of the creek, won't win any prizes for its design, but its prices are lower than other malls with the same stores. Shopping covers everything you might need, from groceries to Persian carpets. The range of shopping opportunities here attracts a cross-section of customers from all nationalities and walks of life. Mainstream outlets dominate, but the newer wing, Bin Hendi, has more cutting-edge boutiques and a selection of eateries. Deira City Centre Mall also has an RTA office that issues temporary Dubai driver's licenses, which you'll need if you want to rent a car and don't have an international driver's license.

**The Electronics Souk** (⊠*South of Sikkat Al Khail Rd., opposite the Perfume Souk* ☎*No phone*) contains hundreds of dusty neon-lit shops that stock everything from mosque-shaped alarm clocks to MP3 players. Some of the stock has been here for years, but the kitsch value is sky-high.

**ASK BEFORE YOU BUY.** Warranties offered on electronic goods, cameras, and computers may have a limited geographical coverage—be sure to ask because many warranties are only valid in Dubai.

**Festival Waterfront Centre** (⊠*Dubai Festival City, Festival Blvd., off Rebat St., south of Business Bay Bridge* ☎*4/232–5444*) covers 2.8 million square feet at this airy mall—a large, two-floor semicircle with 600 stores to add to the city's retail mix. Residents flock to the giant IKEA and to ACE Hardware for barbecues and DIY essentials. The main mall has a selection of upscale international labels, anchored by a Marks and Spencer, as well as a dedicated gold souk. Opening to the western side onto the creek's promenade, it has eateries and a range of craft kiosks, so you can shop and then dine (or vice versa) in delightful waterfront surroundings.

**Reef Mall** (⊠*Salahuddin St., Al Muraqqabat* ☎*4/224–2240*) is a two-story structure with a selection of high-quality street and youth brands, including Athlete's Foot, Bench, Elle, Samuel and Kevin, and Nine West. The largest store is a Home Centre, making it popular with expat homemakers. In addition, Fun City has games and activities for kids of all ages, from tots to early teens.

**OPENING SOON.** Dubai will soon be home to the two largest shopping malls in the world. Mall of Arabia in the Burj Dubai complex will open with 10 million square feet of retail space before the end of 2008, and Dubai Mall at Dubailand will top that with 12.1 million square feet when it opens in 2009 or 2010.

## JUMEIRAH BEACH

**Mall of the Emirates** (⊠*Off Interchange 4, Sheikh Zayed Rd.* ☎*4/409–9000*), currently Dubai's largest shopping center at 2,399,480 square feet, has more than 450 shops and department stores, with a comprehensive combination of designer and main street brands, fashion, housewares, and a souk for souvenirs. Department stores Harvey Nichols and Debenhams have their largest stores in the Middle East here, and more than 60 stores have made their Middle Eastern debut in this mall. A large Carrefour supermarket sells food, inexpensive clothing, and other domestic essentials. The complex was designed to be more than just a retail heaven, with sporting events, arts, and entertainment in addition to shopping. Ski Dubai (*see* ⇨*Chapter 1, Exploring Dubai*), is the first indoor slope in the Gulf area. There's also a multiscreen cinema complex, Magic Planet (*see* ⇨*Chapter 6, Nightlife & the Arts*), a children's adventure and play area, and a community theater company.

Images of **Mercato Mall** (⊠*Jumeirah Rd., Jumeirah 1* ☎*4/344–4161*), with its Italian Renaissance style, make it into most publicity brochures and travel guides about Dubai. This mall jump-started the themed shopping center craze.

By today's standards it's small, with fewer than 100 stores, including Gap, Mango, and Top Shop, as well as many independent stores. The largest store is a Virgin Megastore, and the mall is anchored by a Spinney's supermarket.

**Souk Madinat Jumeirah** (⊠*Al Sufouh Rd., Al Sufouh* ☎*4/366–8888*), the Jumeirah group's modern take on the traditional Arabian souk, is a beautiful labyrinth of narrow alleyways packed with fine souvenirs, including high-quality carpets, arts and crafts, jewelry, and clothing. Goods often clutter the walkways, giving the feel of an authentic Eastern bazaar where a million and one shiny items catch the eye. Most boutiques here are independent, but you will find a Tommy Bahamas and Oxbow as well. The waterside cafés are a great place to relax with a drink.

**Town Centre** (⊠*Jumeirah Rd., next to Mercato Mall* ☎*4/344–4161*) is a petite mall with a selection of stores that includes such international outlets as Naturalizer and Nine West, as well as a health food store. Or stop off at Feet First, a reflexology and massage center, that will help you find relief for your worn-out tootsies.

**The Village Mall** (⊠*Jumeirah Rd.* ☎*4/394–4444*), with many independent stores selling one-of-a-kind items and smaller brand labels, is the place to shop if you want to leave mass-market products behind. It's designed to mimic a Mediterranean village where you can stroll through such stores as Luxcouture, which stocks clothing by Brian Reyes and Christopher Deane, and Chic Oz Design, which carries items by emerging Australian designers. Peekaboo has a range of activities for kids up to seven years old, so you can leave the little ones to play while you shop. For pampering, Sensasia (*see* ⇨*Chapter 7, Sports & Activities*) is one of the best independent spas in Dubai.

## WORLD TRADE CENTRE & BURJ DUBAI

**Boulevard** (⊠*Emirate's Towers, Sheikh Zayed Rd.* ☎*4/330–0000*) is Dubai's most exclusive retail address. This bijou (jewel) of a mall of less than 50 outlets is packed with luxury brands. It's quieter here and not as family-friendly as the major shopping centers. Boulevard is serious spending territory, with YSL, Bvulgari, and Gucci on the lower level and Armani, Emelio Pucci, and Jimmy Choo on the upper mezzanine. Clientele is a mixture of expats working in the business district, conventioneers from Russia, India, and Southeast Asia, and wealthy Emiratis.

**Holiday Mall** (⊠*below the Crowne-Plaza Hotel, Sheikh Zayed Rd.* ☎4/331–7755) is a workaday mall where you can pop in for shampoo and deodorant or diamonds and Persian carpets. This is a good option for postcards and cheap mass-produced souvenirs. There's a multicultural buzz about the place, as taxi drivers come in to buy cigarettes and convention-goers from around the world seek out gifts for their families back home.

## DUBAI MARINA

**Jumeirah Walk** (⊠*Al Sufouh Rd., Dubai Marina* ☎4/366–5000), a community shopping center, occupies the ground level of the multitower Jumeirah Beach Residence complex, a new narrow island between the marina and the sea. The mall opens onto the outdoor waterside corniche for a European-style shopping experience with cafés and casual eateries interspersed among the stores—more than 400 in total.

**Ibn Battuta Mall** (⊠*Off Interchange 6, Sheikh Zayed Rd.* ☎4/362–1900), Dubai's most visually stunning shopping structure, has stores divided into six different courts. Each is designed in the style of one of the countries or regions visited by the great Islamic traveler and diarist Ibn Battuta, who lived during the 14th century. From the azure tiles and fountains at Andalusia Court, you'll wander through Tunisia, Egypt, Persia, India, and finally to the life-size junk boat on display at the China court. Artisans were brought from across the globe to design the mall's decorative elements, including the ornate blue and gold enameling in the dome of the Persian court and the detailed wooden fretwork of the Egyptian souk. There are more than 200 stores here, such as department stores Debenhams and Fitz & Simons and a large Géant supermarket. The sprawling mall is all on one level, so the management provides golf cart transportation (there are several stops with frequent, regularly scheduled service) to give your tired feet a rest.

**DUBAI SHOPPING FESTIVAL.** One of the major events on the annual calendar here, the Dubai Shopping Festival runs from mid-January to mid-February each year. Retailers around the city reduce prices by up to 75%, and malls host a mix of big prize draws, beauty contests, talent shows, and cultural events. In 2007, the Dubai Shopping Festival brought to the emirate 3.5 million visitors, who spent a total of AED 10.2 billion, or $2.8 billion.

## AROUND THE EMIRATE

**Dragon Mart** (✉*International City, Al Awir Rd., Al Awir* ☎*4/368–7208*) is considered to be the biggest trading space for Chinese-produced goods outside of mainland China. Dragon Mart is definitely a great place to make large-scale commercial purchases. Need 600 copies of a teapot, heavy-duty farm machinery, or 100,000 tiles for a building project? These deals are made here. More than 1,000 Chinese storekeepers are on hand to sell numerous mass-produced and one-of-a-kind items. Dragon Mart is a retail mall, but it doesn't attract many browsing families or shopping groups. However, it's definitely a different kind of experience in this emirate.

**Dubai Outlet Mall** (✉*Route 66, the Al Ain Rd.* ☎*4/367–9600*), Dubai's first foray into the world of outlet shopping, is one of the few completed attractions at the vast Dubailand complex and, at the moment, it's a bit out of the way—taxi fare totals about AED 80 one-way from downtown. The mall has 240 stores with such brands as Diesel, Guess, Mango, Max Mara, Reebok, Ted Lapidus, and Timberland. There's also a food court and a small children's entertainment center with rides, bowling, and an ice rink.

# SPECIALTY STORES

## ART

**Art Space Gallery** (✉*Fairmont Dubai, Sheik Zayed Rd., World Trade Centre & Burj Dubai* ☎*4/332–5523*), with a changing roster of exhibitions of Middle Eastern artists, is at the forefront of the growing interest in contemporary arts in the region. Art Space is a great stopover for current and budding collectors.

**B21** (✉*Opposite the Spinneys Warehouse, off Interchange 3, Sheikh Zayed Rd., Al Quoz 3, Jumeirah Beach* ☎*4/340–3965*) represents more than 15 local and international artists, and mostly stocks contemporary Arabian art across a range of genres. B21 also offers consulting services for collectors.

**Gallery One** (✉*Souk Madinat Jumeirah, Al Sufouh Rd., Al Sufouh, Jumeirah Beach* ☎*4/368–6055*), is a mixed art and photography gallery. Owner Gregg Sedgewick took many

## CLOSE UP

# Barter Your Way to a Bargain

Malls in Dubai work on a fixed-price system—though it's possible to get a small discount simply by asking if the ticket actually denotes the best price. However, bartering is an accepted part of life in the souks, where the price is mutually agreed on by purchaser and merchant. Even if bargaining doesn't come naturally to you, there's no need to be nervous about it. If you are buying an expensive souvenir like a carpet or a precious stone, you often will pay more than you should if you consent to the storekeeper's first figure.

You can follow a few easy tips to make bartering in all souks more successful and enjoyable. First, act cool about the specific item you want. Look at several items and narrow down your choice while building a rapport with the vendor. Usually they'll offer a drink—coffee, tea, or soda. This is standard and by accepting their offer, you show you're serious about negotiating. Your first offer should be about half of the vendor's first figure, then increase your offer little by little as the vendor lowers his. If you decide that the price range is still too high, simply tell the shop owner and walk away. You never know, he may call you back with a lower offer.

Never verbally agree to a price you are not willing to pay. If you do, it is considered very bad manners to change your mind!

of the images of Dubai that are for sale, which can be an evocative souvenir of a trip to the emirate.

**Kenza Art Gallery** (⊠*Souk Madinat Jumeirah, Al Sufouh Rd., Al Sufouh, Jumeirah Beach* ☎*4/368–6603*) is a showcase for local artist Sumaira K. Isaacs, who displays her unique approaches to traditional Islamic shapes, forms, and colors.

## BOOKS & MAGAZINES

**Magrudy's** (⊠*Jumeirah Rd., Jumeirah 2, Jumeirah Beach* ☎*4/344–4193*) is the place to come if you're looking for maps or coffee-table books of Dubai, international newspapers, the latest paperbacks, and stationary or postcards. The store has five bookstore/newsstand branches across the city in BurJuman Centre, Deira City Centre Mall, Ibn Battuta Mall, and Al Wahda Mall. This location is the branch that's closest to the main beach resort area.

DUBAI DUTY FREE. The duty-free shopping at Dubai International Airport is consistently voted the best in the world. One huge mall, it stocks a vast selection of cosmetics and perfumes, liquor, cigars and cigarettes, gold and precious stones, and cameras and computers. You can even buy toasters, bread makers, and other kitchen appliances here. The prize drawings offered by Dubai Duty Free include tickets to win a million dollars, luxury vehicles, and real estate.

## CAMERAS & ELECTRONICS

**Jumbo Electronics** (✉*Opposite Al Ain Centre, Bur Dubai, Bur Dubai & the South Bank* ☎4/352–3555) the largest company for consumer electronics in Dubai, has 15 outlets around the city. Its products range from PCs, cameras, hi-fis, MP3 players, and all sorts of video games. The details shown here are for the largest six-floor store. Other branches can be found at the Bur Juman Mall, Deira City Centre Mall, Dubai Festival City, Ibn Battuta Mall, Mall of the Emirates, and Wafi City Mall.

**Plug Ins** (✉*Dubai Festival City, Festival Blvd., off Al Rebat St., Deira & the North Bank* ☎4/206–6777), with four locations in Dubai, has an ample choice of cameras for still or moving images, mobile phones, and small electrical household appliances and personal-care products. Other branches can be found at the Bur Juman Mall and Souk Madinat Jumeirah.

## CARPETS

**National Iranian Carpets** (✉*Souk Madinat Jumeirah, Al Sufouh Rd., Al Sufouh, Jumeirah Beach* ☎4/221-9800) will meet your needs for a wide selection of Persian handmade carpets in various sizes and colors. Knowledgeable staff members will be happy to explain the traditional patterns and different qualities of carpets, so you can choose the one that's right for your budget and home decor. There are branches at Dubai Festival City, Deira City Centre, and Mercato Mall.

## GOLD & DIAMONDS

**Damas** (⊠*Damas Les Exclusives, Wafi City Mall, Wafi City, off Sheikh Rashid Rd., Oud Metha, Bur Dubai & the South Bank* ☎*4/324–2425*), a UAE-based company with locations in more than 15 countries, offers a range of high-quality jewelry in gold and precious stones. Individual design collections are displayed alongside more mainstream styles, as well as designer watches. Damas has divided its stores into brands—Les Exclusives is the most upscale, followed by Semi Exclusive, 22ct, and 18kt. Branches are located in most malls and major hotels.

## FOOD

**Tea and More** (⊠*Souk Madinat Jumeirah, Al Sufouh Rd., Al Sufouh 1, Jumeirah Beach* ☎*4/366–8888 [general number for mall]*) sells numerous teas from around the world, which line the shelves here and are sold in attractive tins and practical packets. There are exotic mixes and good quality single blends. The "More" eludes to the shop's tea accessories, including elegant pots and china cups.

## NATURAL PRODUCTS

**Caravella Trading** (⊠*Souk Madinat Jumeirah, Al Sufouh Rd., Sufouh 1, Jumeirah Beach* ☎*4/366–8888*) specializes in essential oils, creams, and potions, which are made here from recipes perfected in India. Products are for all ages and genders, and cleanse and moisturize the whole body.

## TAILORS

**Dream Girls** (⊠*Behind Satwa Health Centre, Satwa Rd., Satwa, World Trade Centre Area & Burj Dubai* ☎*4/349–5445*) is doubtless one of Dubai's favorite tailoring shops. Dream Girls will make you anything from a simple shirt to a fabulous gown, or you can take in a beloved item of clothing and they'll make a copy of it. There are catalogues full of products that they can make to your exact measurements in whatever material you choose.

# Nightlife & the Arts

**WORD OF MOUTH**

"Buy *Time Out* at the airport after changing money at a bank there and read it front to cover to get a feel for what is going on in the city."

—Lincasanova

By Lindsay
Bennett

**DUBAI IS PARTY CENTRAL FOR** the Middle East. Expats here work hard and play hard, so there's no excuse for sitting in your hotel room watching reruns of *Friends* dubbed into Arabic. The city has action of every type—ultracool bars with multihued cocktails, romantic terraces for sharing a glass of champagne, sports bars and pubs with monumental flat-screen TVs and nachos, and nightclubs where you can dance until nearly dawn. Dubai is a favorite for celebrity DJs with regular one-night-only appearances.

But like everything else in this city, the scene changes rapidly. A new must-see place opens almost every week, and the in-crowd flits from launch to launch like a skittish flock of starlings looking for an evening roost.

You may have to refinance the mortgage to pay for a serious night out in Dubai. Alcohol is served only on licensed premises—usually attached to international hotels—and the prices are exorbitant.

Classic performance arts have a thin presence in comparison with the thriving party scene. Most of the offerings are local, and a few independent galleries stand out as beacons. However, the future debut of Dubai's Culture City may change this. Rising from the south bank of Dubai Creek just beyond Garhoud Bridge, it will include a majestic Dubai Opera House, a focal point for the genre in the Gulf region.

Movies are also popular entertainment for all sectors of Dubai society. At least a dozen large multiplex centers show the latest blockbusters from Hollywood and Bollywood, as well as films from around the Arabic-speaking world and martial-arts favorites from Hong Kong.

**PARTY OFF?** During the month of Ramadan, the hedonistic nightlife scene tones down. Many nightclubs close their doors, and live bands lay down their instruments. Don't visit Dubai during Ramadan if you are looking to party.

CLOSE UP

## Grown Up & Dressed Up

Bars and clubs have age limits and you'll need to show ID if you look underage. You have to be 21 to order drinks or stand in bar areas where alcohol is being served. Some clubs restrict entry to those over 25. In addition, some popular clubs restrict entry to clients based on their appearance. People love to dress up in Dubai, so be sure to break out the latest fashions for your evening of clubbing; otherwise you may be left on the curb.

# WORLD TRADE CENTRE AREA & BURJ DUBAI

## BARS & CLUBS

**6**

**The Agency** (⊠*Boulevard at Emirates Towers, Sheikh Zayed Rd.* ☎*4/319–8088* ⊕*www.jumeirah.com*), a favorite with corporate types for working lunches, offers a sophisticated take on the tapas experience. With a list of more than 400 wines—all displayed in wall cabinets—there's no doubt that you'll find something to your taste, and the dark wood tables and low lighting give the interior the feel of a French-style wine cave. It's a place to sip and savor, not quaff. The menu leans toward charcuterie-style nibbles, but there's a set menu of roast meat every lunchtime. The Agency has also opened a branch at Souk Madinat Jumeirah.

**Aussie Legend's** (⊠*Rydges Plaza Hotel, Al Diyafah St., Satwa Roundabout* ☎*4/398–2222* ⊕*www.rydges.com*) is an Australian-themed bar where the tubes (or beers) are cold and the TV always shows sports. Good beer, pool tables, and friendly regulars make it one of Dubai's best pub experiences. Occasionally, there's live music.

★ **Cin Cin** (⊠*Fairmont Dubai, Sheikh Zayed Rd.* ☎*4/332–5555* ⊕*www.fairmont.com*), an ultratrendy venue for groups of friends or first dates out to impress, has a massive wine wall behind the bar—which no doubt adds to its success. Metal, glass, and glowing light walls of luminescent color are the main design features. The seating here can match your mood, with high tables and stools for chatting and scanning the room, and low tables with black-and-white leather love seats for a more intimate experience. Cin Cin attracts a cross section of Dubai's expats, and it's a good place to put your finger on the pulse of the city's scene.

At **Double Decker** ( ⊠ *Al Murooj Rotana Hotel and Suites, Al Saffa St., off Interchange 1, Sheikh Zayed Rd.* ☎*4/321–1111* ⊕*www.rotana.com*), the signature two-story bus of swinging London, merges with the flamboyance of the Rotana Al Murooj hotel here—all pink stucco and white-frosting trim. From the moment you spot the suits of armor and red telephone box you'll know where you are. It's not quite so flashy as Austin Powers, but it's as clichéd as you can get. Premier League soccer games are broadcast on the big screens and accompanied by pints from the UK. A bit later every night there's live music or DJs spinning their favorite tracks.

**Harry Ghatto's** ( ⊠ *Boulevard at Emirates Towers, Sheikh Zayed Rd.* ☎*4/330–0000* ⊕*www.jumeirah.com*), a popular, bustling Japanese restaurant during the early evening, turns into a tiny club after 9, and an hour later provides the best karaoke experience in the city. It has an excellent reputation for authentic cuisine served in a maze of cozy dining spaces, and the 5-foot-by-5-foot stage sits next to the bar. So grab the mike and belt out your favorite tunes. Based on what you choose, you can immediately convert the space to a Parisian café or a New Orleans blues bar.

**iKandy** ( ⊠ *Shangri-La Hotel, Sheikh Zayed Rd.* ☎*4/343–8888* ⊕*www.shangri-la.com*) transforms the pool area of the Shangri-La Hotel into a chic open-air club (and, yes, you can swim if you like). As the name suggests, it's a pretty place frequented by pretty people. Acres of billowing cotton create cozy areas furnished with sofas and vast cushions, and lighting is vivid in blue and pink neons. Enjoy a *shisha* (water pipe), cocktails, and the finest cognacs and tequilas while listening to trance-style vibes. A good place to chill.

**Lotus 1** ( ⊠ *Convention Tower, Dubai World Trade Centre, off Sheikh Zayed Rd.* ☎*4/329–3200* ⊕*www.lotus1.com*), A chameleon of a place—sometimes a restaurant and later a club—epitomizes the Dubai scene. Elegant Asian-fusion dishes are served at intimate tables among teak and stainless steel design elements. The bar is heavy on neon colors with funky chairs that hang from the ceiling, and the dance floor is made of glass. It's a favorite hangout for the "it" crowd on weekends.

At **Maharlika Café** (✉*President Hotel, Trade Centre Rd., Bur Dubai* ☎*4/334–6565* ⊕*www.presidentdubai.com*), the Filipino band is what makes crowds of people—not just expat Pinoys—flock to Maharlika instead of other dance clubs. With covers of everyone's favorite songs, it's part sing-along bar and part dance hall. Inexpensive beer and vodka-infused juices come by the pitcher, making it a cheap night out by Dubai standards.

**Oscar's** (✉*Crowne-Plaza Hotel, Sheikh Zayed Rd.* ☎*4/331–1111* ⊕*www.icehotelsgroup.com*), one of the new generation of wine bars, takes the mysticism out of the oenophile experience, with sampling menus (a selection of four or five wines) at reasonable prices, accompanied by genuine Spanish tapas, including cured meats, olives, and passable cheese. You can enjoy a good range of old- and new-world wines by the glass or bottle. Oscar's looks like a traditional Spanish bodega, complete with terra-cotta floor tiles and huge barrels for tables.

**Trader Vic's** (✉*Crowne-Plaza Hotel, Sheikh Zayed Rd.* ☎*4/305–6399* ⊕*www.tradervics.com*) has been serving mai tais and its American-style menu since 1994, making it a Dubai veteran. It continues to be a hit because of its fun, relaxed style, and you don't have to dress to impress. The funky, colorful, Polynesian-themed decor is straight out of the '90s. The look is a bit past its sell-by date, but Trader Vic's is still an enjoyable spot with a live Cuban band that plays nightly. There's another location at Souk Madinat Jumeirah.

★ **Vu's Bar** (✉*Emirates Towers Hotel, Sheikh Zayed Rd.* ☎*4/319–8088* ⊕*www.jumeirah.com*), on the 51st floor of the swanky Emirates Towers Hotel, screams sleek 21st century, with a vast metal and glass canopy wall that overwhelms the space. The magnificent view—across the business district, downtown to the north, and the Marina to the south—should get accolades, but the modern cathedral-like space and its striking clientele keep the eye focused inside. Fashionistas will love it here, but wannabes need not apply. The designer labels on display are the real deal. For those who come in more relaxed attire, you'll need to pass the shirt, slacks, and shoes (no sandals) test to get through the door.

**Zinc** (✉*Crowne-Plaza Hotel, Sheikh Zayed Rd.* ☎*4/331–1111* ⊕*www.ichotelsgroup.com*), an intimate basement club with pale metallic walls, gives the illusion that this space is bigger than it is. The long central bar is the main focus, though you can shake it to the latest chart toppers on the diminutive dance floor. This is one of Dubai's most relaxed clubs, where folks come to have fun rather than preen and pout. Laughter Factory hosts a stand-up comedy evening here once a month.

# BUR DUBAI & THE SOUTH BANK

## BARS & CLUBS

**Crossroads Bar** ( ⊠ *Raffles Dubai, off Sheikh Rashid Rd., Umm Hurair 2* ☎ *4/324–8888* ⊕ *www.dubai.raffles.com*) may remind you of the historic Raffles Hotel in Singapore, which is famed for its Singapore Sling cocktail; here, you can sip a Dubai Sling while enjoying the best terrace downtown. The interior space at Crossroads is contemporary Asian fusion, with warm-toned hardwood fretwork and teak floors that contrast with the rich red furnishings. But the terrace is the triumph with tables flowing out toward the hotel's magnificent rooftop gardens. On warm evenings you can wander among the fragrant flowers and herbs and watch the lights of Bur Dubai and Deira twinkling all around.

**Chi@The Lodge** ( ⊠ *Al Nasr Leisureland, off Umm Hurair Rd., Oud Metha* ☎ *4/337–9470* ⊕ *www.lodgedubai.com*) is one of Dubai's oldest venues, but Chi is its latest manifestation. It has four interconnected areas, each with its own style—one of which is a garden that's popular with party animals who like to dance in the open air. An ever-changing list of guest DJs keeps the music fresh and the young clientele excited. This venue is all the rage, so lines can be long.

**Elegante** ( ⊠ *Royal Ascot Hotel, Khalid bin Waheel Rd., Bur Dubai* ☎ *4/352–0900* ⊕ *www.royalascothotel-dubai.com*), Bur Dubai's largest club, is a multispace venue with a huge dance floor. The club has gimmicks, including state-of-the-art light shows and nitrogen effects, an excellent sound system, and a lineup of the current in-demand DJs.

**Ginseng** ( ⊠ *Wafi City Mall, Oud Metha* ☎ *4/324–8200* ⊕ *www. ginsengdubai.com*) is part bar, part nightclub, part eatery, where you'll be surrounded by Asian style at this versatile venue. The dance floor hums to a great mix of tunes. There's an ample cocktail list plus a menu of new-world wines to accompany the Asian tapas menu, including plates of dim sum and sushi. Weekends can get very busy, so arrive early or be prepared to wait in line.

**Jimmy Dix** (✉*Mövenpick Hotel, off Za'abeel Rd., Oud Metha* ☎*4/336–8800* ⊕*www.moevenpick-hotels.com*) is Dubai's take on the 1920s speakeasy. Jimmy Dix has survived an onslaught of modern bars and remains as popular as ever. It's an unpretentious venue where people can relax rather than worrying about what designer names they're wearing. Tex-Mex food in ample quantities plus great live music are added attractions. The crowd can be lively and a little young, especially on weekends.

**MIX** (✉*Grand Hyatt Dubai, off Sheikh Rashid Rd., Umm Hurair 2* ☎*4/317–1234* ⊕*www.dubai.grand.hyatt.com*), downtown Dubai's super club, is a multilevel venue that uses circles as a design feature, with curved bars and a circular dance floor. It's been on the scene for a while and some of the fixtures are showing their age. But the slightly careworn look doesn't stop regulars from packing the dance floor every night, though there's ample room in the upper mezzanines to separate yourself from the crowds if you prefer. Or listen to live music in a separate room or chill out in the laid-back lounge.

**PlanB** (✉*The Fort, Wafi City, off Sheikh Rashid Rd., Umm Hurair 2* ☎*4/324–4777* ⊕*www.wafi.com*) is an eclectic spot that has a vodka and champagne bar, as well as a sushi counter, on the upper floor. The club on the lower floor has a tapas-style menu. The modern minimalist decor is accented by neon lights—very new millenium. Dance music from the '80s, '90s, and today throbs throughout the space, and the resident DJ specializes in funk and house.

**Waxy O'Connor's** (✉*Ascot Hotel, Khalid bin Waleed Rd., Bur Dubai* ☎*4/352–9819* ⊕*www.ascothoteldubai.com*), an atmospheric Irish bar, comes complete with sepia-toned walls and a dusty pool table. Pints of stout, strong Irish coffees, and generous plates of rib-warming food are the staple servings here. Waxy's offers an inexpensive Friday brunch that has a loyal following. The bar can get raucous if the heavy-drinking crowd drops in.

## CULTURAL ORGANIZATIONS

**Sahary Gate** (✉*Bastakia Quarter, Bur Dubai* ☎*4/353–5660* ⊕*www.saharygate.com*) acts as a cultural portal between East and West, holding meet-and-greet events, such as coffee mornings, where visitors can experience the Arab world's traditions. Women can discuss family and community life with Arab women, and business clients can get acquainted with regional customs to improve their understanding of the commercial environment. The organization also has classes teaching Arabic skills, such as calligraphy, and conducts guided walks of Bastakia.

**The Sheikh Mohammed Centre for Cultural Understanding** (⊠*Bastakia Quarter, Bur Dubai* ☎*4/353–6666* ⊕*www. cultures.ae*), founded by the current sheikh to promote cross-cultural understanding, has a range of activities, including cultural breakfasts and lunches and walking tours of Bastakia. It also organizes tours of Jumeirah Mosque (*see* ⇨*Chapter 2, Exploring Dubai*), the only mosque in the emirate that allows entry to non-Muslims.

## GALLERIES

★ **Majlis Gallery** (⊠*Bastakia Quarter, Bur Dubai* ☎*4/353–6233* ⊕*www.majlisgallery.com*) is run by interior designer Alison Collins, who moved to Dubai in the 1970s and raised three children in this Bastakia mansion. She converted the property during the regeneration of the quarter, and since then it has become a major venue for emerging artists from around the Arab world. Exhibitions change constantly, lasting about two weeks each, and genres cover the whole gamut of visual arts, from oil painting to tapestry. Majlis also has an artist-in-residence program and an excellent commercial gallery.

★ **XVA** (⊠*Bastakia Quarter, Bur Dubai* ☎*4/353–5383* ⊕*www. xvagallery.com*) provides an interface between visitors and contemporary Islamic art, with an ever-changing calendar of thought-provoking exhibitions from artists around the region. The owners of XVA play an important role in marketing the arts throughout the emirate, organizing numerous arts fairs and cultural soirees. The gallery is a consulting agency for commercial organizations, has corporate events, and also operates a chic boutique hotel (*For more information see* ⇨*Chapter 4, Where to Stay*) from the gallery location.

# DEIRA AND THE NORTH BANK

## BARS & CLUBS

**Belgian Beer Café** (⊠*Crowne-Plaza Festival City, Festival City* ☎*4/701–2222* ⊕*www.ichotelsgroup.com*) is definitely not the most imaginative name in the city, but at least you know what you'll get here. There's an excellent choice of beers on draft and in bottles from what's arguably the world's greatest brewing nation. Just as in Belgium, each beer has a specific glass for serving—the most unusual of which might be the Kwak glass with a rounded base that comes in a wooden casing. The café's style is straight from Belgium, too, with wooden tables set in small wooden booths around a long bar studded with brass. Brasserie-style food is served.

★ **Irish Village** (⊠*The Aviation Club, off Al Garhoud Rd., Garhoud* ☎*4/282–4122* ⊕*www.aviationclub.ae*) is a popular venue for a taste of the Emerald Isle, often an old-fashioned pint of Irish stout and a plate of stew and potatoes. Sports fans gather to watch their favorite tournaments and relax in the traditionally styled pub, with dark wood interior and matching wainscoting. Outside is a large terrace where you can watch the ducks paddling across the pond to the manicured gardens.

**Issimo** (⊠*Hilton Dubai Creek, Baniyas Rd., Deira* ☎*4/227–1111* ⊕*www.hilton.com*) melds together metal, granite, and black leather in one of the more contemporary bars in Deira. Neon lighting marks the transition from day to evening here, when the clientele changes from business lunchers to the party crowd. The only downside might be the lack of a view beyond the glass walls, but all the pretty people inside give you plenty to look at.

**Up on the 10th** (⊠*Radisson SAS* ☎ ⊕) has as its initial draw the view from this 10th-floor bar, but the cool jazz music gives a reason to stay beyond the first drink. This is a classic grown-up space where gimmicks are eschewed for the simple elegance of a Manhattan loft and melodic piano tones or the resonance of plucked double bass strings. The signature drink here is a champagne cocktail.

**Vista** (⊠*InterContinental Festival City, Festival City* ☎*4/701–1111* ⊕*www.ichotelsgroup.com*) is one of the most spacious bars in Dubai, spread out across the cathedral-like lobby of the Intercontinental Hotel and spilling onto the wooden decking where you can see far-reaching views of Dubai Creek. Glass walls make the scenery from inside to outside seamless. The decor is minimalist contemporary with a long city-style bar, and there's a discreet piano for those who prefer a spot of music with their evening cocktail.

# DUBAI MARINA

## BARS & CLUBS

★ **Fodor'sChoice Barasti Bar** (⊠*Le Méridien Mina Seyahi Hotel Beach Resort & Marina, Al Sufouh Rd., Dubai Marina* ☎4/399–3333 ⊕*www.starwoodhotels.com*) is one of the most popular venues on the nightlife circuit and remains packed on weekends for good reason. Set on a large wooden jetty right on the water, it's a wonderful place to relax with a drink, listen to live music, and survey the coastal views and developments on Palm Jumeirah. The atmosphere is decidedly easygoing and attracts all ages. Barasti serves food and also has shisha, but it's most renowned for its evening cocktail scene.

★ **Fodor'sChoice Buddha Bar** (⊠*Grosvenor House Hotel, Dubai Marina* ☎4/317–6000 ⊕*www.buddha-bar.com*), part of a chain, is casting its net around the world, and where better to establish a presence than in hot Dubai? One of the largest venues in the city, the terraces overlook the mouth of Dubai Marina and the comings and goings of the multimillion-dollar gin palaces (yachts or sailboats). Subdued lighting and rich reds lend an Asian feel to the interior, which is divided into a number of intimate corners and niches for romantic tête-à-têtes. Buddha Bar attracts the über-cool and monied crowd, and it's a great place to strike a pose.

**Icon Bar** (⊠*Radisson SAS Hotel Dubai Media City, Dubai Media City, Al Sufouh 1* ☎4/366–9111 ⊕*www.radissonsas.com*), in the heart of Dubai's Media City, is the spot where cool executives and creative designers get together after work. Many conversations revolve around the day's business activities. The contemporary metal style of the long cocktail bar mimics current design trends, and there are also big TV screens for sports fans, who tend to get rowdy during soccer and rugby season.

**Kasbar** (⊠*One&Only Royal Mirage, Al Sufouh Rd., Al Sufouh* ☎4/399–9999 ⊕*www.oneandonlyresorts.com*), a wonderfully authentic rendition of pan-Gulf traditional style, is one of the major venues in Dubai on the after-hours cocktails and dancing circuit. However, it attracts late-20s and -30s singles and couples rather than the young crowd. The space ranges over three floors with a chill-out lounge, a main dance floor, and an upper interior terrace where you can relax on one of the plump sofas and watch as the dancers move to popular DJ music below. While lounging, order some cocktails and finger foods. Closed Sunday.

**The Peppermint Club** ( ⊠*Habtoor Grand Resort and Spa, Al Sufouh Rd., Dubai Marina* ☎*4/332–0037* ⊕*www.pepper mint-club.com*) is the kind of club that doesn't need an introduction. The Web site doesn't list an address—but the place is packed every week because of its incredible DJs and electro/trance vibes. Lines are long and the doormen are some of the pickiest, but once you get inside all this will be forgotten.

**Rooftop Lounge** ( ⊠*One&Only Royal Mirage, Al Sufouh Rd., Al Sufouh 1* ☎ ⊕*www.oneandonlyresorts.com*) is a place where you can have a drink on the expansive terrace—a modern rendition of a rooftop *majlis* (traditional Arabic sitting area) complete with billowing cotton-tented seating areas and hundreds of plump cushions, turned brass tables, and gilded Arabian lamps and candles. But it's not the decor that draws people to this sophisticated and intimate date spot; it's its views. Located in the Royal Mirage resort, a truly spectacular tribute to the era of 1001 Nights, the hotel's rooftop *barjeels* (windcatchers) in the subdued light of the evening couldn't be more beautiful.

## THEATER

**Amphitheatre at DMC** ( ⊠*off Al Sufouh Road, Dubai Media City* ☎*4/391–4555*), with a capacity of 15,000, hosts some huge mainstream acts and was the focal point for the 2007 Dubai Desert Rhythm Music Festival, featuring Kanye West and Joss Stone. Most headliners who make their way to Dubai in the next few years will likely play here.

# JUMEIRAH BEACH

## BARS & CLUBS

**360°** ( ⊠*Jumeirah Beach Hotel* ☎*4/406–8769* ⊕*www.jumei rah.com*), the circular rooftop bar on the Jumeirah Beach hotel marina, has an amazing view out to the Burj Al-Arab hotel just offshore. It's a great place for a sunset drink, where you can watch the light play across the Burj's exterior curves as day turns to night, while you enjoy a shisha or a refreshing drink. The decor is a riot of white—from the comfy beanbags to the chunky seats and tables. There's live music every Friday and Saturday night, but you'll need to reserve a spot on Platinumlist.com (⊕*www.platinum listdubai.com*), a guest-list management site.

**Après** (⊠*Mall of the Emirates, Sheikh Zayed Rd.* ☎4/341–2575 ⊕*www.malloftheemirates.com*), one of Dubai's "pinch yourself to believe it" locations, is a lodge-style bar and the place to come for an après-ski *vin-chaude* (warm wine), just like you would in the Alps. Après has great views across the slopes of Ski Dubai and prides itself on its range of drinks. Entertainment includes seemingly never-ending showings of snowboarding DVDs. Not only for skiers, it's also favored by expat women taking a break from their shopping sprees for a chilled chardonnay or two.

**The Apartment Lounge & Club** (⊠*Jumeirah Beach Hotel, Jumeirah Rd., Umm Suquim 3* ☎4/406–8000 ⊕*www.jumeirah. com*) is furnished with black and gold for a luxurious feel. There are only two rooms here, but the intimate club is a popular late-night venue. You can try salsa dancing, with free lessons on Tuesdays, or join in the hip-hop Wednesdays. The resident DJ mixes with guest spinners on the weekends when The Apartment is a must-visit address. Dress to impress the doorman or you may not pass the threshold.

★ **Bahri Bar** (⊠*Mina A'Salam Hotel, Madinat Jumeirah, Al Sufouh Rd., Al Sufouh 2* ☎4/366–6730 ⊕*www.madinat jumeirah.com*), set amongst the rose-colored barjeels of Madinat Jumeirah with splendid views across the complex, is a good spot to slip off your shoes and relax. Rich earth tones and gold hues give the space a sumptuous feel, especially in the soft lighting after dark. From the terrace you can watch the *abras* (boats) ply the canals and listen to the distant bustle of the souk while making the most of your private vantage point. The tapas-style menu is perfect for a light dinner or snack to accompany your drinks.

**Boston Bar** (⊠*Jumeira Rotana Hotel, Al Diyafah St., Al Bada'a* ☎4/345–2235 ⊕*www.rotana.com*) is an American pub based on the one in the TV show *Cheers,* with warm wood wainscoting, art-deco-style glass lampshades, and a large central bar great for chatting over beer and pretzels. Theme nights add to the fun, and include a Boston brunch on Fridays and mellow music nights on Saturdays.

**Boudoir** (⊠*Dubai Marine Beach Resort and Spa, Jumeirah Rd., Jumeirah 1* ☎4/345–5995 ⊕*www.myboudoir. com*), an over-the-top homage to the French burlesque club (without the dancers), is a riot of deep burgundy and blue, with padded walls and a candelabra. The champagne flows freely here, just like it did at the Moulin Rouge in Paris's heyday. Boudoir is broken up into a number of intimate rooms that are usually filled with the Dubai elite. You'll need to look the part to be invited into this ultrahip spot, so dress to attract attention.

**JamBase** (✉*Souk Madinat Jumeirah, Madinat Jumeirah, Al Sufouh Rd., Al Sufouh* ☎*4/366–6730* ⊕*www.jumeirah. com*), a self-styled supper club, gives you a feel for the sounds of the Louisiana bayou and the tastes of the Mediterranean basin. There's excellent live jazz and blues music here. Dishes are served in an urban, minimalist, slightly gritty warehouse, which contrasts with the exuberant Arabian flourishes of the rest of the souk.

**Koubba** (✉*Al Qasr, Madinat Jumeirah, Al Sufouh* ☎*4/366– 8888* ⊕*www.madinatjumeirah.com*) is a beautiful lounge off the lobby of the Al Qasr hotel, usually frequented by suited businesspeople discussing deals over coffee and ladies taking afternoon tea. But as night falls, it attracts a thriving bar scene as the sun sets on the facade of the Burj Al-Arab hotel, seen from the outdoor terrace. It's great for pre- or postdinner drinks.

★ **Sho Cho** (✉*Dubai Marine Beach Resort and Spa, Jumeirah Rd., Jumeirah 1* ☎*4/346–1111* ⊕*www.dbxmarine.com*), a favorite haunt for beautiful people—who can occasionally be spotted checking their profiles in the reflections of the aquariums lining the walls—this Japanese-style bar is a unique place for a cocktail or two. Contemporary pale leather accents combine with bright steel, and a sail-like roof over the terrace bar is illuminated with azure lights. The sleek decor melds easily with the dance/trance soundtrack, attracting a clientele in their 20s. Nonswimmers may feel a bit out of place surrounded by hundreds of colorful fish, but it's a striking sight that's well worth a look.

**Sky View Bar** (✉*Burj Al-Arab Hotel, Jumeirah Rd., Jumeirah 2* ☎*4/301–7777* ⊕*www.burj-al-arab.com*), the finlike structure at the top of the stylish Burj Al-Arab Hotel, has fantastic views along the Dubai coastlline, no matter what time of day you choose to visit. The bar has a lunch menu (brunch on Fridays) and is a hot spot for afternoon tea. If you'd rather take in the sunset here, you can watch as the natural light fades and the city's neon glow takes its place.

If you're not staying at the hotel, you'll need to make a reservation before you visit.

## GALLERIES

**Dubai International Art Centre** ( ⊠ *St. 75b, Villa 10, off Jumeirah Rd.* ☎ *4/344–4398* ⊕ *www.artdubai.com*) was founded in 1976 by a group of ex-pats. This arts center has become the most influential community-based organization in Dubai. For members, the heart of the center beats with numerous classes offering hands-on experiences, and there's a regular program of exhibitions by local and international artists. Gallery 67, the commercial outlet, is a forum for the international contemporary visual arts.

★ **Total Arts** ( ⊠ *The Courtyard, St. 4, Al Quoz Industrial Area 1, off Interchange 3, Sheikh Zayed Rd., Al Quoz* ☎ *4/347–5050* ⊕ *www.courtyard-uae.com*), a cathedral-like vaulted gallery, is the work of Dariush Zandi, a local architect and designer who supports local artists by giving them work spaces and exhibitions. In addition, there's a permanent display of more than 300 works. The gallery is a part of The Courtyard, an eccentric place to spend an hour or two. A collection of design studios and art/furniture importers are set around a cobbled, covered atrium. The facade of each enterprise features architectural designs from around the world—including Roman temples and Arabic barjeels. There's also a café on-site.

**Traffic Design Gallery** ( ⊠ *Sarasota Building [behind Tamweel HQ], off Interchange 4, Sheikh Zayed Rd., Al Barsha* ☎ *4/341–8494* ⊕ *www.viatraffic.org*), a cutting-edge design studio that caters to corporate and private clients, showcases works by avant-garde designers of furniture, home accessories, and jewelry in its 7,000-square-foot space. It also hosts exhibits of emerging designers from around the world. There's a great gift shop on-site where you can buy contemporary one-of-a-kind items.

# Sports & the Outdoors

## WORD OF MOUTH

"I used Arabian Adventures when I went on my desert safari, and I was able to book same day. I went in November, and there must have been a convoy of a dozen or more Arabian Adventures 4x4s on the dunes—they follow one another in a long convoy and some-times peel off to fly up and down the dunes. It's a lot of fun and ends in a very touristy faux bedouin camp with decent food, camel rides, sandboarding, craft sales, henna booths, etc."

—thit_cho

By Lindsay Bennett

**DUBAI IS AN EXCELLENT PLACE TO GET ACTIVE.** Aside from the suffocating heat of high summer, it has balmy weather that's ideal for outdoor activities. Warm calm seas lap the shores so you can take to the water year-round.

Because Dubai concentrates on the luxury end of the hospitality market, sports and activities follow suit. Investors have put billions of dirham into the ambience of the hotels here, but the facilities have not been ignored in the push for image. Most major resorts have been built in the last five years—and the paint is just now drying on many more—so facilities here are state of the art and completely current. Ballrooms are out and spas are in, and you've never felt so good as you will after a few days of treatments in Dubai.

Major sporting events punctuate the Dubai calendar. The government has been proactive in investing in athletic facilities and high-prize competitions to attract sports stars at the peak of their game, particularly in golf and tennis. The elite sports of horse racing—the so-called sport of kings—and polo are also at the forefront here.

The power of the group also makes Dubai a great place for an active holiday. With 180 nationalities, like-minded people have formed clubs and leagues in a wide range of activities. Canucks, Swedes, and Russians race it out on the ice; English, Aussies, and South Africans scrimmage on the rugby field; and Indians, Sri Lankans, and Pakistanis bowl on the cricket pitch. The white-collar expat lifestyle centers around the idea of the "club," whether it be the golf club, the fitness club, or the country club—and this is something visitors can also tap into.

# BEACHES & WATER SPORTS

Dubai's eastern coast is lined with a ribbon of fine white, gently shelving sand lapped by warm cerulean seas. It was this pristine unexploited resource that kick-started the tourist industry in the 1980s, as well as the fact that you can take in the rays and enjoy great water sports almost year-round—though the intense heat of July and August is a bit too much to bear for most people. Jumeirah district, close to downtown, had the first resort developments. But by the turn of the millennium, the Jumeirah strip's hotels extended more than 20 mi, and the wild sections of dunes and grass that once characterized the coastline were squeezed to a narrow section around the Abu Dhabi border. The building of several landmark projects has focused attention in certain sections of the strip—Burj Al-Arab, the neighboring Madinat Jumeirah complex, and the Dubai Marina—all of which are now well known by tourists for their excellent resort hotels.

However, the 43 mi of natural coastline would never support Sheikh Mohammed's extensive plans for turning Dubai into a tourism hot spot, so he set to work on the offshore islands. Currently the three Palm projects and The World have increased the coastline to 453 miles, and the Dubai Waterfront will add a colossal 510 more miles. Each palm frond in the three Palm Islands complexes and every island in The World will be fringed by soft golden sand. Public access will be limited here—the beaches will only be open to villa owners, renters, and hotel and beach-club guests—and water sports will be top notch.

**WHAT TO WEAR.** On the beach and around the hotel pool, you can wear what you would while vacationing in Florida. Swimsuits and bikinis are perfectly acceptable—going topless is not. It's also inappropriate to wander through the hotel in swimwear. Cover up once you leave the beach or poolside.

## PUBLIC BEACHES & BEACH PARKS

Several beaches along the strip are designated as free public-access facilities. However, public beaches in Dubai can be a little brutal and are certainly not recommended for children or the fair-skinned. With little shade, there's nowhere to hide when the sun gets too hot, and refreshments are few and far between. Arm yourself with something to cover your skin, plenty of water, and some snacks. All public beaches are open every day.

Dubai authorities have set aside valuable real estate for beach parks, and these are much better family facilities. For a small fee, parks provide beachfront sun beds and non-motorized water sports. Inland from the beach are lawns, shady trees, cafés, barbecue areas, showers, changing facilities, and children's play areas. Beach parks are incredibly popular with all sectors of society and are particularly busy on weekends (Friday and Saturday) when families come to spend the day in the fresh air. Each beach park has one day set aside for women and children only, and some have women-only sections.

## DEIRA

**Al Mamzar Beach Park** (⊠*Deira Corniche, Al Mamzar* ☎*4/296–6201* ⊡*AED 5 per person, AED 30 per vehicle, AED 200 per day for chalet rental, AED 10 for pool* ☺*Sun.–Wed. 8–11, Thurs.–Fri. 8–11:30 [Wed. for women only]*) is Dubai's largest beach park. It's 244 acres and covers the southern bank of the Al Mamzar lagoon outlet on the Sharjah border at the northernmost point of Dubai. Al Mamzar has four main seaward facing bays with shallow inlets for swimming and generous green spaces. The park has a swimming pool. You can rent one of 15 small chalets for the day where you can keep a store of food and a change of clothing. There are cultivated gardens to relax in and 6,500 square yards of lawns. Only women are admitted on Wednesday.

## JUMEIRAH BEACH

**Jumeirah Beach Park** (⊠*Jumeirah Rd., Jumeirah 2* ☎*4/349–2111* ⊡*AED 5 per person, AED 20 per vehicle* ☺*Daily 8–11 (Mon. for ladies only)*) is Dubai's most popular public beachfront park, with a sandy strip that stretches nearly two-thirds of a mi. A lifeguard is on duty throughout the day with a first-aid and resuscitation center, and sun beds and parasols can be rented on the waterfront. Inland, the 32-acre park has grassy lawns and shady trees, cafés, and barbecue pits for cooking. Toilets and showers and a children's play area complete the facilities. Many Sheikh Zayed Road and Bur Dubai hotels run free shuttle buses to the park. Monday is for ladies only.

**Kite Beach** (⊠*Jumeirah Rd., Jumeirah 2* ☎*No phone*) is the section of public beach just south of the Dubai Offshore Sailing Club, and this is a real action beach. Known to many expats as Wollongong Beach (it's close to the old campus of the Dubai branch of Wollongong University), this is where the beach dudes and hot bodies hang out watching kitesurfers and board surfers as they ride the waves.

**Russian Beach** (⊠*Jumeirah Rd., Jumeirah 1* ☎*No phone*), also known as Open Beach, is Dubai's most popular public beach, which sits at the northern end of the Jumeirah strip. A long asphalt track is great for jogging and rollerblading. You can rent sun beds and umbrellas from kiosks, and there's a lifeguard on duty.

**Umm Suqeim Beach** (⊠*Jumeirah Rd., Umm Suqeim 2* ☎*No phone*), which has incredible views of the Burj Al-Arab Hotel offshore, is a favorite of touring groups that briefly step onto the sand to snap pictures before climbing back on the bus for the next stop on the itinerary. Umm Suqeim Park isn't exactly a beach park as it has no sunbathing facilities or direct beach access, but it's just across the road from Umm Suqeim Beach and has play areas for children and a café. Ladies days are Sunday, Monday, and Tuesday.

## BOAT CHARTERS

The emirate currently has four main marina areas, but the area occupied by marinas is set to grow through 2020, with the continual unveiling of top-notch facilities on the offshore islands. Chartering is growing in popularity, as many people want to venture offshore to see what's happening at the construction sites. Still, a sunny day on the water is a great way to simply relax or try some sport fishing.

**HOOK YOUR FISH.** Offshore fishing is a year-round sport here in Dubai, with good numbers of bottom-feeding grouper and snapper sharing the waters with tuna, barracuda and larger sailfish, kingfish, and even a few sharks. The larger species are more prevalent in the cooler months (September to April). Between June and August, fishing is restricted to the early mornings before the waters become too warm for the fish to feed.

### DEIRA & THE NORTH BANK

**Dubai Creek Golf & Yacht Club** (⊠*Off Baniyas Rd., Port Saeed* ☎*4/295–6000* ⊕*www.dubaigolf.com*) offers fishing charters by the morning or by the day.

### BUR DUBAI & THE SOUTH BANK

**Bluesail** (⊠*Atrium Building, Bank Street, Bur Dubai* ☎*4/374–5145* ⊕*www.bluesailyachts.com*) offers skipper training and yacht and boat charters from marinas along the Dubai coast. You can charter by the hour, day, or week, with crew or without.

**Dusail** (⊠*Nashwan Building, Mankool Road, Bur Dubai* ☎*4/398–9146* ⊕*www.dusail.com*) has sailing yachts, cruisers, and speedboats available for short- or long-term charter. Two-hour cruises along the coast depart from Dubai International Marine Club. Dusail also has deep-sea-fishing trips.

7

### WORLD TRADE CENTRE & BURJ DUBAI

**M E Charter** (⊠*Grosvenor House, Sheikh Zayed Rd.* ☎*4/ 329–8467* ⊕*www.mecharter.com*) has several sizes of craft, from 33-foot fishing boats to 86-foot cruisers. You can head out to fish or tour the offshore waters, and enjoy a cocktail at sunset. Different craft have varying minimum rental periods, from three to eight hours.

### JUMEIRAH BEACH

**Dubai Voyager** (⊠*Fishermen Port 2, Jumeirah Rd., Jumeirah Beach* ☎*4/348–1900* ⊕*www.dubaivoyager.com*) has a small fleet of 39-foot fishing boats for day, morning, or afternoon charter.

### DUBAI MARINA

**Bristol** (⊠*Marina Walk, Dubai Marina* ☎*4/366–3538* ⊕*www.bristol-middleeast.com*), a yacht management company, offers charters, water sports, and evening cruises around the marina area on a wooden dhow.

**Dubai Marina Yacht Club** (⊠*Nuran Office G4, Al Majara 4, District 4, Dubai Marina* ☎*4/362–7883* ⊕*www.dubaimarina yachtclub.com*) can accomodate up to 12 passengers on a splendid 50-foot motor yacht with a skipper and crew.

**El Mundo** (⊠*Dubai International Marine Club, Al Mina Seyani* ☎*4/882–0920* ⊕*www.elmundodubai.com*) offers fun, regularly scheduled day cruises as well as private charters, or you can head out on a night cruise to nearby Musandam peninsula in Oman.

**Park Lane Yachts** (⊠*Dubai International Marine Club, Al Mina Seyani* ☎*4/338–9915* ⊕*www.parklaneyachtcharter. com*), a luxury charter company, can arrange charters that include a chef, a wine waiter, or a masseur if you so desire. The outfit also rents sports cars and limousines, so you can valet park at the Burj Al-Arab hotel in an Aston Martin or a Ferrari.

**Xclusive Yachts** (⊠*Dubai International Marine Club, Al Mina Seyani* ☎*50/451–4584* ⊕*www.xclusiveyachts.com*) has scheduled morning and sunset cruises, as well as tours of the islands of The World. The company also offers private charters, which can include a creek cruise with appetizers, lunch, or dinner.

## DIVING AND SNORKELING

Diving in Dubai usually takes place at one of a number of wreck sites in relatively shallow waters between 32 feet and 100 feet below. The main species seen on dives are turtles, eels, octopus, snapper, and parrotfish, with more occasional large pelagic species like rays and sharks. However, many hope that the artificial reefs making up Dubai's offshore islands will provide new environments for sea life to flourish. Unfortunately, in the short term, construction work in these locations causes water clarity to vary considerably, and sea life also may be disturbed.

The best diving in the region is around the horn of the Gulf at Musandam in Omani waters, but this involves a full day trip from Dubai by boat to travel, dive, and then return in the evening. It's a popular option with divers who want to combine the great underwater experience of Oman with the hot social scene of Dubai.

### JUMEIRAH BEACH

**Al Boom Diving** ( ⊠*Al Wasl Rd., Al Bada'a* ☎*4/342–2993* ⊕*www.alboomdiving.com*) offers PADI regulated training and guided dives for qualified divers. The company has a small dive operation in Oman, which is a quick jumping-off point for Musandam dives.

**Scuba Dubai** ( ⊠*St. 26, off Umm Suqeim St., Sheikh Zayed Rd., Interchange 4* ☎*4/341–4940* ⊕*www.scubadubai.com*), a one-stop shop for Scuba gear, training, and advice, sells equipment and rents gear to qualified divers who don't want to do group dives or take more training.

**Pavilion Dive Centre** ( ⊠*Jumeirah Beach Hotel, Jumeirah Beach Rd.* ☎*4/406–8828* ⊕*www.jumeirah.com*) is Dubai's major dive operator, a 5-star PADI training center and a National Geographic–accredited operator. The only dive center in the emirate with a private artificial reef just offshore, it's a great place to learn to dive or fit a short dive into an otherwise packed itinerary.

## KITE SURFING

This fledgling sport is making a tentative start in Dubai, but authorities are wary of giving kite surfers free license along the beach. You must be a licensed member of Dubai Kite Club to kite surf in Dubai. Temporary membership lasts one month, and you'll need passport photos and a copy of your passport to obtain it (current price is AED 200).

The club has seven IKO-approved instructors but doesn't have kites for rent. **Kitepeople** (☎50/843–8584 ⊕*www.kite people.net*) offers rental equipment. The sport currently is restricted to one beach, Kite Beach (or Wollongong Beach), south of the Jumeirah Offshore Sailing Club. Kite surfing is not allowed on Fridays, the Muslim Holy Day.

### DUBAI MARINA

**Dubai Kite Club** (✉*Mina Seyahi Marina, Al Sufouh Rd., Suf-ouh* ☎50/455–9098 ⊕*www.dubaikiteclub.com*).

## POWERBOAT RACING

Dubai has seen a great amount of success in Class 1 of the powerboat-racing formula, which is the pinnacle of powered water-sports. The government-sponsored Victory team was World Champion in 2007. These sleek craft have a 10-meet series between March and December, and the boats can be seen plying the waters off the emirate at the end of the season in early December.

TRYING SOMETHING NEW. **Want to give something new a whirl? You can be sure that whatever sport or activity you want to try—from skiing to yoga—the quality of instruction and supervision will be good, and English is the standard language for instructors.**

## SAILING AND WINDSURFING

Dubai has benign waters, and winds follow a set forecast-able pattern for most of the year. These conditions are perfect for sailing and even the smallest craft allows you to explore the inshore waters in your own time. Several clubs and water sports centers offer sailing tuition to beginners and boat rental to visitors with a ticket. Large resort hotels usually rent windsurfing gear but not all absorb the cost.

### JUMEIRAH BEACH

**Jumeirah Beach Hotel** (✉*Jumeirah Beach* ☎4/348–0000 ⊕*www.jumeirah.com*) has a selection of catamarans, Lasers, and Pico craft for rent. Windsurf equipment is available, as well as instruction up to advanced level. You'll need to be a guest of the hotel or a Beach Club member to enjoy the facilities. Day beach club membership is available during summer and fall.

**DUBAI MARINA**

**One&Only Royal Mirage** (⊠*Al Sufouh Rd., Al Sufouh 1* ☎*4/399–9999* ⊕*www.oneandonlyresorts.com*) has Hobie Cats for rent and other nonmotorized water sports, which are free for registered guests.

**Le Royal Méridien Beach Resort and Spa** (⊠*Al Sufouh Rd., Dubai Marina* ☎*4/399–5555* ⊕*www.oneandonlyresorts. com*) rents Hobie Cats and windsurfing equipment, and there's windsurfing instruction on-site.

**Sheraton Jumeirah Beach Hotel & Towers** (⊠*Al Sufouh Rd., Dubai Marina* ☎*4/399–5533* ⊕*www.sheraton.com*) has Lasers, Hobie Cats, kayaks, and bodyboards for rent by the hour.

# BOWLING

A popular sport for all sectors of society, you'll meet players and families of many nationalities at the alleys.

**DEIRA & THE NORTH BANK**

**Dubai Bowling Centre** (⊠*Off Al Wuheida Rd., opposite Century Mall, Hor al Anz East* ☎*4/296–9222* ⊕*www.dubai bowlingcentre.com*) is the main bowling venue of the city; it has 36 lanes, two eateries on-site, a billiards area, and a Thai massage spa.

**BUR DUBAI & THE SOUTH BANK**

**Al Nasr Leisureland** (⊠*Off Umm Hurair Rd., Oud Metha* ☎*4/337–1234* ⊕*www.alnasrll.com*) has an eight-lane bowling alley with computerized scoring, but the draw of Al Nasr Leisureland is that it offers many more activities on-site (*see* ⇨*Chapter 2, Exploring Dubai*).

**WORLD TRADE CENTRE & BURJ DUBAI**

**Thunderbowl** (⊠*Off Interchange 1, Sheikh Zayed Rd., Al Wasl* ☎*4/343–1000*), a 20-lane facility with a pool and snooker hall and a few restaurants, is a popular social spot for many nationalities.

# DINNER CRUISES

A dinner cruise on Dubai Creek is a much-publicized excursion, though with the choice of excellent restaurants, bars, and clubs in the emirate, it may not be the most exciting way to spend one of your evenings. The Creek is only 14 km (9 mi) long and the upper stretch is currently made unnavigable by the floating bridge linking Garhoud with Oud Metha, which is taking the strain until a new bridge is completed. For the moment, these vessels simply pass the same stretch of creek bank several times while you have your meal, and the view soon loses its appeal. For those who want to try this experience, the following boats offer the best quality options.

### DEIRA & THE NORTH BANK

Of several traditional wooden dhows offering evening dinner cruises, **Al Mansour Dhow** ( ⊠*Boat is moored on the Deira bank outside the Radisson SAS, Baniyas Rd., Deira* ☎4/222–7171 ⊕*www.radissonsas.com*) is regarded as the top choice. The style of the craft can't be beat, with its wooden hull, rich Arabian carpets, and soft furnishings. The food is local Lebanese with Indian additions, and it's served buffet-style (as all the dhow cruises are), which means you'll need to walk around the craft with plates full of food.

### BUR DUBAI & THE SOUTH BANK

**Bateaux Dubai** ( ⊠*Al Seef Rd. [boat is moored on the Bur Dubai bank opposite the British Embassy]* ☎4/399–4994 ⊕*www.bateauxdubai.com*) offers the only fine-dining cruise on the creek, a limited menu of four or five dishes per course, but the food is well cooked and served by an efficient team. Bateaux Dubai is also unique because of its design. The wide modern glass-canopied craft—similar to the one that plies the River Seine in Paris—has excellent views from every table.

# EXCURSIONS AND ADVENTURE SPORTS

For many visitors, getting out of Dubai city is the highlight of their trip. Much of the emirate is made of miles and miles of sand where the latest sports of dune-bashing (driving up and down dunes in powerful 4WD vehicles), wadi-bashing (driving along dry river valleys and watercourses in even more powerful 4WD vehicles), and sand-boarding (like snowboarding or boogie-boarding) make a great break from the culture and the shopping.

The traditional Bedouin lifestyle can also be celebrated, though the experiences are pure tourist excursion rather than a genuine living community. Still it's fun to see how the majority of Emiratis lived just a couple of generations ago.

Most Bedouin "experiences" involve a camel trek, falcon show, and an alfresco meal in a tented camp. These can be combined with the adventure sports mentioned earlier.

The companies included below operate throughout the city. Book them direct or through your hotel concierge.

### BUR DUBAI & THE SOUTH BANK
**Sunflower Tours** (⊠*Umm Hurair Rd., Karama* ☎*4/334–5554* ⊕*www.sunflowerdubai.com*) organizes group desert safaris, camel safaris, dune surfing, overnight safaris, and adventure sports. The company also acts as a booking agent for deep-sea fishing and evening creek cruises.

### WORLD TRADE CENTRE & BURJ DUBAI
**Arabian Adventures** (⊠*Sheikh Zayed Rd., Interchange 2* ☎*4/303–4888* ⊕*www.arabian-adventures.com*) operates across the UAE. In Dubai it's possible to take a desert safari, sundowner safari, or go wadi- or canyon-bashing. Arrangements can be made to Jumana show (*see* ⇨*Nightlife in Chapter 8, Around the Emirate*), Wild Wadi Water Park (*see* ⇨*Chapter 2, Exploring Dubai*), and evening cruises on Dubai Creek.

★ **Voyagers Xtreme** (⊠*Dune Centre, Al Diyafah Rd., Satwa* ☎*4/345–4504* ⊕*www.turnertraveldubai.com*) offers golf lessons, self-driving tours, and camel safaris. You can take to the air in a tandem skydive or more sedately by balloon. Desert safaris and overnight camping trips are the gold-medal desert adventure. The ultimate extreme is "One Wild Week in the Emirates," a package filled with land, sea, and air excursions.

**Desert Rangers** (⊡*Box 37975* ☎*4/340–2408* ⊕*www.desert rangers.com*), a well-established adventure company with a good reputation amongst Fodor's forum members, has a varied portfolio to get you out and about in the emirate, including safaris by dune buggy and camel or overland in 4WD vehicles. Try sand-boarding or hit the dunes in a desert-driving course.

**Gulf Ventures** (⊡*Box 1515* ☎*4/209–5568* ⊕*www.gulfven tures.ae*) caters to incentive groups and covers the entire UAE, but offers a good range of desert activities for individuals, including dune-bashing and dune buggy rides. Less active choices include dune drives and drinks at sunset or dinner in the desert.

# FENCING

Getting to the point, this sport may sharpen your reflexes. The **Dubai Fencing Club** (✉*Mina A'Salam, Madinat Jumeirah, Al Sufouh Rd., Jumeirah* ☎*4/366–8888* ⊕*www.dubaifencing club.com*) is the premier venue in the UAE and offers classes from beginner to expert levels led by the Kouzeva family—a husband and wife team who both were on the Bulgarian Olympic team in earlier years. You can book individual sessions.

# GOLF

With seven golf courses and at least two more in planning stages, Dubai is the center of golfing in the Arab world. Despite the arid conditions, courses are kept in immaculate condition and offer interesting desert hazards and plenty of natural bunkers. Interest in the sport is high, spurred by the government funding of the Dubai Desert Classic tournament, which features the finest players as they compete for the lucrative first prize. Tiger Woods, Ernie Els, Colin Montgomerie, and Nick Faldo are just four professional golfers who have chosen to design courses in Dubai, which can only improve the status of the sport here in the future.

Golfers are expected to show proof of handicap before being allowed on main courses. If you are looking to work on your swing, facilities at all major courses are excellent.

### DEIRA & THE NORTH BANK

★ **Deira Creek Golf & Yacht Club** (✉*Deira Creek Yacht and Golf Club, off Baniyas Rd., Garhoud* ☎*4/295–6000* ⊕*www. dubaigolf.com*) has a par-71, 6,857-yard course spread out along Dubai Creek and played host to the Desert Classic tournament in 1999 and 2000, though the course was redeveloped in 2005. The degree of difficulty is partly psychological, because the final holes are squeezed between the water and punishing bunkers. The academy offers the V1 Golf Swing Analysis system and the Trackman radar plotting system to improve your game.

**Four Seasons Golf Club** (✉*Four Seasons Hotel, Rebat St., Al Badia* ☎*4/601–0101* ⊕*www.fourseasons.com*), designed by Robert Trent Jones II and opened in 2005, is a par-72, 7,303-yard course on a desert oasis that really takes advantage of those conditions. Sand provides "wadi"-style hazards, and there are ample lakes and water features.

The golf academy has Motional Analysis by TaylorMade (MATT) and Science and Motion PuttLab systems to analyze all aspects of your game.

### WORLD TRADE CENTRE AREA & BURJ DUBAI

**Dubai Country Club** (⊠*Hatta Rd.* ☎*4/333–1155* ⊕*www.dubaicountryclub.com*), which is home to Dubai's first golf course, is a 9-hole, 2,270-yard, par-32 course with browns rather than greens as they are made of sand. There's also a floodlit driving range and a golf clinic. Nonmembers are invited to play at off-peak hours.

### DUBAI MARINA

★ **Fodor's**Choice **Emirates Golf Club** (⊠*Emirates Hills* ☎*4/380–2222* ⊕*www.dubaigolf.com*), with two 18-hole courses and a par-3 challenge, is the premier facility in the emirate. The Majlis course was the first grass course in the Middle East, earning it the epithet of "the desert miracle." The par-72, 7,211-yard course is the current home of the Dubai Desert Classic tournament and incorporates sand dunes as hazards in the design. The second course, The Wadi by Faldo, opened in 1996 but was redesigned in 2006. The golf academy has four professionals and indoor and outdoor swing analysis technology.

At **The Montgomerie Dubai** (⊠*The Montgomerie, Emirates Hills, Dubai* ☎*4/390–5600* ⊕*www.themontgomerie.com*) professional Colin Montgomerie and his collaborator Gordon Muirhead created this links-style course in the desert, achieved by interspersing slim fairways with 11 man-made lakes. Holes 13 and 18 (formed in the shape of the UAE) are particularly challenging, as they are surrounded by water. The par-72 course has lengths of between 5,404 yards and 7,308 yards depending on degree of difficulty.

7

# ICE-SKATING

Surprisingly, there is more than one place to put your blades on for a spin on the ice.

### BUR DUBAI & THE SOUTH BANK

**Al Nasr Leisureland** (⊠*Off Umm Hurair Rd., Oud Metha* ☎*4/337–1234* ⊕*www.alnasrll.com*) has an Olympic-size rink and hosts ice shows and ice-hockey games, as well as leisure skating. Check with Al Nasr about schedules, which vary by week. Individual and group lessons are available for 30 minutes. Skate-hire is available.

**Dubai Mall** (⊠*Dubai Mall, Doha Street, Downtown Burj Dubai, Sheikh Zayed Rd.* ☎*4/362–7500* ⊕*www.dubaimall. com*), at the heart of the Carnival Grove entertainment complex, is Olympic standard and is the centerpiece of numerous shows and sporting events, including ice shows and speed-skating races. At other times, it's a popular family attraction for mall-goers.

# SPAS & WELLNESS

The first decade of the new millennium has been all about wellness, detoxing, and destressing, and few places in the world have a better range of spas at such high quality than Dubai. Many hotels have gorgeous facilities with well-qualified staff and products from the world's most renowned cosmetics houses. Private spas are also top-notch and cater to busy people with executive lifestyles. Dubai has a few expert holistic ayurvedic centers, which consult on all aspects of health and well-being, that are quite popular with workers from the Indian subcontinent.

Combined spa and fitness centers, with gym and other sports facilities on the same site, are becoming popular. Private clubs sell yearly memberships, but those listed below also offer day or temporary memberships to visitors.

## DEIRA & THE NORTH BANK

★ **Akaru Spa** (⊠*The Aviation Club, off Sheikh Rashid Rd., Garhoud* ☎*4/282–8578* ⊕*www.akaruspa.com*), a large private spa with 14 treatment rooms, a sauna, and hammam (Turkish bath), has a range of treatments available. Alongside a list of mainstream massages and facials, it offers more complex treatments. Microdermabrasion strips the upper layers of the dermis to allow new skin to regenerate and is used to improve minor skin conditions. Try a session in the Pure Oxygen Capsule where your body is immersed in oxygen, said to detox and revitalize. Akaru Spa uses Thalgo products, made of beneficial marine algae, in many of its treatments. Other partners include Guinot and Payot cosmetics houses in Paris. There's a dedicated floor for men. The Aviation Club also has a hair salon and a nail spa for a total image package.

**Amara Spa** (⊠*Park Hyatt Hotel, Dubai Golf & Yacht Club, Off Sheikh Rashid Rd., Garhoud* ☎*4/602–1234* ⊕*www. dubai.park.hyatt.com*), surrounding a palm-shaded pool, offers eight luxury pavilion spa suites with living area and terrace, hammam, and aromatic steam shower for residential stays, along with simpler treatment rooms. The style is Arabic-Andalusian with vivid blue ceramic-tiled interiors and domes contrasting with whitewashed walls in the public areas, and soothing earth tones in the treatment rooms. Treatments concentrate on massage—with a choice of 10 options—facials, including nonsurgical face-lifts, and body treatments. The spa uses Shiffa, Carita, Anne Semonin, and Aromatherapy Associates products.

**Club Olympus** ( ⊠*Hyatt Regency Dubai, Corniche, Deira* ☎4/209–1234 ⊕*www.hyatt.com*) is a day-sports club with a good range of varied indoor and outdoor activities. Step outside for swimming, tennis, and a jogging track. Inside, the gym is equipped with Nautilus machines (more than one of each type), and there are regular aerobics classes. The club also has squash courts, a sauna, steam room, Jacuzzi, massages, and a spa with separate areas for women and men.

**Inter-Fitness Dubai** ( ⊠*Radisson SAS Hotel, Baniyas Rd., Deira* ☎4/222–7171 ⊕*www.ichotelsgroup.com*) is a day facility with a range of indoor and outdoor activities, including a tennis court and pool, a small gym and spa, and two squash courts.

**Natural Elements Spa & Fitness** ( ⊠*Le Meridien Dubai, Airport Rd., Garhoud* ☎4/217–0000 ⊕*www.starwood.com*), an all-around fitness facility, has nine treatment rooms and more than 50 treatments for the face and body. There are specialist hydrotherapy suites for water treatments. Products are by Pevonia-Botanica. The fitness center has three pools, including a 25-meter swim lane for cardiovascular workouts. The gym is fully equipped with Life Fitness and Nautilus machines and free weights, and instructors hold spinning, yoga, and boxing classes. Personal instruction and long-term fitness support are available.

★ Fodor'sChoice **Taj Spa** ( ⊠*Taj Palace Hotel, Al Riqqa St., Al Muraqqabat* ☎4/223–2222 ⊕*www.tajhotels.com*), designed with the principles of Vastu Shastra—the traditional Indian philosophy of harmonious interior design—combines the ancient therapies of ayurveda with 21st-century cosmetics technology. More than 20 treatment options range from Indian massage and Indonesian body exfoliation to European seaweed body wraps. Products are 100% natural, with herbs and essential oils, and all are sourced in India. There are separate men and women treatment areas.

**VASTU SHASTRA.** Combining the Sanskrit words vastu (building or house) and shastra (instruction), Vastu Shastra is the traditional Hindu treatise on harmonious urban planning and interior design. The tenets offer a plan to positively control *Prana*, the life force that Hindus believe flows around the earth, to promote healthy living.

### BUR DUBAI & THE SOUTH BANK

**Cleopatra's Spa** (⊠*The Pharaoh's Club, Wafi City, Oud Metha* ☎*4/324–7700*), one of the largest day spas in the UAE, is more like a genuine Turkish bath, or hammam, than an opulent resort spa in Dubai. There are many private members, and it has separate treatment areas for men and women. Both sexes have the opportunity to use a steam room, sauna, Jacuzzi, and plunge pool. Elemis products are used in the treatments, many of which must be prebooked.

**The Grand Spa** (⊠*The Grand Hyatt Dubai*, ☎*4/317–1234* ⊕*www.dubai.grand.hyatt.com*) is certainly grand, both in size and decor, with voluminous spaces such as the lap pool, which sits in a conservatory-style building flooded with light. The public areas have warm dark wood details that highlight the oriental design. There are six treatment rooms offering massage, detox, enzyme facials, and body treatments. June Jacobs and Bella Lucce products are imported from New York for treatments. Fitness features include a jogging track with exercise stations, and squash and tennis courts.

**Al Karama Healthcare Centre** (⊠*Al Khazna Centre, Karama Park* ☎*4/335–5288* ⊕*www.alkaramahealthcare.com*) is a holistic medical center concentrating on the principles of ayurveda. The practitioners here offer diagnostic services and long-term therapy programs and are licensed by the Illinois Department of Public Health. Day therapies include massage, yoga, and natural skin treatments.

**AYURVEDA.** An ancient system of well-being developed in the Indian subcontinent and said to have been passed down by Lord Shiva to the Hindu gurus, *ayurveda* loosely translates to "knowledge of life" or "life knowledge." Ayurvedic principles touch all aspects of the human condition or work in a holistic way. There are eight branches of the philosophy and these combine to form a healthy body, healthy mind, and healthy soul. The branches most well known in the west are the yoga and massage therapies.

**RafflesAmrita Spa** (✉*Raffles Dubai Hotel. Sheikh Rashid Rd., Wafi* ☎*4/324–8888* ⊕*www.raffles.com*) opened in early 2008, combining six private treatment suites with a gym and use of the hotel's expansive pool area and sundeck. The interior design combines ancient Egypt with the colors and textures of the four elements; the public areas are bright, and the treatment zones are more neutral. Many treatments carry through the Egyptian theme, including the Eye of Horus eye treatment and Egyptian Gold body treatment. The menu is extensive, but the kooky names make it a bit difficult to identify what the treatment involves. In addition to face and body treatments, the spa has manicures, pedicures, and waxing. A unique extra for guests is the 2.4-acre rooftop botanical garden, where you can relax surrounded by therapeutic fragrance.

## WORLD TRADE CENTRE & BURJ DUBAI

At **The Big Apple** (✉*Boulevard at Emirates Towers, Sheikh Zayed Rd.* ☎*4/319–8660* ⊕*www.jumeirah.com*) fitness is what it's all about. Lines of machines and several collections of free weights fill the gym, and fitness instructors keep you on track. There's an eclectic range of fitness classes and set workouts from Body Pump with weights, RPM for the cardiovascular system, Hapkido—a Korean martial art—and Bollywood dance moves.

To reach **CHI The Spa** (✉*Shangri-La Hotel, Sheikh Zayed Rd., World Trade Centre* ☎*4/405–2441* ⊕*www.shangri-la. com*) you cross the marble bridge over soothing pools, a symbolic departure from everyday stress. Biodroga and Futuresse products are predominantly used in treatments here, and the signature treatment is the Futuresse caviar deluxe facial treatment. The spa has nine rooms and the adjoining fitness club has a gymnasium, Jacuzzi, squash court, and tennis court.

**Gems of Yoga** (✉*White Crown Building, Sheik Zayed Rd., World Trade Centre [behind KFC]* ☎*4/331–1328* ⊕*www. gemsofyogadubai.com*) has well-qualified Indian ayurvedic and hatha practitioners running its programs. Yoga is used to treat medical conditions in line with ayurvedic principles and lifestyle regimes, and classes are also run for recreational students. Yoga courses run for 20 sessions. Trial and one-on-one sessions are available.

**The Health Club** (✉*Emirates Towers Hotel, Sheikh Zayed Rd., World Trade Centre* ☎*4/319–8888* ⊕*www.jumeirah. com*) combines a fitness center, a pool area, and a ladies' spa; it's a contemporary club option in the heart of the business district. The pool offers a lap area and a children's splash facility. The spa has fewer treatments than many others in the city.

**Pilates Studio Dubai** (✉*DNI Building, Sheikh Zayed Rd. [behind RAK Bank]* ☎*4/343–8252*) offers classes for varying levels of Pilates students, from total beginner to intermediate. Founded by Dr. Catherine Lehmann, a leading Pilates specialist, the studio is now registered as a specialist rehabilitation center in addition to running a program of classes. Private one-hour sessions are available.

PRACTICING PILATES. Invented by Joseph Pilates in the mid–20th century, Pilates is a discipline that focuses on concentration, centering, balance, breathing, and natural movement to improve fitness and well-being. The core muscles involved in posture are the main targets, from which muscular form and mental calmness are said to follow as students achieve a union between mind and body.

★ FodorsChoice **Willow Stream Spa & Health Club** (✉*The Fairmont Hotel, Sheikh Zayed Rd., World Trade Centre* ☎*4/332– 5555* ⊕*www.fairmont.com, www.willowstream.com*), a large spa, combines classic design from ancient Greece and Rome with state-of-the-art treatments and techniques. Magnificent colorful mosaics ground the decor—the two swimming pools are unique in Dubai for their colorful mosaic floors. Inside the 40,000-square-foot spa, colonnades around the Jacuzzi offer an image direct from any Roman baths. There's also a fitness center on site with yoga and tango instruction, and personal trainers monitor progress and give advice.

### JUMEIRAH BEACH

At **Elche** (✉*St. 10, off Jumeirah Beach Rd. [behind Jumeirah Plaza]* ☎*4/349–4942* ⊕*www.elche.ae*) Ilsci Molnar, a Hungarian biochemist and botanist, has spent a lifetime creating the herbal therapies. All the plants are picked by hand and quality controlled by Elche. The spa offers a range of body massages and facial treatments. Elche also has a beauty parlor offering cosmetic tattooing, waxing, and intense pulse light (IPL) hair removal.

**The Pavilion Marina & Sports Club** (✉*Jumeirah Beach Hotel, Jumeirah Beach Rd.* ☎4/406–8800 ⊕*www.jumeirah.com*) is a great all-around fitness and spa facility that attracts many expat annual members. It is part of the Jumeirah Beach Hotel but is housed in a separate building overlooking the beach and marina. The large gym has several of each machine with a free-weights area. Personal trainers can supervise personal training programs. You can join classes in yoga, karate, balance, combat (strength), and pump (cardiovascular), or book a game of tennis or squash. The spa has a sauna, massaging hot tub, steam room, and a plunge pool. Day membership is available for nonguests out of peak season.

**Sensasia Urban Spa** (✉*The Village Mall, Upper Level, Jumeirah Beach Rd.* ☎4/349–8850 ⊕*www.sensasiaspas.com*) is a favorite of expat wives, who come to luxuriate in contemporary surroundings. The decor is cool Southeast Asian with low lighting that accents water features and Buddhist statues. Sensasia has a wide range of treatments using natural products like honey, coconut, and green tea. A choice of massages is on the menu, including special treatments for young moms and busy execs.

★ **Talise** (✉*Madinat Jumeirah, Jumeirah Beach Rd., Al Sufouh 1* ☎4/366–8888 ⊕*www.madinatjumeirah.com*) is a beautiful day spa with treatment pavilions set among verdant tropical gardens. There are separate facilities for men and women. The attention to detail here speaks of luxurious pampering, with contemporary Asian artwork on the walls and sumptuous sofas in the dayroom where you can snuggle in your ultrathick robe. There's a long list of spa treatments for face and body, using Sodashi products, a 100% natural range from Australia. After treatment, relaxation options include a private plunge pool or sauna. For the more active, visit the gym and yoga studio. The Magnolia restaurant serves à la carte vegetarian dishes and organic champagne.

## DUBAI MARINA

**Angsana Spa & Health Club** (✉*Level 2, Marina Walk, Dubai Marina* ☎4/368–4356 ⊕*www.angsana.com*) is managed by the Banyan Tree Spa company in Singapore, and brings a tropical Southeast Asian spa concept to the desert with lush greens and vivid welcoming yellows. The highest quality of training and finest natural ingredients has contributed to numerous awards for their locations around the globe. All Angsana Spas have treatment rooms or private pavilions for extra space. There are four Angsana Spas in Dubai; others are at Arabian Ranches, The Montgomerie, Emirates Hills, and Angsana Hotel and Suites (also at Dubai Marina).

**Elixir Spa & Health Club** (⊠*Habtoor Grand Resort & Spa* ☎*4/399–5000* ⊕*www.habtoorhotels.com*) is a luxurious spa, where each separate treatment station is individually styled—the hammam in Turkish style, for example, is a marble-walled steam room. Treatments touch on ayurvedic and Asian philosophies. There are special treatments, including a dry flotation water experience, a Tibetan scalp massage, and a *rasul* (clay detoxification treatment) mud room. The spa uses Karin Herzog's products.

★ **Fodor'sChoice** **Givenchy Spa** (⊠*One&Only Royal Mirage Hotel, Al Sufouh Rd., Al Sufouh 2* ☎*4/399–9999* ⊕*www.oneandonlyresorts.com*) is a lavish and expansive spa where no expense has been spared. You are invited to immerse yourself in the world of the Arabian Orient. Elegant, understated pale greens and blues combined with earth tones and marble dominate the spa, which has 12 treatments rooms. The hammam is an authentic Turkish bath with high domes and a central marble massage table where you can enjoy a classic experience. Spa products come from the renowned house of Givenchy, which prides itself on the quality of its staff training. The spa also has a Bastien Gonzalez foot clinic and an Alexandre Zouari hair salon. There are separate opening times for men and women.

**BASTIEN GONZALEZ. A unique approach to feet and a few secret recipes have turned Bastien Gonzalez into the podiatrist of the rich and famous. His no-liquid polish puts a brilliant sheen on nails that can last up to three months, making your toes feel and look like a million dollars.**

★ **Ritz-Carlton Spa** (⊠*Ritz-Carlton Dubai, Al Sufouh Rd., Dubai Marina* ☎*4/399–4000* ⊕*www.ritzcarlton.com*) is a large spa and fitness facility decorated in a classic, conservative style. Terra-cotta highlights in the treatment rooms contrast with the blue mosaic and carved fretwork in the pool area. The massages utilize mainly Indonesian and Thai techniques. Carita cosmetics, a family-owned company in Paris, supplies the face and body products. The fitness center offers tennis, squash, swimming, and a supervised gym with free weights and cardiovascular machines.

# SPECTATOR SPORTS

## RUGBY

The **Dubai Exiles Rugby Football Club** ( ✉ *Off Ras al-Khor Rd. near Dubai Country Club, Bukadra* ☎ *4/333–1198* ⊕ *www. dubaiexiles.com*) was founded in 1969 for the enjoyment of mainly British and British Commonwealth and ex-Commonwealth country citizens (Canadian, Australian, New Zealanders, and South Africans) for whom rugby was a favorite game from school years into adulthood. Perhaps it also gives those expats the chance to get together every weekend to share a few beers! The season runs from September to March with weekly games. The Rugby Sevens Competition is the highlight of the season with more than 150 teams arriving from around the globe to compete in the tournament, which takes place in late November and early December.

## GOLF

Several regional amateur and PGA tournaments are held in Dubai during the year. Inaugurated in 1986, the Dubai Desert Classic has become a major golfing event attracting the world's finest players. After being held at various courses around the emirate, the classic found a permanent home at the **Emirates Golf Club** ( ✉ *Emirates Hills* ☎ *4/380–2222* ⊕ *www.dubaidesertclassic.com*) on the Maljis course. The 2008 prize fund was $2.5 million and the winner, Tiger Woods, took home just under half a million dollars. The Dubai Desert Classic runs from late January into early February.

## TENNIS

Since the first Dubai Men's Open in 1993, the reputation of this competition has only grown. The Women's Open came on board in 2001. Both tournaments are held at **The Aviation Club Tennis Centre** ( ✉ *Off Al-Garhoud Rd., Garhoud* ☎ *4/216–6444* ⊕ *www.dubaitennischampionships.com*). The high-value fund now attracts top talent with such names as Federer, Nadal, Davydenko, and Roddick on the men's list and Henin, Kuznetsova, Ivanovic, and Jankovic on the women's list. The two tournaments run consecutively and take place in late February and early March.

## ICE HOCKEY

Yes, this rough, tough game of northern climates has found a home in the heat of Dubai. Emiratis have taken to this sport in a big way—the UAE national team even won the Asian Ice Hockey Championship in 2007, its first attempt. The season runs from October to March with scheduled evening games every week, many of which are played at **Al Nasr Leisureland** ⊠*Off Umm Hurair Rd., Oud Metha* ☎*4/337–1234* ⊕*www.dubaimightycamels.com, www. alnasrll.com.* The Dubai Mighty Camels Ice Hockey Club has seven different teams competing in league and cup competitions. The CAE International tournament, an 18-team competition, is held in mid-April.

# TAKING TO THE SKIES

Many of Dubai's new developments are best seen from the air. It's only from bird's-eye level that the amazing constructions of The Palm islands and The World move from imagination to reality. A flight also highlights just how small the city is, and you can choose your craft depending on whether you prefer speed and power or elevation.

## AIRPLANE & HELICOPTER FLIGHTS

**Aerogulf Services** ( ⊠*Dubai International Airport* ☎*4/220–0331* ⊕*www.aerogulfservices.com*) has regular contracts for offshore oil rig transfers and desert survey work, but it also runs a Fly Dubai tour around the main attractions.

★ FodorsChoice **Seawings** ( ⊠*Based at the Marina at Jebel Ali Golf Resort & Spa, Jebel Ali* ☎*4/883–2999, 800/SEAW-INGS toll-free within UAE* ⊕*www.seawings.ae*) offers pleasure flights by seaplane in a seven-seat amphibian Cessna Caravan. The company offers 30-minute tours along the coast to take in Dubai Marina, Palm Jumeirah, Burj Al-Arab, The World, and Burj Dubai. The company also accepts charters for groups and families.

## HOT-AIR BALLOONING

You'll have to start early while the air is cool and conditions are at their most benign, but this slow and gentle method is an incredible way to see the emirate. Pilots cannot absolutely guarantee the trajectory of each flight, but you'll have fantastic views in whichever direction the balloon takes you.

The pilots at **Balloon Adventures Dubai** (✉*Box 76888* ☎*4/285–4949* ⊕*www.ballooning.ae*)have a combined experience of 50 years in the aviation business and run two other operations in Germany and New Zealand. Enjoy a five-hour adventure with an hour in the skies—the rest of the time you'll help set up and dismantle the balloon. Balloon Adventures arranges transfer from most major hotels in the emirate. No flights June through September.

With **Voyagers Xtreme** (✉*Dune Centre, Al Diyafah Rd., Satwa* ☎*4/345–4504* ⊕*www.turnertraveldubai.com*) you can book a balloon flight in the morning, then link in with one of its desert-safari or desert-camping experiences.

# TENNIS

Most of the major resort hotels have tennis facilities, though usually only one court. The Jumeirah Beach Hotel has several at its sports club, but they are only open to hotel guests and members. Tennis is a popular sport with expats, and most fitness centers (not including gyms) have courts. The following list has courts and lessons.

### DEIRA & THE NORTH BANK

**The Aviation Club** (✉*Off Al-Garhoud Rd., Garhoud* ☎*4/216– 6444* ⊕*www.aviationclub.ae*) has been used during the Dubai Tennis Championships (*for more information, see* ⇨*Tennis in Spectator Sports, below*), so you can play on the same court as Roger Federer and other star athletes. There are eight courts here, and nonmembers can play as part of the day-pass fee. The club does not have equipment rental, but the on-site shop offers a range of racquets, balls, clothing, and footwear at duty-free prices.

### DUBAI MARINA

**Dubai Tennis Academy** (✉*American University of Dubai, off Sheikh Zayed Rd., Interchange 5 [next to the Hard Rock Cafe], Dubai Internet City* ☎*4/399–4539* ⊕*www.dubaitennisacademy.com*) was the first of its kind in Dubai when it opened. The Academy offers a range of programs for all ages, the most useful of which for visitors are the private lessons and group clinics. There are ladies-only and mixed clinics.

# Around the Emirate

**WORD OF MOUTH**

"About our amazing night in the desert.
. . . We had one of the best nights of
our lives."

—aussiedreamer

By Lindsay Bennett

**CONSIDERING THE SPRAWLING** forest of construction cranes marking Dubai City, it would be easy to assume that it is only an urban development. While this is true in part, the emirate also is home to numerous natural attractions. For instance, if you take the road east, concrete will soon give way to a flat, almost featureless landscape—the northernmost tip of the Arabian Desert where acacias stand sentinel and feral camels graze.

The desert was the home of the Emirati until a few generations ago. Now it's become the Emirati playground. Local families visit to connect with their Arab roots or, in huge contrast, race across the sand in powerful 4WD vehicles. You can explore Dubai beyond the city on two legs, four legs (by camel or horse), or on four wheels. But remember, if you have a rental car it won't be insured for off-road driving—something you shouldn't do without a good map and backup water supplies. To be extra careful, hire a reliable tour company to take you on an off-road adventure.

There are also several desert resorts located outside Dubai City.

## EXPLORING THE EMIRATE

★ Fodor'sChoice **Arabian Desert/Big Red.** Dubai's largest dune
❷ and the highest natural point in the Emirate aside from the Hajar Mountains, Big Red is more than 100 feet of terra-cotta-colored sand that takes on a deep rose as the sun drops. The dune has developed into an adrenaline-fueled playground, with sand buggies and roll-top jeeps that hurtle up the slopes and 4WD vehicles ploughing furrows in the sand along its flanks. *On Hwy. E44 (road to Hatta), between the villages of Al Haba and Al Ghifirah, around 30 minutes from downtown Dubai.*

★ Fodor'sChoice **Hajar Mountains.** Running like a sinewy spine
❺ from north to south through the Arabian Desert, the Hajar Mountains (also spelled Hajjar) are the highest range in the UAE. Their peaks have always been a natural boundary with what is now Oman to the east. The border between Oman and Dubai threads an invisible line around their peaks. The Hajar Mountains are not very high, around 6,000 feet at most, but the stark treeless ridges and golden, red, and ebony hues of the igneous rock present dramatic vistas. The many wadis and dry valleys within the Hajar

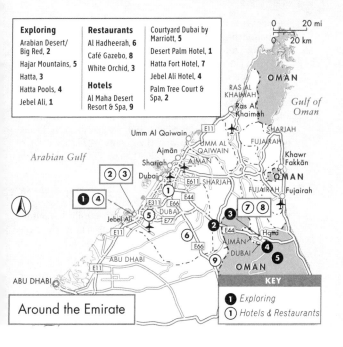

**Around the Emirate**

**KEY**

❶ *Exploring*

① *Hotels & Restaurants*

range are a natural playground for adventure excursions from Dubai. ⊠*3.2 km (2 mi) east of Hatta.*

❸ **Hatta.** A sleepy final stop on the road to Oman, this gorgeous town is nestled in the foothills of the Hajar Mountains. Hatta is an oasis where the fresh water allows fruits, vegetables, and acres of date palms to flourish. The town site was strategically important, as it's located at the end of one of the few easy mountain passes. Hatta was fought over and passed between Oman and Dubai, until it was firmly established that Dubai had control at the end of the 19th century. Today the 100-year-old residential quarter is being renovated, and much of its population is living in a nearby modern suburb.

In 1896 the Al-Matkoums ordered a fort built in Hatta. It and a handful of surrounding buildings have been restored under the banner **Hatta Heritage Village.** Each building is dedicated to a different traditional skill that was practiced by local people just a couple of generations ago. A simple family home sits alongside a potter's workshop, a blacksmith's forge, tobacco-drying sheds, a textile-dying and weaving area, and a palm factory where palm wood and palm fronds are processed into various practical items. Gurgling water that flows along a restored traditional irrigation system provides a cooling backdrop. Climb up through the village to the topmost tower for views to the east across the town and the desert. A gallery in one of the towers displays photographs of the fort during its heyday and provides written background on the border disputes. Life-size figurines with rifles kneel against the tiny look-out window, as if awaiting the enemy. ⊠*Hatta Village* ☎*4/852–1374* ⊠*AED 3* ⊙*Sat.–Thurs. 8 AM–8:30 PM, Fri. 2:30 PM–8:30 PM.*

❹ **Hatta Pools.** A source of fresh water all year round in this arid region, the Hatta Pools are a popular destination for tour companies and picnicking Emirati families. Technically these pools, known as Wadi Khamees in Arabic, are situated just inside Oman, but it's an unpopulated area where the border is barely enforced.

The Hatta pools lie in a stark and dramatic wadi, or river valley. Sandstone walls have been worn into smooth sinuous tracks by eons of running water, the shapes and colors of which swirl together like the lines of a surrealist painting. In some places, the water on the surface pools deeply enough for swimming. In other areas, the water rushes along narrow gullies that are 20 feet deep and its thundering rumble is the only clue to its location. Hatta's popularity causes several environmental problems that may spoil the natural beauty for some visitors. Graffiti marks the walls of the watercourse. In addition, there is no trash collection service and few people remove their garbage, so litter can be a common sight. The Hatta Pools are not signposted out of Hatta and can only be reached on non-asphalt roads, so take a guide or book a tour rather than risk getting lost in the mountains. ⊠*Southeast of Hatta Village along unmade tracks, not signposted.*

❶ **Jebel Ali.** Until the beginning of the new millennium, Jebel Ali was the last stretch of unspoiled beach—protected for many years as it lay beyond the Jebel Ali Free Port on the southernmost section of the Dubai coastline, bordering Abu Dhabi. Inevitably, the beautiful beaches have fallen under the spotlight and it's now in line for wholesale reclamation and development. The Palm Jebel Ali, the third in Nakheel's triumvirate of offshore Palm islands, has already broken

## CLOSE UP

# Al Maktoum International Airport

Work has already begun on the Al-Maktoum International Airport at Dubai World Central, which will be the largest in the world when completed. Just inland from Jebel Ali, the airport is a $33 billion project that aims to serve 120 million passengers annually—nearly four times the number of passengers at Dubai International Airport, which experienced the highest growth in traffic in the world in 2007 and now services more than a quarter of all passenger traffic in the Middle East. In addition, Al-Maktoum International will process 12 million tons of cargo a year, three times the amount that travels through the current largest cargo airport in Memphis. The adjoining Aviation City will be the world's biggest maintenance and overhaul facility, and a business center that will handle leasing and chartering jets, with a projected 100,000 movements a year. Al-Maktoum International will be the focus of a self-contained city of residential neighborhoods, shopping malls, and recreational facilities, including a golf course and resort. Dubai World Central, a 44-square-km (17-square-mi) free zone dedicated to global import/export activities, will surround this area. It is less than 30 minutes away from the world's largest cargo port at Jebel Ali, which will allow for seamless transitions from air to sea or sea to air.

**8**

ground. However, it's overshadowed in size and audacity by the Dubai Waterfront.

Amid all the long-term restructuring over the next decade is the Jebel Ali Wildlife Sanctuary—it's unclear whether or not the redevelopment will affect it. Extending through nearly 31 square mi of dunes and shoreline plus a narrow stretch of offshore waters, the sanctuary protects rare turtle-breeding sites and whale transit routes in the narrowing seas around the Gulf. You'll need a permit to visit the sanctuary, so be sure to obtain one from the Environmental Department of Dubai Municipality. ⊠*Jebel Ali* ☎*4/206–3631, 4/800–900 toll-free.*

CLOSE UP

## Coming Soon to Jebel Ali

Jebel Ali will undergo a complete transformation over the next decade. Dubai Waterfront is the emirate's most imaginative land reclamation project yet—a city district of a billion square feet curving out from Dubai's border with Abu Dhabi and pointing back towards Dubai Marina and the Jumeirah beaches. The designers drew inspiration from the shape of the crescent moon, an important symbol in Islam. In the embrace of the crescent is a small island designed like a star shining in the blue of the ocean firmament. Two-hundred-and-fifty resorts, and residential and business communities will occupy the shoreline and offshore islands, with homes projected for more than 500,000 people. Madinat Al Arab is the interface between the current mainland shore and the rest of the Dubai Waterfront, and it will be completed first. The showpiece of Madinat Al Arab will be Al Burj, a tower that will be the highest in the world when it's finished.

# WHERE TO EAT

**$$$$**  ✕**Al Hadheerah.** A truly impressive setting, this establishment seems like it came straight from the pages of *A Thousand and One Nights*. It's possible to imagine Sinbad stocking up for his next voyage in the alleyways of this authentically recreated oasis town, complete with a souk, belly dancers, falcon displays, and camel rides. The food here is no second thought. The restaurant has a sumptuous Arabian buffet with several cooking stations, where you can eat your fill of *mezze* (traditional Middle Eastern small plates) and grilled meats and choose from an array of tasty desserts. The evening under the stars is absolutely one you'll remember. (Food and entertainment are included in one fixed price.) ✉*Bab al Shams Desert Resort and Spa* ☎4/809–6100 ☐*AE, DC, MC, V* ☽*No lunch.*

**$**  ✕**Café Gazebo.** This verdant terrace overlooking the restaurant pool with the Hajar Mountains beyond is the prettiest spot in the area for lunch. The menu has a range of dishes. Crunchy salads come in hearty portions, and the fried fish is light and crispy. Or enjoy a simple sandwich with a range of trimmings. Lunch is served until 4, so it won't matter if your hunger pangs strike late. The café has an air-conditioned dining area if the heat is too powerful. ✉*Hatta Fort Hotel, Dubai/Oman Rd., Hatta* ☎4/852–3211 ☐*AE, DC, MC, V* ☽*No dinner.*

$$ ✕**White Orchid.** The menu here skips from Japan to Beijing to Singapore, giving visitors a wide sampling of pan-Asian dishes. If you like sushi, there's a small table devoted to its preparation, or you can sit in the wider dining room, which is divided into two tiers and flanked on one side by large windows. Chopsticks don't come with the place settings, and you'll be given a plate rather than a bowl; however, this can be quickly resolved if you ask the waitstaff for more authentic utensils. White Orchid has a delightful terrace and cocktail bar with comfy white chairs and sofas for relaxing over a post-meal coffee or digestif. ⊠*Palm Tree Court and Spa, Jebel Ali Golf Resort and Spa, Jebel Ali* ☎4/883–6000 ⊟*AE, DC, MC, V* ☉*Closed Sun. No lunch.*

# WHERE TO STAY

★ **Fodor'sChoice** ⛁**Al Maha Desert Resort & Spa.** This award-win-
$$$$ ning luxury eco-resort sets new standards in the region with its conservation programs. Located on 86 square mi of protected desert landscape, the accommodation is modeled after modern Bedouin tents, with luxurious interiors complete with their own swimming pools. A fine-dining restaurant and spa, housed in the Arabian-style main building, add to the relaxing delights. The suites have an *Out of Africa* feel with wooden decks that connect the pool to the generous 800-square-foot living space. Enter through French doors into a seating area decorated with hand-crafted furniture and Bvlgari toiletries in the bathroom. Al Maha's eco-credentials extend beyond the rooms to its population of rare Arabian oryx that roam free throughout the grounds. Knowledgeable field guides are part of the full-time staff and offer camel safaris, nature tours, and falconry displays. **Pros:** incredible desert luxury; beautiful natural environment. **Cons:** remote location. ✛*Turn off 4.7 km (2.9 mi) after Interchange 8 on the Al Ain Rd., then 4.5 km (2.8 mi) to Al Marqab* ☎4/303–4222 ⊕*www.al-maha. com* ⇆*42 suites* △*In-room: safe, DVD, Wi-Fi. In-hotel: restaurant, room service, bar, pool, gym, spa, laundry service, parking (no fee), no children under 12, no-smoking rooms* ⊟*AE, DC, MC, V* ⍟*FAP.*

$$ ⛁**Courtyard Dubai by Marriott.** This large modern hotel would be a real treasure if it wasn't located so far outside the tourist mainstream. Much of the clientele here is made up of business travelers. Located in one of Dubai's expat suburbs, the hotel is surrounded by lakes and a community downtown area that has a selection of shops and eateries.

**8**

The generous lobby and range of facilities, including a pool and sundeck, make it competitive with higher priced options, and the modestly sized rooms are well equipped and comfortable. **Pros:** good quality facilities for the price range. **Cons:** remote from the main tourist attractions. ⊠*Green Community* ☎*4/885–2222, 800/321-2211 toll-free in the U.S. and Canada* ⊕*www.marriott.com* ⚲*155 rooms, 10 suites* ⚅*In-room: safe, refrigerator, Ethernet. In-hotel: 3 restaurants, room service, bar, pool, gym, spa, laundry service, concierge, public Wi-Fi, airport shuttle (fee), parking (no fee), no-smoking rooms* ⊟*AE, MC, V* ⦾*EP, BP, MAP.*

$$$$ 🖭**Desert Palm Hotel.** A boutique hotel surrounded by verdant polo fields brings exclusivity to the Dubai desert at a price point that doesn't require cashing in your Fortune 500 stocks. The style here is minimalist—almost Bauhaus—with wood accents and glass panes that allow light to flood into the public spaces. In the rooms, the ivory- and stone-colored Asian-inspired decor is complemented by colorful contemporary artwork and bold satin cushions. The Desert Palm has "residences" that suit families and groups, but the hotel is better for couples and singles who want to relax between forays into the city. **Pros:** luxury retreat. **Cons:** a good distance from the city. ⊠*Al Awir Rd.* ☎*4/323–8888, 800/525-4800 toll-free in the U.S. and Canada* ⊕*www.desertpalm.ae* ⚲*24 rooms* ⚅*In-room: safe, refrigerator, DVD, Wi-Fi. In-hotel: 3 restaurants, room service, bar, pool, spa, laundry service, concierge, parking (no fee), no-smoking rooms* ⊟*AE, DC, MC, V* ⦾*MP.*

$$$ 🖭**Hatta Fort Hotel.** Expats take a break from the dust, traffic, and construction of the city at this hotel located in the clean, cool air of the Hatta Mountains. The Hatta Fort Hotel makes the most of its oasis location by offering a lush interlude among jagged arid hills where you can relax and listen to the birds sing. Rooms are lined up side by side, with stone walls and wooden ceilings that combine safari and mountain lodge elements. Restaurants, bars, and the pool are located inside and surrounding a central building. **Pros:** birdsong can be heard in the morning; lovely mountain views. **Cons:** some road noise from the main Dubai/Oman highway. ⊠*Dubai/Oman Rd., Hatta* ☎*4/852–3211* ⊕*www.jaihotels.com* ⚲*50 rooms* ⚅*In-room: safe, refrigerator, Ethernet (some). In-hotel: 2 restaurants, bars, golf course, pool, gym, spa, no elevator, laundry service, concierge, parking (no fee), no-smoking rooms* ⊟*AE, MC, V* ⦾*EP.*

$$$ ⚇**Jebel Ali Hotel.** At one time, this hotel was a retreat far from the noise and grit of downtown. But the city is quickly encroaching as Dubai Marina continues to expand and the new international airport was constructed only 15 minutes away. The seven-story resort, located on a sheltered stretch of sand, has 128 acres of expansive grounds, including a marina, golf course, equestrian center, and a spa. In addition, a number of peacocks roam wild on the property. The resort caters unashamedly to tourists and is a popular package offer for travel agents from around the world—a multinational crowd gathers in the restaurants and bars at night. **Pros:** excellent resort facilities; relatively quiet (away from major construction projects). **Cons:** distance from mainstream attractions; small, one-person balconies. ⊠*Off Route D53, Jebel Ali* ☎*4/883–6000* ⊕*www.jebelali-international.com* ⌂*260 rooms* ⌂*In-room: safe, Ethernet (some). In-hotel: 5 restaurants, room service, bars, golf course, tennis courts, pool, gym, spa, beachfront, diving, water sports, children's programs (ages 4–11), laundry service, parking (no fee), no-smoking rooms* ⊟*AE, MC, V* ⦿*EP, BP, MAP.* .

$$$$ ⚇**Palm Tree Court and Spa** Sharing the 128 acres of the Jebel Ali Resort and Club, the Palm Trees Court and Spa offers a private beachside oasis surrounded by lush greenery. Gardens, ponds, and streams break up the space between the two-story buildings and attract a range of birds and butterflies. The large, open, wood-and-glass reception area has all the amenities, including bars and restaurants such as the White Orchid Pan-Asian eatery. The rooms are decorated in the tropical colors of marine blue and soft, lemon-yellow. Each room has a terrace or balcony—generously sized by Dubai standards. The hotel spa is on site, and there's a shuttle to Dubai Marina and the main shopping malls. **Pros:** tropical oasis setting; cheerful colorful decor; the sporting and dining facilities of Jebel Ali Golf Resort are also on-site. **Cons:** distant from Dubai attractions. ⊠*Off Route D53, Jebel Ali* ☎*4/883–6000* ⊕*www.jebelali-international.com* ⌂*134 suites* ⌂*In-room: safe. In-hotel: 2 restaurants, room service, bars, golf course, tennis courts, pool, gym, spa, beachfront, diving, water sports, children's programs (ages 4–11), laundry service, parking (no fee), no-smoking rooms.* ⊟*AE, MC, V* ⦿*EP, BP.* .

# NIGHTLIFE & THE ARTS

**Jumana—Secret of the Desert** (✉Al Sahra Desert Resort, Dubailand ☎4/367–9500, 800/58–62–62 toll-free ⊕www. alsahra.com) is an open-air show that takes you on an evening adventure featuring a kidnapped princess and a good prince battling evil. At this specially built desert venue, there will be an international cast of dancers and acrobats, as well as light and fireworks displays by Groupe F (choreographers of the Olympic Games ceremonies in Athens and the millennium celebrations in Paris). A tasty Lebanese buffet is served before and after the show. The show is generally booked as an excursion through a tour operator or your hotel concierge and will include round-trip transportation.

# SPORTS & THE OUTDOORS

## BOAT CHARTERS

At **Jebel Ali Marina** (✉Jebel Ali Golf Resort and Spa, Jebel Ali ☎4/883–6000 ⊕www.jebelali-international.com) you can charter fishing boats and other motor boats from the southernmost marina in the emirate.

## SAILING & WINDSURFING

**Jebel Ali Golf Resort & Spa** (✉Jebel Ali ☎4/883–6000 ⊕www. jebelali-international.com) has catamarans, Lasers, and windsurfing equipment for rent by the hour at its beach club. Instructors are also available if needed.

## SPAS

**The Spa** (✉Jebel Ali Golf Resort & Spa, Jebel Ali ☎4/883–6000 ⊕www.jebelali-international.com) strikes the right note between Arabian style (mosaic and gold leaf) and modern contemporary decor. The honey-hued walls offer a relaxing backdrop, and there are 10 treatment rooms, a well-equipped wet area with sauna, a steam room, and a hammam. Elemis is the favored product supplier, though Wild Earth treatments use herbs and essential oils from Tibet.

## GOLF

**Arabian Ranches Golf Course** ( ⊠*Arabian Ranches, Emirates Rd., Dubailand* ☎*4/366–3000* ⊕*www.arabianranches golfdubai.com*), which was designed by professional Ian Baker-Finch in association with Nicklaus Design, plies an extended route through the desert, wrapping around the dunes. The configuration places the first tee and final greens in the shadow of the clubhouse for grandstand tournament finishes. The Emirates Amateur Open is played here amongst other members-only and open tournaments. The academy has a well-lit driving range, digital swing analysis and putting, chipping, and bunker practice zones.

**The Els Club** ( ⊠*Dubai Sports City, Dubailand* ☎*4/425–1010* ⊕*www.elsclubdubai.com*) was designed by professional golfer Ernie Els, and the 7,538-yard course bears his name. Opened in January 2008, the course allows players of several abilities to play from varying tee positions. Els incorporated natural landscape elements, including sand dunes and native vegetation, into the design to allow local wildlife to thrive.

**Jebel Ali Golf Resort & Spa** ( ⊠*Jebel Ali Golf Resort and Spa, Jebel Ali* ☎*4/883–6000* ⊕*www.jebelali-international.com*) has a 9-hole, par-36 course that sweeps alongside the sand dunes of the Jebel Ali coastline, the marina, and large salt lakes. Movable tees make it easy to extend to 18 holes, which the professionals did when competing in the Dubai Desert Classic Tournament during the 1990s. Academy facilities include a 27-hole putting green, air-conditioned swing room, and an A-Star video swing analysis system.

## ORSEBACK RIDING & ALL THINGS EQUINE

Fine horseflesh plays an important part in R&R in Dubai, and horses have a special place in the history of the Arab Bedouin. Just think about the traditional tales of the Bedouin prince riding across the desert on his magnificent stallion to rescue his princess. There's certainly something exhilarating about riding a horse through the sand or along the beach. The riding centres here are large and well equipped, often with the ability to train to a very high standard. You can simply rent an animal for an afternoon ride or take lessons. Polo facilities are particularly well established here.

**Club Joumana** (⊠*Jebel Ali Golf Resort and Spa* ☎*4/883–6000* ⊕*www.jebelali-international.com*) caters to everyone from beginners to experienced riders, with lessons, dressage, and jump arenas. The hotel is surrounded by verdant grounds for trekking. Or you can take your mount to the beach or surrounding desert.

**Dubai Polo and Equestrian Club** (⊠*Arabian Ranches, Emirates Rd., Dubailand* ☎*4/361–7111*) is a top-ranked equestrian center with a neighboring polo facility that has lessons for all levels, including specialist dressage and polo skills. There are extensive private stables, and the complex has been designed with Andalusian architecture in mind in homage to the renowned horse skills fostered on the Spanish mainland.

**Emirates Equestrian Centre** (⊠*Off Muscat Rd., Nad al-Sheba, Meydan* ☎*4/336–1394* ⊕*www.emiratesequestriancentre. com*), established in the 1980s as a regional center of excellence, is set on 80 acres with 12 separate arenas and cross-country courses with jumps. Instruction here covers almost every horse-based discipline, including show jumping, dressage, and eventing. If you simply want to canter on the grounds, you can do so by the hour.

## MOTOR SPORTS & GO-KARTING

Motor sports are growing in Dubai with new money invested in the Dubai Autodrome in Sports City, one of the key projects of Dubailand. It already holds professional meets for two and four wheels. Taking to the wheel couldn't be easier for amateurs here, whether it be automobiles, karts, or bikes.

**Dubai Autodrome** (⊠*Emirates Rd., Dubailand* ☎*4/367–8750* ⊕*www.dubaiautodrome.com*), Dubai's FIA-certified, 3.34-mi racetrack, is a state-of-the-art facility designed to draw motor-sport excellence to the region. Check the Web site for professional race dates. Amateur Franchitis and Hamiltons also get to play here, with special driving days and local competitions. You can take courses in an Audi TT or RS4, a sporty Subaru, or a single-seat FIA Formula sports car. There are half-day and full-day programs.

**Kartdrome** (⊠*Dubai Autodrome, Emirates Rd., Dubailand* ☎*4/367–8744* ⊕*www.dubaiautodrome.com*), a 0.74-mile circuit, is a dedicated CIK-approved track with 17 corners, a tunnel, and a bridge to test your skills. In addition, there are floodlights for racing after dark, and the track can be shortened if the full race length is too tough. Racers are broken into two age groups, 7 to 12 years and more than 12 years. You can pay by the hour, and there are facilities for families or groups to run full-length competitions, with pit lanes for up to 24 teams. All the equipment you need is included in the rental price, but be sure to wear closed-toe shoes because you aren't allowed to race in sandals.

**The Emirates Karting Centre** (⊠*Beside the entrance to the Jebel Ali Golf Resort and Spa* ☎*4/282–7111* ⊕*www.emsfuae. com*) is marked out among the coastal dunes close to Jebel Ali Beach. The Emirates Kart Track is a small-scale affair at 800 meters, but is good fun for an hour or so of high-speed action with karts for juniors and adults. The site has floodlights so you can race after dark.

## SHOOTING

Not a mainstream sport, certainly, but the clay-pigeon shooting opportunities are worth mentioning because of the quality of the club here.

**Jebel Ali International Shooting Club** (⊠*Jebel Ali Golf Resort & Spa, Jebel Ali* ☎*4/883–6555* ⊕*www.jaihotels.com*) is an Olympic-standard shooting club that attracts many locals and visitors. The club has outdoor ranges for the seven clay pigeon disciplines and an archery range. Inside, there's a firearms simulator room where you can analyze your technique and accuracy. Professional instruction and all equipment are supplied for single or group lessons.

# SPECTATOR SPORTS

## HORSE RACING

A favorite sport of the Al-Maktoums, the sheikh and his brothers have invested millions of dollars in the bloodlines of their successful Godolphin stables. What better way is there for the family to celebrate its passion than by funding the world's richest horse race—with a prize fund of more than $21 million? The season runs from November until late March, when the Dubai World Cup is the climax and the city's grandest social event.

The **Nad al-Sheba Racecourse** (⊠*Off Muscat St., Nad al-Sheba* ☎*4/327–0077* ⊕*www.dubairacingclub.com*) is Dubai's main horse track at this writing, but a new racecourse is being developed closer to Nad al-Sheba. It is not expected to open until 2010.

## CAMEL RACING

On a huge flat expanse north of the Nad al-Sheba horse track, a small grandstand pinpoints the location of the **Camel-Racing Arena** (⊠*Off Muscat Street*). The camels speed over the course as dust billows around their feet; it's always a tight competition. Races take place on Thursday and Friday mornings during the winter, starting at sunup, and are completed by 8:30 AM. An impromptu market sets up around the meets selling whatever camel owners might need. Look out for handmade blankets for a practical and inexpensive souvenir. Although not a common organized excursion, most tour companies that do custom tours can organize a trip to the camel races, and this is the route taken by most tourists; it is usually easier to book this kind of activity through the concierge at your hotel.

THE AUTOMATIC CAMEL. Traditionally, lightweight, prepubescent boys were the preferred camel jockeys. However, an international outcry put an end to this when campaigners proved that many young boys were being taken from their homes in Pakistan by force to race in this dangerous sport. The UAE authorities banned racing with child jockeys in 2005, and camels now ride with computerized mechanical jockeys on their humps.

# Dubai Essentials

## PLANNING TOOLS, EXPERT INSIGHT, GREAT CONTACTS

There are planners and there are those who, excuse the pun, fly by the seat of their pants. We happily place ourselves among the planners. Our writers and editors try to anticipate all the issues you may face before and during any journey, and then they do their research. This section is the product of their efforts. Use it to get excited about your trip to Dubai, to inform your travel planning, or to guide you on the road should the seat of your pants start to feel threadbare.

# GETTING STARTED

We're really proud of our Web site: Fodors.com is a great place to begin any journey. Scan Travel Wire for suggested itineraries, travel deals, restaurant and hotel openings, and other up-to-the-minute info. Check out Booking to research prices and book plane tickets, hotel rooms, rental cars, and vacation packages. Head to Talk for on-the-ground pointers from travelers who frequent our message boards. You can also link to loads of other travel-related resources.

## ▌ RESOURCES

### ONLINE TRAVEL TOOLS

Transport **The Roads and Transport Authority** (⊕www.rta.ae) has an excellent Web site with information on roads, buses, taxis, and abras (boats) in the city. There's also a regular update on progress on the new metro system.

Government and Municipality **Dubai Municipality** (⊕www.dubai.ae) has a lot of information in English, which may be useful to both visitors and residents.

Press and Magazines **Gulf News** (⊕www.gulfnews.com) offers domestic, regional, and international news in English.

**Khaleej Times** (⊕khaleejtimes.com), an English-language daily, has local and international news.

All About Dubai **We Know Dubai** (⊕www.weknowdubai.com) is a Web site designed and written by expat residents who have their collective finger on the pulse of the emirate. The blog on the site has an interesting perspective on all kinds of Dubai news.

### VISITOR INFORMATION

The Dubai government, through the Department of Tourism and Commerce Marketing (DTCM), has funded a series of glossy brochures that look impressive but give little practical information to help plan a visit. The government's Web site is much more useful, with information about culture, activities, sports, and nightlife. It also offers online hotel booking for various price categories, though this part of the site does not always function correctly.

A 24-hour information desk at the airport can book hotel accommodations for you, and there are smaller information kiosks at BurJuman Mall, Deira City Centre Mall, Hamarain Mall, Mercato Mall, Mall of the Emirates, and Wafi City Mall.

Before You Leave **Dubai Tourism** (☎212/575–2262 ⊕www.dubaitourism.ae).

In Dubai **DTCM** (✉Baniyas Square, Naif district, Deira ☎4/228–5000 ⊘Sat.–Thurs. 9–9, Fri. 3–9 ✉Sheik Zayed Rd. ☎4/883–3397 ⊘Sat.–Thurs. 9–9, Fri. 3–9).

## ▍ THINGS TO CONSIDER

### PASSPORTS & VISAS

All visitors entering the UAE need a valid passport, and it must be valid for at least six months beyond their stay in Dubai. American, Canadian, UK, and EU citizens entering the UAE for tourism purposes will be presented with a free 60-day One Entry Visit visa when they enter the country. Frequent visitors should enter the country on a regular visitor's visa and then apply for the Multi-Entry visa while in the country.

Transit passengers with at least an eight-hour layover between flights at Dubai International airport are entitled to a free 96-hour transit visa provided they have confirmed onward booking for a third destination. This can be arranged on arrival at Dubai International Airport.

**Information Department of Naturalization and Residency–Dubai** (✉Next to Bur Dubai Police Station, Al Jaffliya District ☎4/398–0000 ⊕www.dnrd.gov.ae).

### TRIP INSURANCE

We believe that comprehensive trip insurance is especially valuable if you're booking a very expensive or complicated trip (particularly to an isolated region), or if you're booking far in advance. Comprehensive travel policies typically cover trip cancellation and interruption, letting you cancel or cut your trip short because of a personal emergency, illness, or, in some cases, acts of terrorism in your destination. Such policies also cover evacuation and medical care. Another type of coverage to look for is financial default—that is, when your trip is disrupted because a tour operator, airline, or cruise line goes out of business. Generally you must buy this when you book your trip or shortly thereafter.

If you're going abroad, consider buying medical-only coverage at the very least. Neither Medicare nor some private insurers cover medical expenses anywhere outside of the United States (including time aboard a cruise ship, even if it leaves from a U.S. port). Medical-only policies typically reimburse you for medical care (excluding that related to preexisting conditions) and hospitalization abroad, and provide for evacuation. You still have to pay the bills and await reimbursement from the insurer, though.

Expect comprehensive travel insurance policies to cost about 4% to 7% or 8% of the total price of your trip (it's more like 8%–12% if you're over age 70). A medical-only policy may or may not be cheaper than a comprehensive policy. Always read the fine print of your policy to make sure that you are covered for the risks that are of most concern to you. Compare several policies to make sure you're getting the best price and range of coverage available.

# Trip Insurance Resources

| INSURANCE COMPARISON SITES | | |
|---|---|---|
| Insure My Trip.com | 800/487-4722 | www.insuremytrip.com |
| COMPREHENSIVE TRAVEL INSURERS | | |
| Access America | 800/729-6021 | www.accessamerica.com |
| CSA Travel Protection | 800/873-9855 | www.csatravelprotection.com |
| HTH Worldwide | 610/254-8700 | www.hthworldwide.com |
| Travelex Insurance | 800/228-9792 | www.travelex-insurance.com |
| AIG Travel Guard | 800/826-4919 | www.travelguard.com |
| Travel Insured International | 800/243-3174 | www.travelinsured.com |
| MEDICAL-ONLY INSURERS | | |
| International Medical Group | 800/628-4664 | www.imglobal.com |
| International SOS | | www.internationalsos.com |

# BOOKING YOUR TRIP

For experienced travelers and those used to using the Internet to buy services, booking a trip to Dubai is easy and stress-free with reliable information being offered by the major hotels, tour operators and airlines, and secure Web sites for online bookings. However, rack rates for hotels are high, and this is a disadvantage for independent travelers. A travel agent should be able to secure you a better overall package price.

**Dubai Travel Agents Friendly Planet Travel Inc.** (☎800/555–5765 ⊕www.friendlyplanet.com) conducts tours of countries and regions worldwide, including a trip called Dazzling Dubai.

**Al Tayer Travel Agency** ( ✎Box 2623, Dubai, United Arab Emirates ☎4/223–6000 ⊕www.altayer-travel.com), also known as ATTA, offers a program of full tour booking and concierge services such as car rental, guided tours, and side trips.

**DNATA** ( ✎Box 2623, Dubai, United Arab Emirates ☎4/316–6748 ⊕www.dnata.com) is a government-owned travel agency for incoming and outgoing travel.

**Kanoo Travel** (✉Box 2190, Dubai, United Arab Emirates ☎4/393–8400 ⊕www.kanoogroup.com) offers incoming help with pleasure and business travel.

## ▍ AIRLINE TICKETS

Emirates Airlines offers an Arabian Airpass with cheap flights from Dubai to 12 destinations in the Gulf and Middle East region. The closest city to Dubai covered by the Arabian Airpass is Muscat in Oman, and the farthest is Alexandria in Egypt. Arabian Airpasses are priced according to zones on a per-journey basis. The closest zone (A) is priced at U.S. $50 and the farthest zone (C) is priced at U.S. $150, both for economy class. Coupons for Arabian Airpass flights cannot be purchased online and can only be purchased at Emirates offices in the Middle East. Arabian Airpass coupons can only be used in conjunction with international tickets purchased outside the Middle East with a minimum value of $350.

**Air Pass Info Emirates Airlines** (⊕www.emirates.com).

## ▍ RENTAL CARS

Dubai's roads have been proven as some of the most dangerous in the world. Traffic density is high, and blatant disregard for speed limits and traffic regulations is widespread. Add to this a constantly changing road layout due to construction around the city, and driving is a minefield for visitors. So it's best to avoid renting a vehicle, unless you are a confident driver and have experienced widely different driving styles in the past.

Many of the international car rental companies in Dubai are licensed offices of local companies. Smaller vehicles include a mixture of European (Peugeot), Far Eastern (Mazda, Nissan, Toyota, Honda), and U.S. (Chevrolet) options. Larger vehicles tend to be European, including BMW, Audi, and Mercedes, but MPVs are becoming an increasingly popular choice for families and those who want more comfort/ safety. Four-wheel-drive vehicles are available, but most car-rental companies prohibit off-road (dirt or sand roads) or desert driving as part of their contracts.

Minimum age ranges for rentals are usually 21 years old for compact vehicles and 25 for larger and 4WD vehicles. The maximum age is usually 75. Visitors must have an international driving license, or a temporary Dubai license to rent a vehicle. Your national driver's license alone will not be accepted.

It's advisable to get insurance for Oman if you intend to explore the eastern desert area or head to Hatta. The border between Oman and Dubai meanders across the area and is not always signposted. This isn't a problem in terms of you passing backwards and forwards (no border guards, except at the official road border to the east of Hatta town), but for your vehicle rental there will be financial implications if you have an accident because you will be uninsured. If you simply intend to explore Dubai city and the coastal strip, you won't need this insurance extension.

If you are dropping off your rental at Dubai International airport, the rental office is inside the complex so it doesn't take too long. Traffic congestion across the creek may cause you delays on your return to the airport from Sheikh Zayed Road, Jumeirah Beach, and the southern districts. Allow 30 minutes extra on the journey from these areas at peak times (Mon.– Thurs. 7–9 and 5–7).

### CAR-RENTAL INSURANCE

Although not compulsory, CDW is advised because of the high accident rate in Dubai. Personal accident coverage is optional, and you should look at your level of existing coverage on your own insurance before accepting or declining this cover with your rental agreement.

■ TIP→ You can decline the insurance from the rental company and purchase it through a third-party provider such as Travel Guard ( ⊕ *www. travelguard.com*)—$9 per day for $35,000 of coverage. That's sometimes just under half the price of the CDW offered by some car-rental companies.

## ▌ VACATION PACKAGES

It may be worth researching what packages are available for your trip to Dubai. Hotels have high rack rates and travel agents can often get reduced prices through bulk buying power. One disadvantage may be that travel agents have relationships only with certain hotel groups and chains, which will limit your options of where to stay. Discuss this with your travel agent before committing to a booking.

## Car Rental Resources

| LOCAL AGENCIES | | |
|---|---|---|
| Autolease Rent-a-Car | 4/224–4900 | www.autolease-uae.com |
| Diamondlease | 4/220-0325 | www.diamondlease.com |
| MAJOR AGENCIES | | |
| Alamo | 800/522–9696 | www.alamo.com |
| Avis | 800/331–1084 | www.avis.com |
| Budget | 800/472–3325 | www.budget.com |
| Hertz | 800/654–3001 | www.hertz.com |
| National Car Rental | 800/227–7368 | www.nationalcar.com |

## ▌ GUIDED TOURS

Guided tours to the region usually include Dubai as part of a seven- or eight-country tour, often under the title "Persian Gulf" tour or "Oman and UAE" tour. Adventures Abroad offers guided tours for small numbers of no more than 21 people to locations including the Persian Gulf and the UAE. Bestway Tours and Safaris operates guided tours, allying Dubai and the UAE with surrounding states, or contrasting states such as Ethiopia or Tanzania in Africa. Bales Worldwide specializes in tours to the Middle East, and Dubai is normally included with neighbor Oman in a two-country itinerary.

Recommended Companies **Adventures Abroad** (☎360/775-9925, 800/665–3998 toll-free ⊕www.adventures-abroad.com). **Bestway Tours and Safaris** (☎800/663-0844 toll-free from Canada and U.S. ⊕www.bestway.com). **Bales Worldwide** (☎0845/057—1819 in the UK ⊕www.balesworldwide.com).

# TRANSPORTATION

Dubai city is made up of more than 100 abutting districts, covering the area north of Deira Creek south to Dubai Marina. The boundaries between these districts are not clearly defined or signposted, especially in the crowded downtown. Street signs and property numbers are not standard because postal services have never offered direct delivery. Residents and visitors alike navigate around the area by describing locations in relation to local well-known landmarks such as a shopping mall, hotel, or major highway intersection.

As the city has grown, more districts have been added to the map, with their associated restaurants, hotels, and malls. The lack of an emirate-wide standard addressing system quickly is becoming a pressing problem. In the absence of exact address information, this guide provides the street and district for the attraction, as well as any nearby landmark commonly used to describe the attraction's location. These are understood within Dubai and are used by taxi drivers and bus drivers to get you where you want to go.

## ▌ TOURIST BUS

The Big Bus Company is part mode of transport, part tourist attraction. Big Bus offers two "hop-on, hop-off" services around Dubai that link major attractions and provide an upper level plat-

form from which to view the city as it passes your window. The red route operates around Deira and Bur Dubai. The Blue route links the city with the beaches and the Festival City area. The two routes overlap at various points allowing you to transfer from one to the other. Tickets also include a walking tour and entrance to a selection of museums and are valid for both routes for 24 hours from first use. You'll find ticket kiosks at Mall of the Emirates, Deira City Centre Mall, Wafi City Mall, Souk Madinat Jumeirah, and BurJuman Centre; you can also buy tickets online or on the bus itself.

**Information** **The Big Bus Company** (☎4/340–7709 ⊕www. bigbustours.com).

## ▌ BY AIR

Flying time from North America to Dubai is around 12½ hours from New York and 15 hours from Houston. From cities in Western Europe it's around 6 hours, and around 7 hours from London. From the Far East, it's 7 hours from Singapore to Dubai and 7 hours again from Hong Kong.

### AIRPORTS

Dubai International Airport (IATA designation: DXB) is the only international airport in Dubai and it sits 10 to 15 minutes east from the Deira Creek front and 30 minutes northeast from the main Jumeirah Beach hotels.

There is no departure tax when leaving the emirate.

On-site Dubai International Hotel has 78 rooms (singles and doubles) that can be rented by the hour. Prices for rooms are U.S. $41 single/U.S. $52 double between 4 AM and 7 PM, U.S. $51 single/U.S. $62 double between 8 PM and 3 AM. Major airlines have their own lounges, and the Department of Civil Aviation has a Business Class lounge that's accessible to all passengers. The DCAL lounge offers rooms with showers by the hour and five workstations with computers and Internet access. There's a separate room for smokers. There are two additional quiet lounges where passengers can rest or sleep between flights. More active travelers can visit the G-Force Health Club, which has workout facilities and a pool.

Although not a satellite within Dubai, Abu Dhabi International Airport in neighboring Abu Dhabi is 90 minutes from downtown Dubai and could be an option for some travelers. However, you cannot obtain a temporary Dubai driving permit unless you have a Dubai entry stamp, so you would have to rent a car in Abu Dhabi if flying into that airport.

**Airport Information Dubai International Airport** (☎4/216–2525 ⊕www.dubaiairport.com)

## GROUND TRANSPORTATION

Dubai Municipality has 30 large buses with extra luggage space that operate in two circular routes between the airport and the downtown area every 30 minutes, 24 hours per day. Route 401 runs into and around the Deira side of the Creek; route 402 runs into and around the Bur Dubai districts. Fares are AED 3 per journey. These buses run close to 80 hotels.

Public bus services link the airport with the main bus stations in Deira and Bur Dubai, from which further services go to districts across the city. Services 4, 11, 15, 33, and 44 connect with Terminal 1. Route C1 links the airport (Terminal 1) with Satwa Bus Station traveling through Deira and Bur Dubai between 6 AM and midnight with a service every 10 minutes. Fare is AED 1.

Most hotels offer airport transfers but will charge a fee unless you have booked an executive floor room, in which case it will be included. If there is no airport transfer, take one of the registered taxis from ranks outside the airport terminals that offer service 24 hours a day. Taxis are metered, so there's no need to haggle the price with the driver. Rates are charged per pickup (currently an AED 20 initial charge from the airport) and then per km (or 0.62 mi). Taxi rates per km rise slightly between 10 PM and 6 AM.

### FLIGHTS

Dubai International is a major hub for east-to-west travel, and more than 80 airlines offer flights here. From the U.S. and Canada, Delta has direct flights to Dubai International via Atlanta and Houston. Emirates Airlines has daily direct flights from New York's JFK Airport and Houston to Dubai International and connecting flights from Houston and Newark via London's Gatwick. Most major European airlines offer connecting service from the U.S. to Dubai through their European hubs.

The national airline of the UAE, Etihad, offers nonstop flights from New York to the international airport at Abu Dhabi—a 90-minute bus transfer to its office on Sheikh Zayed Road in Dubai is included. Etihad has competitive prices when compared with Emirates when flying direct to Dubai International.

**Airline Contacts** **Delta Airlines** (☎800/221–1212 for U.S. reservations, 800/241–4141 for international reservations, 4/397-0118 in Dubai ⊕www.delta.com). **Northwest Airlines** (☎800/225–2525 ⊕www. nwa.com). **Emirates** (☎800/777-3999 for reservations, 4/214–4444 in Dubai ⊕www.emirates.com). **British Airways** (☎800/247–9297 for reservations, 800/441–3322 in Dubai ⊕www.britishairways.com). **Air France** (☎800/237–2747 for reservations, 4/602–5400 in Dubai ⊕www.airfrance.com). **Olympic Airlines** (☎800/223–1226 for reservations ⊕www.olympicairlines. com). **Swiss International Air Lines** (☎877/359–7947 for reservations, 4/294–5051 in Dubai ⊕www.swiss. com). **Finnair** (☎800/950–5000 for reservations ⊕www.finnair.com). **Malaysia Airlines** (☎800/552–9264 for reservations, 4/397–0250 in Dubai ⊕www.malaysiaairlines.com). **Royal Jordanian Airlines** (☎212/949-0060 for reservations, 4/294–2488 in Dubai ⊕www.rja.com). **Etihad Airways** (☎212/554–1300 for reservations, 888/838–4423 toll free ⊕www.etihadairways.com).

## ▌ BY BOAT

Dubai's open-sided *abra* water ferries ply the short distance between the north and south banks of Dubai Creek. They carry up to 100,000 passengers a day and show visitors a unique perspective on the city. This is a must-do activity. There are two nearby stations on the Deira bank (Old Souk station and Sabkha station). The station on the Bur Dubai side has a section for arriving boats and a separate section about 50 feet away for departing boats. It costs AED 1 for the 10-minute journey, and the boats run around the clock (though the number of boats drops between midnight and 5 AM), departing from the quayside when full (around 20 passengers).

A 36-seat air-conditioned water bus service also operates on four lines, reaching further into the creek than the abra. Service B1 runs from Sabkha station to Bur Dubai station, service B2 from Bani Yas station to Old Souk station, service B3 links Sabkha station with Seef station, and B4 connects Bani Yas station to Seef station. The services run daily from 6 AM until 11 PM every 10 minutes at peak times. The cost of the water taxi per journey is AED 4.

Abras can be hired by the hour for creek tours for a price of AED 100 per hour (paid to the abra driver). Abras make the perfect platform for photographing creek-side vistas and enjoying the commercial boating activity on the wharfs.

**Information** **Dubai Road Traffic Authority** (⊕www.rta.ae).

# ▌BY BUS

There's a 62-route inexpensive network of modern air-conditioned public buses running to all parts of the city between 5 AM and midnight, but these are little used by visitors. A confusing route system, crowded buses during peak hours, a lack of information about public transportation at hotels, and very few shaded bus stops (something soon to be changed, as 50 air-conditioned bus shelters are slated to be built around the city) deter visitors.

Board buses at the front and get off at the rear. There is no eating, drinking, or smoking on public transportation. Separate sections on each bus are set aside for women passengers (and for women with children)—they are clearly marked—and men should not sit in these seats, but women and children can (and do) sit with their male relatives in the regular seats. If you are unsure of where to get off, ask the driver for advice.

Fares are paid in cash to the driver, and they do not give change, so have exact fare. Fares are inexpensive with a maximum of AED 2.5 on long journeys to locations such as Bur Dubai to Dubai Marina.

Inter-emirate services link Dubai with its neighbors. Eight routes run to the other five emirates several times per day. Inter-emirate single fares are currently AED 15 for the trip to Abu Dhabi in the south and AED 5 for the journey to Sharjah, Dubai's northern neighbor.

**Information Dubai Road Transport Authority** ( ☎ 4/800–9090 ⊕ www.rta.ae).

# ▌BY CAR

Driving is not recommended for first-time visitors to the area. In addition to questionable local driving standards, the amount of construction work in the emirate means constant diversions and road closures that even taxi drivers have difficulty navigating. Although road signs are generally in both English and Arabic, temporary signs may not be. Gas and parking charges are inexpensive, but finding parking is difficult, especially downtown by the creek.

It's also easy to hire a car with a driver by the day. This may be more expensive than a taxi but may suit visitors who prefer personalized service and want to avoid taxi lines during peak hours. Major car rental companies can arrange for a car and driver, as can hotel concierge desks. You'll pay per six hours or per 12 hours.

Taxis can also be hired by the half day (six hours) or full day (12 hours). These arrangements can be made in advance or on the street. The cost of a six-hour hire is AED 300 and 12 hours is AED 600.

## GASOLINE

Gasoline (or petrol), including unleaded gas, is available in all parts of the city. By international standards it's cheap, but prices have risen several times in the last few years. At this writing the price is AED 6.50 per imperial gallon (the standard measurement for dispensing fuel). Most fuel stations have attendants, who appreciate a small tip (small change or AED 1), especially for services such as windshield cleaning. Gas stations are open daily, 24 hours. Emarat, Emirates Petroleum, and Enoc fuel stations do not currently accept credit cards; payment must be made in cash or company-specific fuel payment card at these stations.

## PARKING

On-street parking is difficult to find. Paid on-street parking and parking lots are the norm, but the sheer number of vehicles makes space scarce. Coin-operated machines are found in all paid parking zones. Prices range from AED 1 to AED 2 per hour, and there may be a time limit on how long you can stay in one parking space (normally four hours). There are prepaid parking schemes. The one most helpful to short-term visitors is the parking card available at post offices, which costs AED 42 for the equivalent of AED 50 worth of parking. Shopping malls have free parking, but hotels may charge.

## ROAD CONDITIONS

Roads across the city range from wide multilane highways to narrow single-lane streets. Road surfaces are generally good, and are excellent on the newest stretches such as at Dubai Marina. Out in the desert there are many unsurfaced routes through the sand that should not be attempted without a 4WD vehicle and a good map (but remember, driving on unsurfaced roads may invalidate your car rental insurance). Traffic is always heavy in Deira and Bur Dubai around the business districts but becomes very heavy during the morning (7–9) and evening (5–7) peak periods. Traffic is generally controlled by lights, though there are traffic circles at some major intersections. Currently the worst bottlenecks are at the top of Sheikh Zayed Road and Al Garhoud Bridge, though traffic can be slow and heavy across the city at any time of day.

Because the emirate is expanding rapidly the existing road system is also expanding, with new intersections and layouts to link new districts to the main road network. Existing road patterns may be changed temporarily, sometimes at short notice, so that even experienced drivers who know the destination can become confused. This can cause erratic driving as drivers must rethink routes and overcome road closures and diversions.

Dubai's roads are some of the most dangerous on the planet. The local driving style is fast and erratic. There is little concern for speed limits and lane dividers on the major highways, stop signs and red lights.

Rainstorms are rare but can cause chaos because they are so unusual and there is no planned drainage around the city.

It's an offense to jaywalk (fine AED 50), but people still do cross the highway when and where they shouldn't. Keep your concentration in downtown areas where the streets can be crowded with pedestrians, especially in the cooler air of the evenings when Dubai comes out to play.

## ROADSIDE EMERGENCIES

All emergency service and breakdown personnel will speak English, so explaining your problem won't be an issue. If you have an accident you must stay with your vehicle (keep yourself safe from other traffic by waiting on the curb or median). Call the police and get an accident report to keep your insurance valid. If renting a vehicle, your rental company should issue you with a telephone number in case of breakdown or accident. Keep this information safe.

**Emergency Services Automobile Association** (☎4/266–9989, 800/4900 toll-free for emergenciesy) offers a 24-hour call-out service for members. **International Automobile and Touring Club** (☎800/5200 toll-free for emergencies) provides call-out and breakdown services to members. **Police** (☎999).

## RULES OF THE ROAD

Road signs and speed limits have information in Arabic and English. Most road signs are internationally understood pictograms. Speed limits are generally decided by road type (one lane or two lane) and whether the road is in a built up area or a rural area.

Driving with any alcohol in your bloodstream is a serious offense. Dubai police do not stop drivers for routine breathalyzer tests, but if they have suspicions that a driver has been drinking they will confis-

cate the vehicle and take the driver into custody.

Speed limits in Dubai are 60–80 kph in urban areas and 100–120 kph on two-lane highways. Exact speed limits are posted on the roadsides. Speeding remains a major problem in the emirate. Taxis in Dubai emit an audible sound if the speed limit is exceeded. You can ask your driver to slow down if this warning sounds regularly during your journey. Other driving dangers are drivers changing lanes suddenly without warning, and drivers not waiting in line on on-ramps or off-ramps but trying to cut in at high speed at the last moment.

The road system uses U-turns as part of its design. Signs at intersections and traffic lights indicate whether or not it is permissible to make a U-turn at that particular point.

Drivers must have an International Driving Permit, or a license (temporary or permanent) issued by the Dubai authorities in order to drive a vehicle in the emirate. Getting a temporary license once you are in Dubai will take at least four hours, so it's much easier to bring an international license with you from home.

Other important rules are that parking is not generally allowed against the left curb (or outside curb) except in designated areas, it is an offense to use your mobile phone while driving unless you have a hands-free device, and children under 10 are not allowed to travel in the front seat of a vehicle.

There are automatic electronic tolls (SALIK) on Sheikh Zayed Road by Mall of the Emirates and on Al Garhoud bridge. Your vehicle must be equipped with an electronic toll tag with sufficient funds recorded on it and AED 4 is automatically deducted from the tag for each pass of the toll machine. SALIK tags can be purchased and topped up at most petrol stations and branches of Emirates Bank and Dubai Islamic Bank—but recent shortages of tags have caused some problems. If you rent a vehicle, you will be responsible for any tolls.

**Information Dubai Police Department** ( ⊕www.dubaipolice.gov.ae).

## ▌ BY SUBWAY

Fifteen-point-five-billion dirham has been set aside to build the Dubai Metro system and the project is ongoing at this writing, with ensuing traffic problems as roads are closed and rerouted to allow tunnels to be dug and viaducts to be built for overland sections of track.

The 32½-mi Red Line will have 29 stations running from the Rashdiva district in the north, and traveling south to Jebel Ali running parallel to Sheikh Zayed Road. The Red Line is due to commence operations in 2009 and will link to the Sheikh Al-Maktoum International Airport in the south of the emirate.

## ▌ BY TAXI

Taxis are the most efficient way to get around the city. Fares are relatively cheap, and most drivers speak English and have a good knowledge of the major tourist attractions and malls.

You can hail taxis in the street or call for one. Taxis can be difficult to pick up in Deira and Bur Dubai because of high demand by business and government officials. Friday afternoons are also a difficult time across the emirate because many taxi drivers are Muslim and they take a break from taxi service to join in the main prayer service of the week. Wait times at malls can be long in the evenings as many expat workers do not own vehicles and will need taxis to get home with their purchases.

Some drivers may refuse to take clients to certain destinations, citing traffic congestion (Deira is a particularly unpopular destination if drivers have to cross one of the creek bridges); however, drivers are not supposed to refuse a fare based on destination.

Licensed taxis are cream-colored with a red roof and the word TAXI in an illuminated sign on the roof and printed along the sides; if the red light is illuminated, the taxi is occupied. There are taxi stands at all the major malls and hotels. You can also hail a taxi in the street by raising your hand.

All taxis are metered. Rates are charged per pickup and then per km (0.62 mi). Currently a pickup from a hailed taxi is AED 3 between 6 AM and 10 PM, AED 3.50 between 10 PM and 6 AM. If a taxi is requested from a dispatcher, pickup rates are AED 6 between 6 AM and 10 PM, AED 7 between 10 PM and 6 AM. There is an AED 20 surcharge for airport pickups. There are also charges for waiting.

Tolls will appear as an extra on your fare. Taxi drivers can supply a receipt if you need one. A gratuity is always welcomed but is not compulsory.

**Taxi Companies** **General Taxi Dispatch** (☎800–9090 or 4/208-0808 for calls and specialist vehicles). **Metrotaxi** (☎4/267–3222). **National Taxi** (☎4/206–5557).

# ON THE GROUND

## ▌ COMMUNICATIONS

### INTERNET

Most hotels have some sort of Internet access for guests, whether it is in-room Wi-Fi or in public areas, Ethernet connection in rooms, or access via a hotel machine in the business center. Most connections are high speed. Some hotels offer free Internet access to all guests; others offer it free to executive floor guests only.

Dubai authorities do censor Web content and will block sites considered unsuitable. It's very difficult to get a handle on how much censorship actually takes place either for moral reasons or for antigovernment criticism, though censorship is not as strict in many other Muslim countries.

Many hotel lobbies, cafés, and coffee shops have Wi-Fi, so traveling with a laptop is relatively stress-free. If you have to pay for access, Etisalat, the UAE telecommunications provider, charges AED 15 per hour for nonsubscription roaming at its Hot-Spot sites.

### Internet Cafés **Cybercafes**
(⊕www.cybercafes.com) lists more than 4,000 Internet cafés worldwide. **Avari Hotel** (✉Clock Tower Roundabout, Deira ☎4/295–6666 ⊕www. avari.com) has an Internet café. **Internet Café** (✉Dunes Centre, Al Diyafa St., Satwa ☎4/345–3390 ⊕www.internetcafe.ae) is open until 3 am every night.

### PHONES

Dubai has reliable landline and mobile telecommuncations. Local prepaid phone cards by Etisalat are the cheapest option for all calls. The Etisalat AED 20 card can be used for local and international calls, and to access Internet services with a laptop at Etisalat Wi-Fi Hot Spots. It can be bought at Etisalat shops and at stores and supermarkets throughout the city.

Buying a mobile phone or a local SIM card for your own mobile is easy. Etisalat shops will be able to help you (take your passport for identification).

When you are calling the United Arab Emirates, the country code is 471; the Dubai emirate code is 4; so to call a number in Dubai from the U.S. you should dial 00–471–4 (plus the seven-digit number).

### CALLING WITHIN DUBAI

Local numbers have seven digits. To call a Dubai number from one of the other emirates in the UAE start this seven-digit number with 04. Public pay phones can be found around the city. Most take only phone cards that can be bought in many shops, gas stations, and supermarkets. Cards are priced from AED 20. For directory assistance ring ☎180. Operators will speak English.

### CALLING OUTSIDE DUBAI

Public phone boxes allow international direct dialing. Once you have inserted your calling card, dial 00 and then the country code. In hotels, you usually have to dial a one-digit number to get an outside line. Once you have an outside line dial 00 and then the country code. For international directory inquiries or help, call ☎180 or 181.

The country code for the United States is 1.

U.S. telecommunications companies providing inexpensive international call services can all be used in the UAE, and each company has an access number that you'll need to dial. Hotels should not block calls to access numbers.

**Access Codes** AT&T (☎9–800–121). **MCI** (☎0–800–111). **Sprint** (☎0–800–131) only works for U.S. phone numbers.

## MOBILE PHONES

If you have a multiband GSM phone, you can probably use your phone in Dubai. Roaming fees can be steep, and you will pay the toll charges for incoming calls.

Cell phone stores are everywhere in Dubai, and mobile phone ownership is widespread. Some car rental companies will rent you a phone during your stay, and there's also a kiosk next to the car rental kiosks just after the customs hall in arrivals at Dubai International, where you can rent for a short term. But it's also cheap to buy a SIM card and get a local number if you have an unlocked phone. Buying a phone and setting up an account, or buying a top-up card in Dubai is also relatively simple.

You'll need to show the entry stamp/visa in your passport when you set up. Etisalat is the national provider and they have a special package for short-term visitors called Ahlan. You'll pay an initial charge of AED 90 (with an AED 35 call credit included) after which local calls cost 50 fils (AED 0.50) per minute. Outgoing international calls are charged AED 2.50 per minute. SMS messages are charged at 30 fils per local message, 90 fils per international message.

A new competitor to Etisalat, Du has a Visitor Mobile Line costing AED 70, set up with an AED 20 recharge card included; it's valid for 90 days (renewable). Calls cost 1 fil per minute local, 60 fils per minute international. Text messages cost 18 fils per message local, 60 fils per message international. Du also sells series of rechargeable cards ranging from AED 23 valid for 10 days to AED 230 valid for 30 days.

**Contacts Cellular Abroad** (☎800/287–5072 ⊕www.cellular-abroad.com) rents and sells GMS phones and sells SIM cards that work in many countries. **Mobal** (☎888/888–9162 ⊕www.mobal rental.com) rents mobiles and sells GSM phones (starting at $49) that will operate in 140 countries. Per-call rates vary throughout the world. **Planet Fone** (☎888/988–4777 ⊕www.planetfone.com) rents cell phones, but the per-minute rates are expensive. **Etisalat** (☎4/004–4101 ⊕www.etisalat.ae) **Du** (☎55/567–8155 ⊕www.du.ae).

## ▮ CUSTOMS & DUTIES

Customs regulations are generally the same as other international destinations except in two important areas. Many over-the-counter and prescription drugs are banned in the UAE (including over-the-counter cold medicines with codeine that are commonly sold in Europe and Australia). The Embassy of Abu Dhabi (another emirate in the UAE) maintains a list of restricted medications on its Web site. Some common substances that are completely banned in the UAE include poppy seeds (even those commonly used on rolls and bagels). You will be allowed to bring restricted drugs into the UAE if they are prescribed to you by your doctor, but must carry a copy of the prescription with you. Although the authorities may be understanding and simply confiscate the items if you can't prove you need them, they can decide to detain you or arrest you for drug smuggling. In addition to pharmaceutical products, there are heavy penalties for bringing recreational drugs into the country, even small amounts for personal use. If found guilty of smuggling, you'll be liable for a jail sentence of three years minimum.

Dubai is the most liberal country in the Gulf, but a very conservative attitude toward pornography still prevails.

You can only bring pets into the country if you have a resident's visa. A permit must then be obtained from the Ministry of Water and Environment (Vet Quarantine Section) before the animal will be allowed into Dubai.

You'll be allowed to bring the following items into the country duty-free: gifts to the value of AED 3,000; up to 400 cigarettes, plus 50 cigars and 500 grams of tobacco (over 18s only); four liters of alcohol (or 48 cans of beer, each of 355 milliliters) or a combination of (over 18s only); cash not exceeding AED 40,000; and items for personal use such as laptops, cameras, and sports equipment.

**Information in Dubai** **Dubai Customs** (📞4/302–3828 🌐www.dbxcustoms.gov.ae). **Embassy of Abu Dhabi** (🌐http://abudhabi.usembassy.gov/restricted_medication_.html).

## ▮ ELECTRICITY

Dubai has a safe and modern electrical system—it needs to with the amount of neon it emits every evening. The electrical current is 220/240 volts and 50 cycles, which is different from the system in the U.S. Appliances brought from North America will need a transformer. Most plugs in Dubai are the three-prong rectangular blade plug—type G—also found in Britain.

**Contacts** **Steve Kropla's Help for World Travelers** (🌐www.kropla.com) has information on electrical and telephone plugs around the world. **Walkabout Travel Gear** (🌐www.walkabouttravelgear.com) has a good coverage of electricity under "adapters."

## ▌EMERGENCIES

**Consulates** **U.S. Consulate**
( World Trade Centre, Sheikh Zayed
Rd. 4/311–6000).

**General Emergencies** **Police and
Ambulance** ( 999). **Fire** ( 997).

**Hospitals & Clinics** **Dubai Hospital** ( Al Khaleej Rd., Al Baraha,
Deira 4/219–5000). **The American Hospital** ( Off Oud Metha Rd.,
Oud Metha, Bur Dubai 4/336–
7777).

## ▌HEALTH

*For information on travel insurance, shots and medications, and
medical-assistance companies,
see Shots & Medications under
Things to Consider in Before You
Go, above.*

### SPECIFIC ISSUES IN DUBAI
There are no serious endemic health
risks to be worried about in Dubai,
though the heat and strong sun are
the major concerns. International
brands of sunscreen can be found
in pharmacies and hotel stores, but
they may be more expensive than
at home.

Dubai has been declared malaria-
free, so there is no danger of serious
illness, but there are still mosqui-
toes. Staying inside can help, and
you can also buy anti-mosquito
creams and sprays in pharmacies
and hotel gift shops.

If you are unfortunate enough to
fall ill, doctors and nurses here
speak English. Your hotel should
have the name of a doctor who
can be called to your room if nec-
essary, and walk-in clinics and hospitals are around the city. Costs can
be high, so it's important to have
health insurance coverage for your
trip.

### OVER-THE-COUNTER
### REMEDIES
Many drugs that can be bought
over the counter in the U.S. are
restricted in the UAE and cannot
be imported into the country without a prescription. These include
codeine, acetominophen (Tyle-
nol), dextromethorphan (found in
decongestants), isotretinion (found
in acne treatments), and prochlor-
perazine maleate (for nausea and
vomiting). Prescription drugs for
depression, anxiety, schizophrenia,
and hormone replacement and control are also on this list.

## ▌HOURS OF OPERATION
Government offices are open 8
AM–2 PM. They close at noon on
Thursday and remain closed all
day on Friday. Stores open long
hours and open every day. Shopping malls stay open throughout
the day all year round, opening at
10 AM (apart from Lamcy Plaza,
which opens at 9 am) and closing
at 10 PM (some close at midnight on
Friday and Saturday). Shops in the
downtown area and in the souks
open at 8 AM and close at 9 PM.
Many stores outside malls close in
the afternoons from around 1 PM
until 4 PM. During Ramadan shops
outside the malls may only open
after sunset. Malls do not close for
major religious festivals but local
stores will close on the day.

Museums open daily but may be
closed in the afternoons and also

have shorter working hours on Fridays. During Ramadan they will alter their working hours.

Most hotel bars stay open throughout the day, but some open around 4 PM. They stay open until around 1 AM, though many operate as bar/nightclubs so will stay open later. True nightclubs open at 9 PM or 10 PM and stay open until 3 AM, but they close promptly at this time.

## HOLIDAYS

Dubai has only two fixed national holidays, New Year's Day on January 1 and National Day on December 2. All other holidays are set by the Islamic lunar calendar. Al-Hijra (Islamic New Year) is usually in late November or December. Mouloud or Mawlid (Birth of the Prophet) is in late February or March. Leilat al-Meiraj (Ascension of the Prophet) is in late July or August. Eid al-Fitr (end of Ramadan) is in September or October. Eid al-Adha (Feast of the Sacrifice) is in late November or December.

## ▌ MAIL

If you need stamps for your postcards, they can be bought at tourist souvenir stores and in most hotel stores. Mail deliveries take at least 10 days from Dubai to the U.S. and Europe, and the service is not always reliable. Most post offices are open daily 8 AM–2 PM; larger branches are open 8–8.

Visitors can have mail sent *poste restante* by using a public P.O. box number. Emirates Post has public box numbers at each post office. Mail in your name can be retrieved for a small fee (50 fils–AED 3

depending on number and size of parcels). Of course, this system relies on knowing the post office nearest your location—not easy for a first-time visitor. The Deira Central public P.O. box number is 111311, Jumeirah is 72800.

If you need to receive mail in Dubai, ask the concierge where you're staying if guests can receive mail at the hotel's P.O. box number. It's better to have important letters and packages couriered rather than relying on postal services.

**Main Branches Dubai Central Post Office** (✉Off Za'abeel Rd., Kerama ☎4/337–1500).

## SHIPPING PACKAGES

Many shops selling handicrafts and particularly carpets will ship goods for you. Services are reliable with the main stores having a good reputation. FedEx has a well-established network in Dubai, but service is very expensive. Emirates Post has a more reasonably priced parcels service for packages. The price for a 5-kilogram package Express Service is AED 284; however, the Emirates Post does not offer insurance on packages to the U.S., and services are slower than with a commercial shipping company. Empost does offer a more expensive express international courier service.

**Express Services FedEx** (☎800/4050). **Empost** (☎4/286–0000 ⊕empostuae.com).

## ■ MONEY

Dubai is an expensive destination by American standards, and accommodations are among the most expensive in the world. Eating in international restaurants is also generally more expensive than in the U.S., though eating in local restaurants is a much cheaper option. Alcohol is available in Dubai but only for a price.

A mid-range hotel room can be around $300 per night. Expect to pay AED 50 for a taxi from the airport to Jumeirah Beach, AED 75 to Dubai Marina. A typical hotel's breakfast buffet may cost AED 70, or a continental breakfast could cost AED 40. Dinner at a mid-range international restaurant is about AED 140 per person, lunch is about AED 60 per person for a sandwich and coffee. It is best to budget at least AED 300 per day for food. A glass of beer costs about AED 45, and a bottle of wine starts at AED 175.

Credit cards oil the wheels of daily life in Dubai and can be used at all malls and major restaurants. Cash comes in for smaller purchases like coffee, taxi rides, and inexpensive items in the tourist souks. Always carry some smaller bills for small purchases, as well as 1 dirham coins for abra drivers.

You can bargain at the souks, where paying in cash can make a difference on high-price items. However, traders in the gold souk say that credit card vs. cash isn't an important issue when it comes to agreeing on a final price.

Prices throughout this guide are given for adults. Substantially reduced fees are almost always available for children, students, and senior citizens.

### ATMS & BANKS

ATMs are widely available in the city at main bank branches, in some hotels, and in shopping malls. Instructions are in Arabic and English. Bank ATMs usually allow transaction limits of AED 3,000, but some free-standing machines have lower limits. ATM machines are stocked with AED 500, AED 100, and AED 50 notes, but if you request a large amount (more than AED 1,000), the machine will give you large bills. Banks are open Sat.–Wed. 8 AM–1 PM, Thurs. 8 AM–noon. Closed Fri. Bureaux de Change are open daily 8:30–1 and 4:30–8:30.

### CREDIT CARDS

Throughout this guide, the following abbreviations are used: **AE,** American Express; **D,** Discover; **DC,** Diners Club; **MC,** MasterCard; and **V,** Visa.

It's a good idea to inform your credit-card company before you travel. Otherwise, the credit-card company might put a hold on your card owing to unusual activity—not a good thing halfway through your trip. Record all your credit-card numbers—as well as the phone numbers to call if your cards are lost or stolen—in a safe place, so you're prepared should something go wrong. Both MasterCard and Visa have general numbers you can call (collect if you're abroad) if your card is lost, but you're better off calling the number of your issuing bank, since MasterCard and Visa usually just transfer you to your bank; your bank's number is usually printed on your card.

Most major credit cards are widely accepted across Dubai in hotels, restaurants, malls, and for excursions, though some organizations do not accept Diners Club, and even fewer accept Discover. Credit cards are unlikely to be accepted in tourist markets such as the one at Kerama, and in some small or local restaurants. Credit card fraud is not a concern in Dubai. Many stores have payment machines where you can insert your PIN to secure your transaction, but you may also be asked to sign a transaction slip.

**Reporting Lost Cards American Express** (☎800/528–4800 in the U.S. or 336/393–1111 collect from abroad ⊕www.americanexpress. com). **Diners Club** (☎800/234–6377 in the U.S. or 303/799–1504 collect from abroad ⊕www.diners club.com). **MasterCard** (☎800/627–8372 in the U.S. or 636/722–7111 collect from abroad ⊕www.master card.com). **Visa** (☎800/847–2911 in the U.S. or 410/581–9994 collect from abroad ⊕www.visa.com).

**CURRENCY & EXCHANGE**
The currency throughout the UAE (including Dubai) is the United Arab Emirate Dirham (AED, or often written HH or Dhs in Dubai). The dirham is divided into 100 fils. The notes come in denominations of 5, 10, 20, 50, 100, 200, 500 and 1000 dirhams. All notes are the same size but have different col-

ors and images on their front and back faces.

Coins are issued in denominations of 1 dirham and 1, 5, 10, 25, and 50 fils; however, the 1, 5, and 10 fils are no longer widely used. The values of the coins are indicated in Arabic letters and numbers. The 50-fils coin is easily recognizable by its fluted outer edge, and the 1-dirham coin has a handled jug or coffeepot embossed on its face. The 25-fils coin is the largest of these three main coins in circulation.

The AED is pegged to the U.S. dollar at a rate of AED 3.6724 to US$1 (or AED 1 = $0.2722); it does not fluctuate. U.S. dollars are usually accepted in souks and malls, but not for low-value items such as a cup of coffee or tea.

**TRAVELER'S CHECKS & CARDS**
Traveler's checks are not normally accepted in payment for goods and services in Dubai. They can be cashed in banks, bureaux de change, and at hotels. Exchange rates are lower for traveler's checks than for currency. Because the dirham's value is linked to the dollar, it's good to carry dollar traveler's checks as rates will remain stable.

**Contacts American Express** (☎888/412–6945 in the U.S., 801/945–9450 collect outside of the U.S. ⊕www.americanexpress.com)

# ▌SAFETY

Dubai is a very safe destination with low levels of theft and muggings, but petty crime is not unknown, so you should always take sensible precautions when it comes to your personal safety and the safety of your valuables. Leave important paperwork such as return tickets and copies of your passport details in the hotel safe. Don't carry more cash than you need on a given day. If traveling by rental car, don't leave any belongings on show when you leave the vehicle.

Although bona fide gold and diamond merchants in the souks and malls are trustworthy, be wary if approached on the streets by people purporting to sell these products. These salespeople will not be licensed and regulated and their products may be forgeries.

■TIP→ **Distribute your cash, credit cards, I.D.s, and other valuables between a deep front pocket, an inside jacket or vest pocket, and a hidden money pouch. Don't reach for the money pouch once you're in public.**

## ▌ TAXES

There is no airport departure tax to pay when you leave Dubai. Hotels apply a municipality tax of 10% on room rates (plus most charge a 10% service charge—totaling 20% on base rates); restaurants also apply a 10% municipality tax to meals (plus many charge a 10% service charge—totaling 20% on meal prices). There is no value-added or purchase tax added to retail prices.

## ▌ TIME

Dubai has only one time zone and is four hours ahead of GMT. There is no daylight saving time.

## ▌ TIPPING

Most hotels and international restaurants add a 10% service charge to the bill; however, it is a common practice to give a few extra dirham in cash directly to the server (perhaps 5%). If service is not included, a 10% tip is the norm.

Bellboys, porters, and valet parking staff should receive small tips between AED 1 and AED 5. Taxi drivers do not expect a tip, but rounding up the fare is common. If you have engaged a driver for a long or complicated journey, round up to the next 5 dirham. Tank fillers at gas stations appreciate some small change.

# INDEX

# NOTES

# NOTES

# NOTES

# ABOUT OUR WRITER

**Lindsay Bennett** discovered her love of travel while backpacking around the world in between studies that led to a degree in politics. Today, she's written more than 40 travel guides on destinations worldwide, from the little-explored wilderness destination to the fashionable urban metropolis, and her passion for setting out to far horizons is as fresh as ever.

Despite shrinking journey times and the development of the information superhighway, she believes there's still a big world out there to be experienced, savored, and described in print. Lindsay often works in tandem with her husband, Pete, a renowned travel and lifestyle photographer. The synergy of words and images they produce is appreciated by an international client list.

Dubai has been a focus for Lindsay for the past few years. Although she's certainly not averse to sipping cocktails at the chic nightspots in Dubai Marina, she's just as happy enjoying a *shwarma* at a street-side café in Deira, surrounded by the hustle and bustle of daily life.

Lindsay divides her time between her homes in the UK and France, hotel rooms around the world, and journeys in her 34-foot-long Winnebago—a vehicle that's traveled a long way, from a factory in Indiana to the Baltic coast to Turkey's eastern border with Syria.

## Acknowledgments

Lindsay Bennett would like to thank the following people for their input and enthusiasm: Rebecca Sageman for her patience and unflappable nature—not to mention her great company—and Farah Zoghbi, whose extensive contact list proved invaluable.

# NOTES